got money?

Enjoy It! Manage It! Even Save Some of It!

got money?

Enjoy It! Manage It! Even Save Some of It!

Financial Advice for Your Twenties and Thirties

JEFF WUORIO

AMACOM

American Management Association

New York • Atlanta • Boston • Chicago • Kansas City • San Francisco • Washington, D.C.
Brussels • Mexico City • Tokyo • Toronto

Special discounts on bulk quantities of AMACOM books are available to corporations, professional associations, and other organizations. For details, contact Special Sales Department, AMACOM, an imprint of AMA Publications, a division of American Management Association,1601 Broadway, New York, NY 10019.
Tel: 212-903-8316 Fax: 212-903-8083

This publication is designed to provide accurate and authoritative information in regard to the subject matter covered. It is sold with the understanding that the publisher is not engaged in rendering legal, accounting, or other professional service. If legal advice or other expert assistance is required, the services of a competent professional person should be sought.

Library of Congress Cataloging-in-Publication Data

Wuorio, Jeff
    Got money? : enjoy it! manage it! even save
some of it! / Jeff Wuorio.
        p.   cm.
    Includes index.
    ISBN 0-8144-8009-8
    1. Finance, Personal. 2. Saving and investment.
    I. Title.
    HG179.W86   1999
    332.024–dc21
                                                    99–30975
                                                    CIP

Printing number

10 9 8 7 6 5 4 3 2 1

For Judy, Meghan and Nathan, for putting up with more nonsense than anyone could humanly deserve.

CONTENTS

ACKNOWLEDGEMENTS

've been fortunate enough to have come into contact with many people over the past 15 years or so who have been happy to share both their time and financial knowledge. Some had a direct hand in helping craft this book. Others may have planted a thought years ago that proved helpful later, but I'm grateful for the assistance, encouragement and friendship they ultimately gave me. When it comes to money—in particular, what you can pick up and read about money—snake oil and absurdity often rule the day. These folks and others like them offer a voice of coherence and balance within that chaos. Thanks, in no particular order, go out to:

- Glen Clemans, for his friendship and assistance in reading various chapters;
- Dave Yeske, who generously lent his time to look over the chapter on mutual funds;
- Edie Milligan, whose insight prompted inclusion of the hundreds of websites this book contains;
- Jill Gianola, not merely for her time in reading the manuscript, but for the many hours she has generously granted me over the past several years;
- Andy Hudick, for looking over the tax chapter;
- Joe Anthony, for friendship and intelligent tax guidance;
- Peter Miller, who lent his considerable expertise to the chapter on real estate;
- Eddie Yandle, for his feedback on the various ways technology and finance cross paths;
- Dave Erland, for his time for reading the insurance and benefits chapters;
- Ray Loewe of College Money, for his considerable knowledge of student loans and other such matters;

- Doug Knights, for his reading of the chapter on IRAs and his generosity over the years;
- To colleagues past and present at Money Magazine, in particular Lesley Alderman, Kathy Drake, Rich Eisenberg, Sian Ballen and Jason Zweig;
- Sheldon Jacobs, for his vast array of knowledge of no-load mutual funds;
- Ken Scott of the National Foundation for Consumer Credit, for generous resources and assistance;
- Spike Bragg, a veritable Mahatma of car shopping knowledge and refreshing email humor;
- Brigid O'Connor and varied members at the Institute of Certified Financial Planners, for help with this and countless other projects;
- My sister-in-law Susan Kaplan for doing her level best to make the pictures come out;
- Finally, everyone at Amacom Books, particularly Ray O'Connell, who helped make this book as rewarding an experience as one could ever imagine.

INTRODUCTION

I worked my way through college by commuting between school in Hattiesburg, Mississippi, and Bourbon Street in New Orleans, where I must say I learned more of what would serve me later in life than I did in Algebra II classes.
—Jimmy Buffett

While the man from Margaritaville is probably talking about, shall we say, somewhat more recreational subjects, the same thing can be said about money. The truth is, money—how we handle it, keep track of it, how it can make us happy instead of miserable—is a subject that doesn't come up all that often in our school years. In high school and college we are educated, trained, or a combination of the two, and, once out of school, we apply those skills in some sort of job or career. But it's rare that someone tells us what we should do with our money once we begin to pull in an income (or at least someone who knows what he or she is talking about—sad to say, there's an abundance of other types of people who are more than happy to share their purported expertise). Nor does it matter what you studied; even the most gifted student of Keynesian economic theory may have no more idea how to shop for a cost-effective bank account than, say, an English major.

During the course of my preliminary research into *got money?*, I got the following e-mail from someone who had seen my on-line posting asking for stories and anecdotes:

> I have been out of college for eight years now, and I'm still erasing debt that I built up courtesy of a company that preys on college students. The company recruited students and organizations to get people to fill out as many credit applications as possible. At Penn State, where I went to school, it was a regular practice for sororities, fraternities, and needy students to raise money this way. We all got these cards, and we used

them just to get through the semester. I had no thought about the future—only survival. I thought I would be able to pay these off as soon as I got out of school and started to earn "real money," but I have been paying for my mistake for the past eight years in the form of high interest and bad credit. Thousands of students are still doing this, but my husband and I have only been able to see the light at the end of the tunnel in the past year. Parents and students should know about this before it happens to them.

To me, that illustrates the hole most of us have in our education and the long-term damage it can cause. And, lest you think I'm putting myself on a pedestal in taking on this subject, not so. When I graduated from college nearly 20 years ago, I usually didn't bother to record checks when I wrote them. Remember, this was in the days before ATMs, so getting cash out of the bank was a bit more involved than it is now. Nonetheless, as often as not I'd just cut the check, take my money from the teller, and head out to buy pizza, beer, cigarettes (now there's a brilliant place to drop unrecorded money), or almost anything else you can name. No one—neither family nor the academic community in which I had spent most of my life to that point—had ever taught me how to deal with money or, for that matter, what money really represented, short of an immediate means to an end. In fact, all I can remember about my money "education" are the angry phone calls from my dad after I had written yet another rubber check, which was generally followed by his agreeing to cover the overdraft.

Sad to say, my dreadful money habits didn't improve as I grew older. After graduating, I continued to ignore such basic money habits as recording checks and deposits, let alone anything beyond that, like saving a portion of what I was taking home in pay. Investments? Insurance? Handling a credit card as if I had half a brain? Not on the agenda; sorry.

It was probably my parents' deaths less than two years after I left school that shocked me out of my money funk. All of a sudden, the financial backstops I had relied on my entire life were out of the picture. I knew that I had better learn all that I could about handling my money more sensibly, or else I would be on the fast track to searching through my sofa cushions for rent and grocery money.

One of the biggest surprises in my subsequent financial education—which included reading everything I could get my hands on and picking the brains of countless financial professionals—was that making the most of your money isn't as complicated as particle physics. Granted, some things are more complex than others, but the lion's share of basic financial ideas and principles are within the intellectual reach of anyone. There are some who argue that many financial institutions have traditionally tried to make money seem more complex than it really is—"You can't get this, kid, so just leave everything in our hands." There may be more than a grain of truth to that, but the fact remains that money is simply not as tough a nut as many might believe. Not only does that knowledge head off some pretty nasty financial pitfalls—mountains of credit card debt, an inability to get a loan or buy a house—but it can also open up some pretty attractive possibilities—vacations that you can actually pay for rather than sloughing them off on a credit card, a nice home in which to live, college for your kids, and, perhaps most appealing of all, financial solvency that lasts, not to mention the absence of a form of ongoing anxiety that has ruined many a life.

Another bit of good news is that an increasing number of colleges and universities are beginning to offer personal finance classes. In one particular school, a course on money basics is the most popular non-major class in the entire school, with students fighting hammer and tong through a lengthy waiting list. This reality signals a growing realization within academia that, in fact, money knowledge has a justified place in a balanced education and that today's students at all levels are increasingly aware enough to realize their need for this kind of help. A far cry from the days of blithely writing checks and ignoring their elders, I must say. And as the Internet continues to grow and expand, an increasing number of Web sites dedicated to cementing your financial well-being are becoming readily available.

Unfortunately, not all is rosy in the financial lives of recent college grads and those about to be. For one thing, as the cost of higher education continues to explode, more and more students are graduating with a mountain of financial debt. Nor is the financial community gun shy about exploiting students' financial needs.

According to the National Foundation for Consumer Credit, roughly two-thirds of all college students have credit cards, with an average balance of $2,100. Nor are a lot of young folks helping themselves—in a recent Consumer Federation of America survey, more than three-quarters of college juniors and seniors didn't know that the actual cost of a loan is based on the interest rate charged.

Despite that grim news, I want to offer *got money?* in the most positive light possible. Rather than just huffing and puffing about the various debacles that can result from bad money management—and I will huff and puff some about them, as I just did in the preceding paragraph—I'd like to spend more time talking about all that smart money habits can achieve. In my view, money means possibilities, not problems, particularly if you keep money in the proper perspective. I hope you'll come to share that viewpoint.

Three organizational points, the first having to do with the role technology plays in our financial lives. As opposed to 20 years ago, when someone who owned a computer might have been looked on as a geek or techie trendoid, computers and the Internet are very much a part of our daily lives now, and there is a plethora of sites that offer advice on how to handle your money. So throughout the book I've included breaks in the text that address Web sites, software, and other sorts of technology that can further your understanding of the particular topic being discussed. As for Web sites, since they tend to come and go as quickly as television shows with so-called celebrities who possess the acting ability of a mailbox, I've tried to focus as much as possible on major sites whose shelf life will, at the very least, last long enough for you to find them—and, I hope, the lesser-known ones will still be around or have referring links in place to steer you toward equally useful sites. I hope they prove helpful as adjunct sources of information, as money tools, and, overall, as ways to take your money education beyond the confines of this book. (Of course, you'll also note that I've thrown in some breaks that involve living, breathing human beings, just so we never lose sight of whom all this wonderful technology is supposed to serve.)

Second, don't assume that you already need to have scads of money to benefit from this book. Far from it, in fact, I've tried to tackle basic issues first, ones that I hope may help free up money where there may have been none before. Admittedly, certain portions of the book may be better suited to readers who have a bit more in the way of funds available, but try not to pass them by. I hope that the contents of this book, if nothing else, get you started toward a time when you find you have more money than you've ever had before.

Finally, I hope to take a subject considered unbearably dry by many and perhaps breathe a little bit of life into it. That's because money really is intrinsic to our well-being—not wealth mongering, but money as a healthy element of a well-rounded life. And that's something that every complete education should include.

Now, to paraphrase Buffett, let's get on with learning some things that should do us all some good.

got money?

Enjoy It! Manage It! Even Save Some of It!

CHAPTER 1

Some Basics

Whether you're still in school or not long graduated, it's critical to go over a few basic ideas to establish a firm basis for your financial well-being. Even if you go no further than setting up a budget that actually works on this planet or getting a grip on saving money, you'll be worlds ahead of many people—including, as likely as not, your parents. So, with the notion of working on something that you can happily lord over them, let's proceed.

By the way, many of the topics discussed in this chapter are covered in greater detail in subsequent portions of the book. Treat their coverage here as a primer, a basic lineup of ideas and suggestions from which almost anyone can benefit. Read them, give them a try, and you'll be well on your way.

Set Up a (Groan) Budget

For many people, it's not happenstance that "budget" and "misery" contain the same number of letters. Even the most financially responsible person equates budgeting with deprivation and unfair constraints—an ongoing decree of all the wonderful stuff you simply can't have because you just don't have the money.

But setting up and sticking to a workable budget doesn't have to be an act of self-torture. By following a few simple suggestions and keeping a reasonable grip on reality, you can create a budget that helps you achieve your goals.

Here's a bit of good news. You may have seen magazine articles and references in financial planning books and Web sites that lay out budget breakdowns—a percentage of your monthly money for rent, so much for car payments, and so on. Well, for my money you can feel free to go ahead and toss 'em. For one thing, they often include categories that simply don't apply to many people, such as alimony and childcare. Moreover, it seems rather unrealistic to lump every living soul within a bunch of abstract parameters— what may seem reasonable to one person may be totally off base for another.

So, instead of worrying if 20% of your monthly spending money is too much for eating out, start the budgetary process from the other end. Track your spending for a month or two to see where your money is actually going. To get the best picture you can, be obsessive about following every penny as closely as possible. Get hold of a pocket notebook, and record every purchase— coffee, snacks, meals out, the works. This exercise is as important to a full-time student on a fixed allowance (I hate that word, but none other really fits) as well as someone who's generating an income. In both cases, you have a limited amount of money to spend, so it pays big-time to know where it's all going.

At the end of a couple of months, add up your spending, and see how the total figure matches the amount you actually have to go around. Once you determine where your funds are actually going, you can then get a sense of what portion of your budget works and what needs trimming. For instance, if you find three weekly trips to the grocery store are consistently stretching your paycheck beyond its means, target that for reduction. By the same token, if you're one of the few who doesn't spend almost every available penny, that may be a signal that you can start living a bit more lavishly—not necessarily à la Michael Jackson, out building full-fledged zoos on a whim, but not like a financial Savonarola, either. Additionally, once you've pinpointed what works and what doesn't in your budget, you can adjust your spending to better reflect your values and priorities, such as putting more money aside to save for a long-term goal that means more to you than eating out one more time a week.

The nice thing about this little exercise is that it can often reveal surprising money leaks. One common revelation in budget tracking is noting the repeated stampedes to the ATM machine, which carry a double whammy—not only is it easy to forget to record ATM withdrawals, but the cash in hand can easily disappear without a trace. So make sure you record each and every ATM foray. They can add up fast and often surreptitiously.

Getting your spending in line then transports you to the pleasant side of budgeting—using those guidelines to establish goals. Knowing where your money is going—and taking steps to control that flow—lets you begin to establish budgetary priorities. For example, if you're apartment hunting but also plan to buy a new car in a year or so, you may choose a slightly less expensive rental to free up additional cash for the car. If you're chomping at the bit about moving out of your parents' home, fewer lunches out or weekends at the coast can make a substantial difference in your ability to rent an apartment of your own or, even better, buy your own place.

Here are some other tips to help you maintain a sane budget:

▶ *Whenever possible, pay with cash.* This may sound like a laughably simplistic idea, but you'd be surprised how much this can do to keep your budget on course. For one thing, if you try to limit your spending to cash, it's simple—you don't have the money, you don't buy something. That's the best kind of discipline there is. Moreover, spending with credit cards tends to blend your expenses. When the monthly bill comes, we all tend to focus on the overall amount we owe, rather than on the individual items. Instead, we should keep an eye on the small items, which tend to add up, boosting the overall amount you owe. And that's made easier by sticking to cash whenever you can.

▶ *Consider using a debit card, where money is automatically removed from an account, instead of a conventional credit card.* Not only does that keep you from spending money beyond your means, but it also offers an excellent way to accurately track your spending habits. The primary caveat about debit cards is that it's almost impossible to challenge a charge. Once the money's taken from the account, you're usually out of luck. With a debit card, therefore, you trade the benefit of having recourse against mistakes to get a tighter rein on your spending. We cover this in greater detail in the section on credit cards, but it's enough of a potential budget saver to warrant mention here.

▶ *Pro-rate nonmonthly expenses and goals.* If your car insurance payment is due every six months, set aside one-sixth of that amount in a separate account so that the bill doesn't sneak up on you all of a sudden. The strategy works equally well with more pleasant forms of spending—if you've got ten months until your next vacation, figure out where you want to go and how much it might cost and save 10% of the total every month. Then, come vacation time, you can take off with your budget intact.

▶ *Watch where you use your ATM card.* A study released early in 1998 showed that an increasing number of banks are charging noncustomers steep additional fees for using their ATM machines. On average, using your card at another bank's ATM costs you $1.23 per transaction. That may not seem like much, but if you make two trips a week to somebody else's ATM, that's $100 a year. So consider the availability of ATM machines when choosing a bank or; if a bank offers you a great deal but little ATM convenience, accustom yourself to going out of your way a bit.

⤢ Useful Web Sites

Here are a couple of handy Web sites that can assist you in drawing up and tracking a workable budget.

American Express offers a budget calculator that's specific to students at http://www.americanexpress.com/student/moneypit/budget/budget.html. The nice thing about this calculator is that it includes items such as grants, scholarships, and other things that other interactive Web sites exclude. The calculator systematically walks you through what you're taking in in income, then what's leaving in the form of tuition, rent, and other expenses. Ultimately, the calculator details whether you're keeping within your budget or whether you need to trim some things back.

American Express also offers a budget calculator geared more to the workaday world (http://www.americanexpress.com). This site lets you plug in things such as mortgages and retirement funding.

A slightly more specific set of calculators can be found at http://www.financenter.com/budget.htm. Here, rather than plowing through a boilerplate calculator, you're offered an array of functions that lets you work through specific problems. For instance, want to know how much you'll save every year if you hold off buying a new car or see two fewer movies a month? There's a calculator just for that. Of course, there's also a more generic calculator that lets you gauge how much you're actually spending compared to how much money you have to go around.

↗ Useful Software

What about using a financial software program such as Quicken or Microsoft Money to help record your financial goings on? Financial software programs can be helpful in setting up and tracking a budget. Depending on the particular package you use, you can produce charts that detail your income and outflow, make projections, and plan and prioritize your spending. So, in that sense, these programs can automate certain features that would involve a lot more effort if you tried to sit down and do the math with a pencil and paper. Software programs can also be very handy for automating tax record keeping.

However, there is one drawback to using financial software. Bear in mind that many such programs let you write checks or bank online (more about this in Chapter 10). With either of these features, most programs allow you to designate a particular payment or bill to a category within your budget. That can make budget tracking fast and easy, since everything you're paying is automatically allocated to your budget. However, if you're sticking with the old checkbook to pay your bills or your software program doesn't offer check writing or online bill paying, you've got to sit down and pound in every single check and every single deposit and withdrawal you make. That's a lot of extra work you have to commit to.

Bottom line: Think carefully about what you'd like to do with financial software. The more you intend to use those functions that interact automatically with others, such as bill paying and budgets, then your money may be well spent. But if you're paying bills by hand and doubt your resolve to keep your budget entries up to date, you may be better off saving your money.

Shop for Cost-Effective Banking Services

Another essential step in financial basics is shopping for the best, most cost-effective banking services you can find. The reason this is grouped under financial basics is that, ironically enough, banking itself really isn't all that basic any more. You may not remember it, but in the banking of yesteryear, folks always went to the nearest branch, a new account earned you a snappy new toaster, and tellers called you by name as they stamped your passbook. Moreover, since banks didn't offer all that much variety to begin with, it was all easy to figure out—you had your checking, you had your savings, and that was pretty much that. In fact, that precedent may prompt your elders to question why you should devote any time to speak of to finding a bank account: "Just go down there and open up the account, by gum! And tell 'em old Virgil says hey!"

Sorry, but the old gray bank just ain't what she used to be. For better or worse, the era of simple banking has gone the way of eight tracks and mood rings (don't even ask). Nowadays, banks offer everything from interest-bearing checking accounts to credit cards to mutual funds. In turn, they impose a bewildering array of fees and charges. And those offerings can lure you to products that, in the long run, may not be the best place for your money.

Start your pursuit of cost-effective banking by asking your bank for a complete schedule of charges and fees. Be prepared for a shock—for instance, banks across the board have increased their fees for overdrafts and monthly maintenance charges. Some banks charge you every time you use a teller for a transaction instead of an ATM. Others levy surcharges if you use a blank counter slip to withdraw money instead of a preprinted withdrawal slip. Some even have the unmitigated gall to charge customers who—gasp—have the nerve to telephone with a question about an account. So, before you sign on the dotted line, check out the fee structure to see what various services will cost you. Keep checking after you've had the account a few months—scan your monthly statements carefully, not only to balance the account but also to keep an eye out for new charges and fees.

From there, it's usually best to keep things simple. Find the lowest-cost checking account possible. If you write lots of checks, look for a bank that charges a flat monthly fee. If you write relatively few checks, an account based on a per-check fee may be cheaper. Some banks waive monthly fees if you keep a certain balance. However, examine your past statements and see what sort of monthly balance you've maintained—if it's consistently below the minimum, opt for the flat-fee account.

"Money in the bank" may have been a credo our parents lived by, but it's an outdated notion today. It's a good idea to keep as little money in your checking account as possible; since it's earning no interest in a simple checking account, it does you no good. And bypass interest-bearing checking and conventional savings accounts, whose returns are anemic—one bank contacted at random quoted basic savings as paying around 2%, with interest-bearing checking roughly half a point lower than that. Adjust that for inflation, and it's akin to burying your bucks in the backyard.

Instead, look into putting your excess cash in a money market mutual fund, whose returns are better than everyday savings and interest-bearing checking (at this writing, about 5%, compounded daily). Once that's in place, keep your money there as long as possible, and move it into checking and investments as you need it. More about this subject in investments in Chapter 4.

Next, check out your bank for a low-cost credit card. Compare interest rates as well as how much the bank will charge you for the card. If you rarely carry a balance from one month to the next, ask for a card suited to consumers who pay in full (the annual fee is often eliminated.) Ask if the card comes with an overdraft provision. To see if your bank is genuinely competitive, check out publications such as *Money Magazine*, which lists the best credit card deals throughout the country.

From there, focus on other fees and services. Track how often you use your ATM card in a given month; if your bank charges per ATM transaction (or levies steep fees for ATM transactions at other locations), consider another bank. If you're interested in an account where a minimum balance eliminates monthly fees, make sure you understand just what the bank means by a minimum. Some banks average out the balance over the entire month, while others levy fees if the balance drops below the minimum even for just a day or so.

Moreover, don't limit your banking services shopping to just banks. If you're employed and your company has a deal with a credit union, look into it. They consistently levy lower fees and offer services unheard of at many banks. For instance, many credit unions provide free checking with interest, regardless of the balance you maintain in the account.

Last, remember that you're in the driver's seat when it comes to shopping for cheap banking services. Banks, credit unions, and savings and loans are in cutthroat competition for your business. Therefore, don't assume every fee is cast in absolute stone. If you think a certain charge is unjustified, ask the bank to reduce or eliminate it. The answer may be a pleasant surprise.

➚ Useful Web Sites

Although you may not come away with a toaster, a trip to the Bank Rate Monitor Web site (www.bankrate.com) may prove far more lucrative than a visit to the corner repository. The site offers an extensive array of banking and consumer services, including a current survey of the best credit card deals available throughout the country and data on auto, personal, and home equity loans. The site also provides current information on the burgeoning online banking industry, including particularly sweet deals on CD returns and money market accounts offered exclusively to online accounts.

> The Bank Rate Monitor is also a great spot to access up-to-date news deal-
> ing with banking and consumer issues—in fact, you can sign up for an
> automatic system that warns you when the national mortgage rate aver-
> age goes up or down by as little as one-tenth of a percentage point. That
> can prove extra handy if you're waiting around hoping to lock in a low
> interest mortgage.

Record What You Need to Record

It may well be the universe's most popular question, probably
because it takes in so many topics within the framework of a single
plea: "When can I finally throw out . . .?"

Feel free to fill in the blank, because, when it comes to financial basics, this is one question we've all posed time and again. As
our money matters become more complicated, so does our record
keeping. Gone are the days when the bankbook and canceled
checks were the only pieces of paper we had to keep and organize. Now, mutual fund statements, savings account records,
deductible expenses, and a tsunami of other papers threaten to
drown us, making effective and efficient record keeping all the
more essential.

The good news is that personal record keeping need not be
a hopeless headache. It's really no big hassle to set up and actually use an organizational system that keeps your financial papers
in order, accessible and, perhaps most important of all, within
reach when that blissful day comes when you can drop them into
the circular file they truly deserve to occupy for eternity. Even better, if you get into the habit of maintaining good records when
your situation is fairly simple, the task of looking after your
records will be less of a chore when things do become more complicated.

There's one critical mass of papers that you need to hang
onto forever. If you've ever filed a federal tax return, keep a copy
permanently. Not only do the returns help establish a long-term
picture of your financial health, but you'll need them in case the
feds target you for an audit. If nothing else, if the IRS asks a ques-

tion about a particular return and you don't have it, they'll charge
you for a copy. That doesn't mean you need to stash your returns'
supporting documents for eternity as well; since the usual statute
of limitations for tax audits is three years (as many as six if the
government has reason to believe you underpaid), it's a good
idea to keep supporting papers with your returns for at least six
years.

Storing bank statements away for the same six-year period
provides further protection from audit hassles. The IRS routinely
conducts what are known as "economic reality" audits, reviews of
taxpayer records that don't seem to jibe with a certain level of
lifestyle. So, if you have a million-dollar house on a $30,000 income
(an admittedly extreme, if not altogether unattractive, example,
but you get the idea), bank records can be critical in proving you
haven't done anything underhanded.

Good bank records can also help out in other ways. Say, for
instance, in the past six years you have $60,000 more in bank deposits
than you declared as income. It turns out you got $10,000 a year in
tax-free gifts from your parents, which is perfectly legal. But that can be
hard to prove with just the tax forms, so bank records can be very helpful in an audit to document a record of cash flow.

Likewise, hang onto annual statements detailing all forms of
investment—again, if you've got them, your home, stocks, bonds,
mutual funds, and other types of investments—for at least three
years after you sell them (items such as quarterly statements can be
tossed as you receive updates). While these, too, can provide much-
needed ammunition in the event of an audit, they're also an essential
element of your tax preparation, since they document how much
you made (or lost) from your initial investment. Moreover, keeping
investment records handy can skirt a major headache, as anyone
who has tried to get financial records in the vicinity of April 15 can
attest to (duplicate statements can take weeks to obtain, and some
fund families and brokerage houses will charge you for the additional
copies).

Of course, all the preaching in the world about the importance of comprehensive financial record keeping rings pretty hol-

low without a strategy to make the task less daunting. Start by breaking down your record keeping into smaller components. Rather than organize your papers every six months (or, even worse, annually), set some time aside every month to put your papers in order. Nor does your task necessarily have to involve some sort of high-tech, New Age organizational mechanism; buy an old fashioned accordion file, and label the various pockets for bank statements, mutual fund statements, credit card records, or whatever is appropriate. Then sit down once a month with all pertinent papers, and put them where they belong.

One overriding principle to bear in mind when organizing your records is to keep everything as visible as possible. The more difficult you make it to locate something, the less successful your search for it later on will likely prove. So, when sorting out your monthly records, take the time to pull the statements from their mailing envelopes before placing them in a file. For even greater convenience, attach a note to each file indicating how long you need to keep those particular papers; that way, you can tell at a glance what needs to stay and what can go. Staple multipage statements together. Otherwise, they have a tendency to go all over the place.

For many who are out of school and working, the challenge of keeping and organizing receipts is perhaps the biggest record-keeping nightmare of all. But there is a simple solution: Use your appointment book or calendar to help keep tabs on what you spent and when. As you pay an expense that affects your taxes, just take the receipt and clip or tape it into your calendar. That handles the tasks of holding onto receipts and tracking when you incurred the expense in one simple step.

Now that you have a strategy in hand, get ready to enjoy the benefits of orderly and accessible record keeping. For one thing, having good records will save you money if you have your taxes prepared by someone else; every moment you take to better organize things on your end will mean less time spent when your tax pro's clock is ticking. If you do your taxes yourself, think of the money you'll save on aspirin knowing where things are. Then there's the psychological comfort in knowing that any question about your finances has an answer—accurate, up to date, and at the ready. And that beats a desperate, headfirst dive into a crumpled mountain of papers any day.

Save, and Ye Shall Be Saved

We've all heard the points ad nauseam—savings are important; it's important to get started on some sort of savings program; we've got to start saving more because Americans are lousy savers, and so on. Well, all those points are probably true, but they do bypass an essential element, one that may help you get started on a savings program: Why? What are you saving for? A home? A car? A trip around the world? An emergency fund that's there in case you lose your job? Maybe something a bit less challenging, such as a collection of CDs or an expensive computer program?

What Are You Saving For?

The first step in getting started with some sort of savings plan—which is undeniably important in and of itself—is to think carefully about what you're saving for. That, in turn, will help you define how much you should plan on saving, as well as where you plan to put your savings. Here's one way to look at it. Basically, there are only five things to do with the money you don't spend: Keep it as money; buy something that keeps its value; lend it to someone; start or buy a piece of a business; or gamble. That's it. And once you know what you want to do with your money, choosing from among those five financial options (or a cross between two or more) becomes simple. Even more to the point, you know why you're saving and are able to put the money where it belongs. By contrast, many a savings program has gone by the wayside because the saver, however noble his or her intentions, didn't know precisely what he or she was saving for. If you lack that focus, it's all too easy to divert your would-be savings somewhere else.

While we'll get into the particulars of various ways to save in later chapters, the point here is the absolute importance of defining why you're saving.

Time Is On Your Side

Once you've nailed down just what it is you're saving for, there's some pretty good news in store. If you're still in college or just out, you have the time to amass a real bundle, thanks to the power of long-term compounding. To illustrate, putting away a relatively modest $25 a month in something paying an equally modest 5% interest a year for 20 years gets you $10,275. Bump the interest rate up, and your take goes up along with it.

The message here is to define your goals, then get started with some sort of savings program as soon as you possibly can, because time is definitely on your side. If you fear you lack the discipline to fork over even a modest amount on a monthly basis, consider an automatic investment program, available at almost every bank, savings and loan, mutual fund family, and at other financial institutions. This kind of program allows you to designate how much you want withdrawn from, say, your checking account every month. Then, without your having to lift a finger, the money is removed every month and put where you want it—in a savings account, money market account, mutual fund, you name it. It's an effective and painless way to put your savings on autopilot.

↗ Useful Web Sites

The essential component of saving—living below your means and setting aside what's left over—is spelled out nicely at http://ourworld.com puserve.com/homepages/Bonehead_Finance/bone4c_s.htm. The site provides some suggestions on where to save and offers strategies to free up money for saving. It even whets your appetite by showing how much money you can amass over time if you regiment yourself to saving regularly. Also handy are links to related sites that detail money saving tips and help with getting yourself out of debt.

Taking the subject of saving a step further, http://www.ed.gov/pubs/Prepare/chart8.html offers a nuts and bolts overview of various savings vehicles, such as certificates of deposit, savings accounts, and money market accounts. Nice, easy to follow format that provides pluses and minuses to each savings choice.

Set Up an Emergency Fund

Having an emergency fund is an essential element of financial basics. All too often, people who think they're making all the right financial moves are suddenly flattened by an unexpected expense— it can be as benign as a fender bender or as traumatic as the loss of a job. The frequent result is that all their noble financial deeds can go down the drain as funds are diverted to meet that expense.

The solution—often overlooked, but critical, nonetheless—is to set up an emergency fund for just these sorts of unforeseen occurrences. Once you have your regular budget under control and operating smoothly, start putting aside a little extra every month into a separate account—one that you can get to in a hurry if need be, like a money market fund or savings account. Equally important to adding to this money on a regular basis is to keep your mitts off it—remember, it's there for emergencies, not for those times when you're a couple of bucks short on a six-pack.

How much should you keep in your emergency account? Conventional wisdom says we all should have as much as three months' living expenses—or even more—in accessible cash. Since conventional wisdom is an oxymoron—particularly when it comes to how humans handle their money—that figure need not be cast in stone. But do try to set aside a certain amount on a regular basis and keep the money handy in a money market fund where it can earn a little interest. That way, should something unexpected happen, your budget doesn't have to go into the tank completely. Put another way, an emergency fund can be a bona fide budget saver.

The Last Word: Inflation

I've included a brief section on inflation in the basics chapter for two reasons—first, what inflation is and isn't is widely misunderstood, and, second and equally important, inflation affects almost every element of your financial life. In so many words, inflation is the effect of rising prices on your purchasing power. It's usually expressed in terms of percentages. In recent years, inflation in the United States has hovered around 3%, which means that, if you have $1 to spend in a year when inflation is running 3%, your dollar will actually be able to buy only 97 cents worth of goods or services at year's end.

While three cents lost every year may seem rather piddling, inflation can cut into your money big-time over the long haul. Using our $1 illustration, if you held onto that buck for 10 years with inflation at 3% each year, it would effectively be worth roughly 70 cents after 10 years. Even worse, our dollar would shrink to about half its original value after 20 years. Although that doesn't seem like much, put that formula to work on hundreds and thousands of dollars at the same time, and it's easy to see why big-ticket items such as college tuition, houses, and cars have exploded in price.

We'll be touching on inflation in later chapters, but bear in mind that it's essential to consider the effects of inflation whenever your money's involved. For instance, if you're thinking about buying a car in five years that costs $25,000 now, tossing inflation into the mix can give you a much better idea of just how much you should be saving. Likewise with investments—a mutual fund that's returned an average of 12% a year for the past five years may seem fine, but lop off 3% for inflation, and an effective return of 9% seems a good deal less attractive.

↗ Useful Web Sites

For a graphic view of inflation's effects, point your browser to http://www.putnaminv.com/frames/e101.htm. The site illustrates how inflation has boosted the cost of groceries, higher education, and other items. It also offers a few quick ideas for savers and investors to counter inflation.

Interested in seeing how inflation has gone for the past 70 years or so? Have a look at http://www.fintrend.com/html/inflation.html, which details month-by-month inflation rates since 1914. While this doesn't really explain why inflation has trended the way it has, it may make you feel a good deal better about the modest inflation rate we're currently enjoying in the United States in the last few years of the twentieth century. So, quit bellyaching—at least you weren't around in early 1920, when the inflation rate topped a staggering 20%.

➚ *Additional Web Sites for Financial Basics*

Whether or not you use Quicken software, a visit to the company's financial planning site at http://www.quicken.com will likely prove time well spent. Within the confines of that single site are a host of financial, money management, and investment tools and information designed to serve the novice as well as the more experienced money manager. For one thing, the site offers an array of articles and discussion on financial basics—in that sense, the site is a great choice if you have a nuts-and-bolts question or want more information on an essential financial topic. Current stock and fund quotes, mortgage shopping, and insurance and retirement planning are all pulled together under one easy-to-navigate Web site. While there are other sites on the Web that may offer comparable and admittedly more sophisticated and comprehensive setups, Quicken's site is nonetheless a worthy stopover for financial basics.

Another great Web site for nuts-and-bolts financial information is Microsoft Money Central (http://moneyinsider.msn.com/home.asp). The site has an astounding array of articles covering a variety of financial topics, including saving, investing, budgeting, taxes, and other essential topics. Equally appealing is Money Central's array of calculators and planning tools that, among other things, let you figure out how much you need to save, whether you're carrying too much debt, and even how long you can expect to live. There are online tests designed to quiz your financial knowledge. You can also research savings rates and mortgages and even hook up with a financial planner in your area.

NOTE: In the interest of full disclosure, know that I have contributed articles and columns to both these sites. But I would have recommended them anyway—they're both that good.

CHAPTER 2

Financial Death via Debt

ebt—in its various, insidious forms—is as basic a financial issue as any of the ones discussed in Chapter 1. The reason that it merits a chapter of its own is, sad to say, that it's so blessed huge. That, and that the ways to attack it are critical enough to warrant special treatment.

The fact is, debt eats away at students and those just out of school with a particularly vicious appetite. In fact, it's a veritable buffet; from student loans to credit card debt to the other types of debt you shoulder as you start your professional life. Many people spend a good chunk of their adult lives climbing out of the sinkhole of debt they first dug in their teens and early 20s.

What makes debt particularly destructive is that it's exceedingly low-key; its effects sneak up on you only in the long term. For instance, taking out loans to pay for school is an out-and-out necessity for most students—when the time comes to pay tuition, they're just happy the money's there. They don't give any thought to how many years they may spend paying it back or how much the loan will actually end up costing them. That's all the more true with credit cards. Not only is their interest rate much higher than that for the average student loan, but there's often no specified period within which the money must be paid back (ah, that fiend the minimum payment. We'll rake him over the coals later). So you pay only what's absolutely necessary, as the amount you owe continues to climb and climb.

The most ironic thing about debt is that, in a very weird way, it's a necessary part of a healthy financial picture. You're no doubt familiar with the classic paradox confronting job seekers—you can't get a job without any experience, but you need a job to get the experience. In a sense, that's also the case with debt, because it's only by handling debt responsibly that you prove yourself capable to the financial powers that be of taking on even greater financial responsibilities, such as car payments and home mortgages. So it's essential to obtain and handle debt as it should be handled. It's only when that debt becomes overwhelming that problems can wash over you. And when that wave hits, it's something that can leave you floundering for the rest of your life.

But no matter how deep in debt you may find yourself (and, I hope, at least some of you reading this will be wallowing in the pure joy of being relatively debt-free), there are strategies to dig yourself out and get back on your financial feet. That's not to say it will be easy or necessarily pleasant. But it is critical to setting the table for your later financial well-being.

The Expansive—But Not Entirely Destructive— World of Student Loans

As we noted earlier, student loans are a way of life for most college students, as well as for those who are not long out of school. As you undoubtedly know, the reason is that a higher education has become not only outrageously expensive but also too costly for most families to foot the bill out of pocket. The average four-year cost of tuition, room, and board at public universities now tops $25,000—more than double what it cost only 20 years ago. And find yourself a comfortable chair or a soft place to fall if you haven't heard the latest figures for private institutions—nearly $65,000 for the same four years. In fact, that figure is actually somewhat misleading, as one-year costs at prestigious schools such as Ivy League colleges now routinely exceed $30,000. In that sense, if you're out of school or nearing the end of college, you should count yourself lucky—costs are likely only going to continue to increase.

↗ Useful Web Sites

For a more complete picture of recent college costs as well as foreseeable trends in the expense of higher education, have a look at http://www.college board.org/press/cost97/970917.html. The site also links you to an interactive map of the United States where you can find recent tuition costs for almost any college and university in the country.

The good news is that the student financial aid market has responded to these stratospheric rises by expanding the availability of student loan programs—federal loan programs alone now provide more than $30 billion in aid to students. The bad news is that—well, the student financial aid market has responded to these stratospheric rises by expanding the availability of student loan programs. That's not to say they shouldn't have, as that would have left untold numbers of students out in the financial cold. But the amount of student debt has skyrocketed as a result. It's not uncommon for students to pursue and receive the absolute maximum amount of financial aid available to them. And that's put students and grads into a deeper financial hole—over roughly the past 20 years, median student loan debt has exploded from $2,000 to more than $15,000.

But there is an irony to all this. Put simply, there are a whole lot of worse ways to get into debt than owing money for your higher education. Moreover, there are various ways to craft your student loan payback to make it easier and more advantageous to your financial well-being. (I won't get into the pluses and drawbacks of various types of loans. Unless you're looking for additional funds or are planning to move onto grad school, that ship has sailed.)

First off, even though the amount of money people owe via student loans has skyrocketed, student loans nonetheless remain a bargain in the otherwise leech-like world of debt. Unlike credit cards, which can carry interest rates as high as 22%, government-funded loan programs such as the Stafford program carry interest rates as low as 7.5% or so. Not only is that a monstrous 14 to 15%

difference, but, thanks to federal legislation enacted in 1998, the interest rate on student loans is now tax deductible.

That makes student loans more of a bargain. Here's an illustration: Say you owe $10,000 at 7.5% with a 10-year payback period. That translates to 10 years of monthly payments of $118.70. In the first year, your total payments would be $1,424, of which roughly $726 is interest. A little number crunching will make a point: Since you're paying $726 in interest, that means you're saving about $109 in federal taxes if you're in the 15% bracket ($726 times .15 = $108.90. More on what brackets mean in the tax chapter—just go with that for now). Put another way, your actual out-of-pocket payback for the year is $1,315, since you're saving $109 on your taxes. Not a bad deal at all.

Naturally, the government being the government, student loan deductibility isn't without its quirks. For one thing, the deduction applies only to the first 60 months of the loan—once you're past the first five years, no deduction. Moreover, you can't claim the deduction if your parents still list you as a dependent. And, as it's written now, the law starts reducing deductibility once you reach a certain income level ($40,000 if you're single, $60,000 if you're married and filing a joint tax return). Still, even though there are limitations, a limited amount of deductibility is better than none at all.

⤢ Useful Web Sites

For the lowdown on the new tax rules regarding student loans, have a look at the Internal Revenue Service's Publication 970, "Tax Benefits For Higher Education," at http://www.irs.ustreas.gov/prod/forms_pubs/pubs/p970toc.htm. There, in addition to the tax deductibility of student loans, you can learn more about use of Individual Retirement Accounts to pay for school, education savings bonds, and how to handle things if your employer is helping to pay your tuition.

In addition to being tax deductible, student loans are generally structured to offer you the lowest monthly payment possible (with the added plus that, unlike credit cards, where monthly "minimums" don't even make a dent in what you owe, student loan interest rates actually let you make reasonable payments that do make a difference). And, referring back to our discussion about the importance of establishing a credit record, student loans can be an affordable means of doing just that, setting yourself up nicely for home mortgages and other forms of credit where a good credit history carries a lot of pull.

Should you try to eliminate your student debt faster than your payment program requires? In many cases, surprisingly enough, the answer is no. With low interest, low monthly payments, and now the added boon of tax deductibility, there's a lot to be said for taking the full term for repayment. The argument becomes all the stronger if, for example, you're able to take the extra money you might have used to pay down your student debt faster and invest it, particularly in some tax-advantaged investment like an IRA or a 401k through your job. To illustrate, let's suppose you invest that money in an IRA that earns 11% a year. That gives you a return four points greater than you would have gotten if you'd put the money toward a 7% debt like a student loan. Add the tax-deductibility of an IRA, and the rationale becomes all the more compelling.

But there are times when reworking or even repaying your student loan may be the better option:

▶ If you have a number of federal loans and are having some problems meeting the various payments, consider consolidating them into one loan. The feds provide several different loan consolidation programs that pool all your loans into one payment. The idea here is that a consolidation program may result in lower monthly payments than you would make if you were to keep the loans separate. This idea is particularly appealing given the recent drops in interest rates, which, coupled with consolidation, may slash not only how much you pay month-to-month but the overall cost of your loan. For further information, call the federal Department of Education's toll-free consolidation number at 800-557-7392.

↗ Useful Web Sites

For additional information on loan consolidation and other ideas that may trim your student loan expenses, check out the Department of Education's Web site at http://www.ed.gov/DirectLoan/consolid.html.

► You may also restructure your loan if your income isn't quite what you expected. The Income Contingent Repayment Plan lets you set up a payment plan based on your income so that your student loan obligations don't cause you undue financial hardship. What you end up paying is based on your annual income, and payments are restructured annually to take into account changes in your income.

↗ Useful Web Sites

For more details on the income-contingent plan, check out the Web site at http://www.ed.gov/DirectLoan/pubs/repabook/.

► If you used a lender associated with Sallie Mae (the nation's largest education finance company) in getting a Stafford loan, be aware that it pays to be timely with your payments. If you make the first 48 payments on time, you'll get two points knocked off your interest rate for the remaining life of your loan. To make certain that your first 48 arrive on time, set up an automatic payment plan where the monthly amount is automatically removed from an account of your choosing. As an added bonus, you'll receive an additional _-point cut in your loan's interest rate.

► Remember the television program *Northern Exposure,* where a young med school grad has his student loans paid off by the state of Alaska in return for a period of what for him amounted to indentured service in the bush? It's not that farfetched a scenario, nor as grim as the television show portrayed. For example, the Nursing Education Loan Repayment Program (4350 East West Highway, 10th Floor, Dept. AACN, Bethesda, Maryland 20814; 800-435-6464) will pay up to 85% of nurses' student loan debt; in return, nurses agree to work for three years in an area where there's a shortage of qualified health care workers.

↗ *Useful Web Sites*

For more particulars on the Nursing Education Loan Repayment Program, check out http://www.gsa.gov/fdac/data/p93908. There you can find out more about repayment provisions, program eligibility, and other details.

Nor are loan forgiveness programs limited to health care. An expected shortage of teachers in the next decade or so has spawned a variety of loan repayment programs for teachers willing to relocate to inner-city or rural areas or who teach what are known as "high need" subjects, such as special education or bilingual studies. Your best bet is to contact your state Department of Education, since such programs are generally state or federally funded. Alternatively, contact Recruiting New Teachers, an organization that specializes in bringing newcomers into the teaching fold. They're located at 385 Concord Ave., Belmont, Massachusetts 02178.

One caveat—as in Joel Fleischmann's case in *Northern Exposure*, loan forgiveness programs can be pure hell if your sole motivation is to have your debt cleared. However, if you're looking to gain some experience in an area you may not have otherwise considered or are looking for something unique or interesting to do before you move on, perhaps to grad school, loan forgiveness programs can prove beneficial in any number of ways, including financially.

One final tip about student loans: Whether you're still shopping around for a loan to pay for school or have graduated and are looking for the best way to handle your student debt, it pays to shop aggressively for the best deal you can possibly get. Compare interest rates, repayment timeframes, and, in particular, the lender's willingness to offer any sort of repayment incentives. It's never too late: If you've left school and your current lender doesn't dangle any carrots for prompt loan repayments—as, for instance, Sallie Mae does—see if you can't move the loan over to another lender that does offer incentives. It never hurts to try, and it may save you some bucks in the long run.

Joe Plastic Lives

Joe Camel may have slunk back into the desert, but an insidious relative is alive and, sad to say, very well indeed.

Consider this the next time you're walking out to the mailbox—unless you're a state-of-the-art deadbeat or a member of a reclusive monastic order, there's a reasonable chance that the day's mail will include a pitch from a credit card company. In some cases, the overture may be a slick-looking invitation to apply; in others, you may already be approved. Just fill out the form, wait for the card to arrive, then hightail it to the store. If you're still in school, the exposure can be ongoing. Like military recruiting outposts on every street corner in time of war, credit card companies are blanketing college campuses with an ongoing presence. Just stop by the friendly kiosk located outside the dining hall, sign up, and join the team. Rah, rah.

What's wrong with this picture? More than many of us can imagine. Americans are drowning in credit card debt, with nary a life preserver in sight. According to the Federal Reserve, we owed $528 billion in credit card debt as of the end of 1997, up nearly $30 billion from the prior year alone. The problem is particularly acute for college students and for those not long out of school. People ages 22 to 33 hold only 18% of all credit cards but contribute 25% to outstanding credit card debt. People in that age group are more likely to carry a balance and, on average, carry a larger balance than other folks. Not only do estimates hold that fully two-thirds of all college students carry some type of credit card, but they're having more than their share of problems handling the cards responsibly. The National Consumer Counseling Service says that more than half of its clients who come looking for help with debt problems are between the ages of 18 and 32. Nor does the credit-card industry show any signs of letting up in its ongoing effort to get as many Americans to use as many credit cards as possible. Estimates are that some three billion credit card solicitations are mailed out every year. So if you do happen to get one in the mail today, you shouldn't feel all that special.

Real-Life Interlude

Think the credit card companies don't know you're out there? Think again. Credit card companies routinely buy millions of names from any number of sources, including Internet sites, financial institutions, and even other credit card companies just for the purpose of trying to lure you over to their credit card. And they're very, very good at slipping very enticing offers under your nose, with precious little consideration paid to your financial responsibility or your capacity to keep up with payments on the card.

As an exercise, I recently went through an online college selection calculator, placing my name in the system as if I were a senior in high school. Not long thereafter—surprise, surprise—there arrived in the mail an invitation to sign up for a credit card. Replete with hip-looking college kids waving their own credit cards around, the flyer touted the fact that the card had no annual fee, that I could receive discounts on so-called "cool stuff," and—if I applied the magic orange sticker where it belonged on the application—I would also receive 3 percent cash back. (Nice to know that the credit-card companies have enough faith in your intelligence to assume you can figure out how to peel and apply stickers. I wonder what would happen if you didn't attach the sticker? Would your application be rejected because that was a warning sign you were too dense to carry a credit card?)

Sweet, right? About as sweet as taking a chomp out of a lemon. I turned the application over and saw on the "credit card information" chart that the annual percentage rate was just under 18%—even subtracting the 3% cash-back perk, that still meant a ridiculous 15% interest. Even worse, any balance that was more than 30 days past due would be subject to 19% interest, minus the 3% cash back.

The lesson: Ignore all the slick malarkey credit card applications throw at you and, instead, seek out the credit card information chart that outlines every charge, penalty, and other responsibility that comes with using the card. More often than not, you'll discover enough outlandish costs to make your hair stand on end.

Before I get too preachy, I'd like to add that it's easy to understand how we all have become so hooked on credit. For some, the lure of plastic is sweet financial denial—when you buy with a credit card, it just doesn't seem like you're really spending money. Moreover, a credit card feeds our hunger to have it now rather than dutifully saving up over time for a big purchase, thanks to plastic we can cart our goodies home today. That can be particularly alluring to a college student or to some-one just out of school who's had enough self-denial to last a lifetime; you may well feel you've worked hard to get where you are and you deserve a reward. On top of that, for many college students and for those just out who are struggling to make ends meet, credit cards aren't some luxury to be used for trips to the theater and other perks; they're a financial lifeboat, enabling their holders to meet expenses for necessi-ties such as groceries and work clothes. Unfortunately,   our depen-dence on credit cards is racking up monstrous expenses. To illustrate: A $3,000 big-screen television bought at 18% interest may have the very appealing monthly payment of $50. Trouble is, it will take 147 months to pay off the expense at that rate and end up costing $7,350, more than double the original price. And, should you skip a payment or be late once or twice, the consequences can be disastrous—credit card issuers are increasingly levying "penalty rates" on card holders whom they deem to be credit risks. In some cases, cards' interest rates can be doubled without any warning to the holder.

⤤ *Useful Web Sites*

> If you're interested in seeing just how long it would take to pay off a bal-ance on a credit card—or you already owe and need to find out what you have to do to dig your way out—check out the "What Will It Take to Pay Off My Line of Credit?" calculator at <u>http://www.smartcalc.com/cgi-bin/smart-calcpro/hel6.cgi/FinanCenter</u>. Once there, just enter the balanced owed, the interest rate, and how much you're able to pay every month, and, in a glance, you'll see where you stand, for better or worse. This is also handy for comparing the impact of various credit card interest rates.

Few in this day and age will deny the usefulness and the occa-sional necessity of a credit card—after all, emergency expenses do come up. And it's also important to start establishing a good credit record for those financial moves that will likely come later in life, such as buying a home and taking on other significant expenses that will require some sort of financing. But there are various strate-gies that can be used to ensure that you use credit effectively and not destructively. Start by limiting the number of credit cards you carry. There is really no need for people to use any more than two credit cards (by horrific comparison, it's not uncommon for people to carry between eight and 10 cards). From there, consider using a debit card rather than charging purchases onto a bill that is paid later as interest accrues, a debit card automatically removes funds from an account when an item is purchased.

Debit cards can be a genuinely effective way of cutting back on the hunger to spend. For instance, if you're worried that you won't have enough money in your account to use a debit card, that's a fairly sure sign that you really can't afford the purchase in the first place. (To give yourself a bit of a cushion, investigate debit cards with overdraft provisions. That way, if an absolute emergency comes up, you can use the card for more than you have in the account.)

Conventional credit cards have one significant advantage over debit cards—if someone steals the card and uses it or you wish to contest any sort of charge, you can do so without actually having your money leave your account. So, if you opt for a credit card, shop aggressively for the best one available. *Money Magazine* prints a monthly list of what it considers the best credit card deals in the country, both for people who carry a balance and for those who pay their bills every month.

↗ Useful Web Sites

As we mentioned earlier, the Bank Rate Monitor (http://www. bankrate.com/universal/rate/content/cchome.asp) offers a world of great information on selecting the best card to meet your needs. The site offers insight into credit cards, debit cards, and teaser rates, as well as the best rates and terms available. The Web site even offers a handy "tip of the week," touching on a particular aspect of credit card use.

Consider several elements when shopping. First, look at the card's interest rate, and see just how long that rate will hold. Be wary of "teaser rates," exceedingly low interest rates designed to lure you into getting a card. While they are attractive at first, the interest rates usually spike up significantly, often after only a few months. If a teaser rate seems too attractive to pass up, look around for cards whose rate lasts at least one year. It's also worthwhile to lock in a low fee for the life of the card. Credit card companies slap various names on these sorts of cards, but they all boil down to your paying a certain amount every year to keep your interest rate relatively low. For instance, Wachovia Bank offers a "prime for life" card that guarantees that, for about $80 a year, your card will carry the equivalent of the prime lending rate (as of this writing, that's about 8.5%). Compare that with conventional cards that smack you with interest rates of 16% and higher, and that 8.5 seems awfully sweet.

However, check carefully to make sure the money you shell out for a lower interest rate is actually worth it. For instance, if you hardly use your card at all, not only does that qualify you for the Guinness Book of World Records, but it also makes a low-interest-rate card senseless. Why pay a premium for something you don't use all that often? By the same token, if you're one of the equally rare breed who's able to pay your credit card balance in full each and every month, stick with a plain old card. Again, you probably won't save enough in interest charges to offset the yearly fee. But if you're like most of us, who carry balances month to month and rack up interest charges along the way, a lower interest rate can prove a real money saver, even with the added cost of an annual fee.

⤴ *Useful Web Sites*

> To help figure out which is the better deal—a higher-rate card with no annual fee or a cut-rate card that imposes a yearly charge—have a look at the interactive calculators at http://www.financenter.com/cards.htm. Select "Is a lower rate worth the annual fee?" and enter whatever numbers apply to your situation. The calculator then identifies which option is best as well as giving you an estimate of just how much you might be able to save by making the right choice.

However, how you actually handle the card is far more important than the card's interest rate. Do your reasonable best to try to pay credit card bills in full every month. More specifically, pay the bill when it arrives, rather than the actual due date—remember, you're charged interest every day that you carry a balance. Paying in full not only lets you avoid interest charges but will prove less expensive over time while lower-interest cards usually have an annual fee, higher-interest rate cards often waive annual charges, making them ideal for a user who pays in full every month.

For those who would like to pay every month but doubt they have the discipline, consider American Express or other similar cards that require balances to be paid every month (interest kicks in only after you're late with a payment). Likewise, cash rebate cards or cards that let you accrue airline mileage or other perks can be great, just so long as you're able to pay off the bill every month, thereby skirting high interest rates.

↗ Useful Web Sites

Rebate cards, dangling goodies such as cash back, airline miles, and even credit toward cars, are all over the place these days. So if one interests you, it pays to check it out to determine just how much you'll be paying in the long run. For a rundown on the best rebate cards, http://www.bankrate.com/brm/publ/rebate.asp offers information on teaser rates, the interest you'll actually pay, annual fees, and a host of other data to help you make an intelligent decision.

If carrying a balance is unavoidable, ignore the minimum monthly payment specified on the statement—that's nothing more than a sure way to bleed to death slowly, since you're only paying the bare minimum and aren't making any dent in what you owe. Instead, try to add something to the minimum every month, thereby paying down the amount you actually owe, not just inter-est. If you owe on several cards, try to target the extra payments to the card with the highest interest rate.

If, on the other hand, all these wonderful suggestions come a bit too late for you because you're already burdened with ongoing credit card debt, don't despair—there are ways out of it, but it takes some real discipline. First, sit down and tally up all that you owe. Then figure out how much more you can pay on the most expensive credit cards, and start targeting extra payments toward those cards. As an alternate strategy, start paying off whatever small balances may be outstanding. Rather than paying off every card bit by bit, you may get a psychological lift by eliminating some of the lesser debts quickly. That can make you feel like you're getting somewhere.

As an alternative, consider consolidating all your credit card debt under one low-interest card. As we noted earlier, you can check out the Bank Rate Monitor Web site for a suitable card for consolidation. However, if you choose to consolidate debt under a low-interest card, be prepared to move aggressively to pay off the debt, since the interest on most low-rate cards will spike up sooner or later.

If consolidation isn't possible or desirable—for instance, you know yourself well enough to recognize that an all-out sacrifice to pay off a card may be asking too much—at least try to work with your current credit card company to see if it will lower the rate on your card. Ask if it will pare down an 18% interest rate to 15% or even lower (you'd be surprised how often this works. Not only do companies want to keep you as a customer, but a lower interest rates lessens the chance of default. And, for credit card companies, as you'll find with most financial institutions, getting something is always better than nothing at all.)

Negotiation can be particularly effective if your card comes from a bank where you have a checking and a savings account. To be blunt, don't be the least bit shy about throwing this fact in the bank's face and making it clear that you'd have no qualms about taking your accounts elsewhere unless the bank is willing to cut you a deal. (Whether you'd actually do that or not is beside the point— just try to come off as someone who would think long and hard about hauling your money elsewhere if the bank doesn't bend.) Again, you may come away surprisingly pleased. There are lots of places to put your money, and banks dearly want to hold onto your business—particularly if you're relatively young and someone whom they're eager to transform into a contented customer for life.

↗ Useful Web Sites

Here are a couple of great Web sites that may prove valuable to folks who just can't seem to get out from under credit card debt and other similar problems:

One excellent source of information on debt, credit cards, and other related issues is the National Foundation For Consumer Credit Web site http://www.nfcc.org/. There, in addition to reams of information on credit and debt, you'll find a handy "debt test" that gives you an idea whether you're handling your credit responsibly or whether debt may have too great a stranglehold on you.

If you want to have a look at other debt-related sites, check out http://members.aol.com/debtrelief/index.html. Sponsored by the Center for Debt Management, the Web site offers counseling and debt services, an extensive online library, and links to other helpful sites on credit and debt.

CHAPTER 3

Investing for Long-Term Success with Stock Mutual Funds

For me, the very best part of successful money management comes now—when you've gotten your finances into good enough shape that you can begin setting some of your income aside on a regular basis and, hopefully, watching it grow. While some folks may equate financial success with being out of debt and having enough money to pay their bills every month (and Heaven knows, that's certainly true), to me limiting money management to that capacity is like treading water. By comparison, investing is like freestyle swimming—if you learn how to do it properly, you're going to move forward.

A few ideas to chew over before we get into the meat of investing (for vegetarians, feel free to replace the aforementioned image with the soy-based product of your choosing). First off, while we've just spent the prior pages hammering over and over about the evils of debt and how it must be controlled and eradicated, you don't have to wait until you're absolutely debt-free before you start investing. For one thing, debt reduction and investing can happily coexist if you set up your system properly and don't place undue emphasis on one or the other. Moreover, if we all waited to be completely out of debt before we started investing, the New York Stock Exchange would have tumbleweeds careening across its floor, because there would be very few of us in that happiest of categories.

Admittedly, this is an issue where temperament plays a role. If you're the type who would feel a whole lot better wiping out any debt completely before investing cent one, that's not the worst thing in the world. But bear in mind that it's awfully hard to stay out of debt completely and consistently (all it takes is one charge with the credit card and, boom, you're technically "in debt"). So, however, noble and worthy your desire may be to wipe the debt slate clean before you invest, it's a difficult state to achieve and maintain. The best approach may be to address debt reduction and investing at the same time. As we discussed in Chapter 2, start by earmarking a few extra dollars every month to help pay down your credit card debt; then invest a similar amount. That way, you're trimming your debt and getting your investment program up and running at the same time.

Another point: Please note the title of this chapter. With very few exceptions, successful investing is predicated on the long-term. Needless to say, that means different things to different people, depending on their circumstances. Someone who is saving and investing for a down payment on a home may be looking at as few as five years. Conversely, a recent college grad looking toward retirement has decades of savings ahead. Moreover, your time frame will have a great deal to do with your choice of investment.

What investing is not is how it's often portrayed in popular culture—the Charlie Sheen-like shyster in *Wall Street* who's hawking stocks left and right in hopes of making an overnight kill. Admittedly, there are some who look at investing in this fashion. One is the stock market timer (for those of you unfamiliar with the term, this is someone who, as the name suggests, tries to time his or her forays into and exits from the stock market on the basis of any number of factors and pieces of information). The market timer, as often as not, has reams of information at his or her fingertips that support his or her decisions and who, again as likely or not, treats stock trading as a full-time business. Then there are folks who are sufficiently deluded to think they can do the same thing with a sliver of the same information and know-how. They may luck out on occasion, but their overall success is predicated on just that— dumb luck. And that's something no thoughtful investor would ever want to bank on. If nothing else, never, ever use the term "play the market" as some do—for all that it is, investing should certainly never be treated as play, unless you want childish results.

⬈ Useful Web Sites

For an eye-opening view that shows that market timing really can't do that much for you even if you hit things right on the nose, have a look at the article "Timing Isn't Everything" at http://www.fundsinteractive.com/ features/vuj07984.html. The piece illustrates that money invested systematically for the long haul doesn't earn much less than what is gained from a series of market-timing hits. Bear in mind while reading this that all it takes is one or two efforts at market timing that go south, and you've shot yourself in the foot.

Just What the #@*&!!! Is Investing?

In its most simplistic sense, investing is giving your money to someone else with the expectation that, over time, he or she will give you back more than you gave them. That's investing—no more, no less. How that definition plays out in reality depends on who gets your money—a bank, a government entity, a company, or another recipient. And just what that recipient does with the money you give it will impact just how much you get back in the long run.

Much of this chapter on investing is devoted to stocks (or, more specifically, to stock mutual funds). Stocks are portions of ownership that a company sells to the public to raise cash for expansion, product development, or any of a number of other needs. In a very real sense, when you buy stock in a company, you own a part of that company. What's also important to you as an investor is that buying a slice of a company that grows and blossoms over time offers you the best opportunity for financial growth. If the company wins, your success is commensurate with the company's success; since you own a portion of a company that's worth more at the end, your share of that company increases in value. There's really no other investment that, by definition, compares.

↗ Useful Web Sites

If you're looking for heaps of statistics about stocks, bonds, and other sorts of investments, don't bypass Investor Home (http://www.investorhome.com/history.htm). There you have access to scads of historical data on all types of investing, showing, among other things, that, over the past 70 years or so, stocks—small stocks in particular— have outperformed every other type of investment (12.5% a year return, on average). But Investor Home is no stock Pravda—it also notes that in the 1980s, bonds actually outperformed stocks, although if you stretch out the time frame further, the opposite is true. The site also offers a variety of links to further information on the history of investing and the numbers behind that history.

By contrast, bonds in their varied forms are a loan—either a company or government agency is borrowing your money on the promise to return it, with interest. While bonds can offer reasonable interest rates (certainly better than those offered by savings accounts or money markets) and while some financial pros will argue to the death that bonds should be a part of anyone's investing plan, the fact remains that the payoff from debt almost never equals what you can get when you own a share of a company. More on this later, but for now, be assured that the best bet for long-term financial growth comes from stocks and nothing else.

↗ Useful Web Sites

Before we move on, here are a couple of additional Web sites that are worth checking out if you're interested in finding out more about the basics of investing:

Investment newcomers would do well to make the American Association of Individual Investor's Web site (www.aaii.org) one of their first surfing stopovers. Unlike other financial sites, it doesn't have an advertisement or investment recommendation anywhere, which is consistent with AAII's goal of unbiased investment information and education. The site is filled with information on stock selection, portfolio management, and nuts-and-bolts guidance on other financial products such as bonds and insurance. There's even a glossary designed to demystify bewildering financial terminology. Nor should more savvy investors bypass AAII, as the site also provides information on advanced stock analysis and screening methodology. But the emphasis here is on education, and that makes this site a gold mine for anyone who wants to know more about making smarter money decisions.

Particularly useful if you have a specific question in mind is The Investment FAQ (www.invest-faq.com). It's easy to look up financial information and guidance according to the subject, such as mutual funds, insurance, and corporate-sponsored retirement plans. The site also offers an easy-to-follow guide to investing and money management for newcomers that touches on investing dos and don'ts and ways to choose a suitable financial planner. As your money knowledge grows, you can tap into The Investment FAQ's more sophisticated areas, such as technical analysis. The site is even gutsy enough to pan—and substantiate its criticism—of self-styled investment "experts" such as Charles Givens and Wade Cook. That alone makes the site worthy of a net browser bookmark.

Stock Funds, Not Just Stocks

Okay, you're saying, now that this guy has gotten me all worked up about stocks, let's get started with talking stocks. Sorry, but I'm not going to do that, at least not in any sort of exhaustive detail. The reason is that I'm a believer in stock mutual funds, not necessarily individual stocks, particularly for someone who's just getting his or her feet wet. There are several good reasons for this. First, as we'll discuss later in greater detail, mutual funds are managed by financial professionals with access to reams of data and analysis, not to mention the time and resources necessary to sift through all that stuff. They are paid (very well, I might add) to pick winners and, conversely, to dump losers with the least amount of damage. Even if you have all the time and wherewithal in the world, it would be hard to argue that you could match the day-in, day-out performance of a talented mutual fund manager.

The second is diversification, something that can be difficult to achieve on your own if you're just starting out or have limited funds to go around. As we'll discuss in more detail later, spreading your money among a variety of investments can limit risk while giving you the best shot at steady growth. Got $500 to invest? Well, that may buy you a few shares in one company, maybe two if you spread yourself thin enough. By comparison, that $500 in a stock fund can buy you ownership in dozens of companies and maybe more, since your money jumps in the pool with money from other investors. (Studies have indicated that investors can achieve "adequate" diversity with portfolios that have as few as eight stocks. Again, however, that can be tough to swing if you're just getting your feet wet in investing—yet another argument for going with mutual funds).

The final reason is that selecting and buying individual stocks is an exceedingly complicated, even convoluted subject. Stock selection theories and strategies run the gamut from exhaustive numbers crunching to what seems out-and-out witchcraft (for instance, I once reviewed an investment newsletter that predicted the movement of the stock market by the tides and lunar sequences. I kid you not.) With so many aspects of stock picking begging to be addressed, I don't think it very responsible to conclude that a single chapter—let alone a portion of a chapter—on stocks offers even a reasonable overview of the subject (there are countless complete books devoted to the subject, a number of them quite good). Moreover, when there are reams of stock mutual funds around that can accomplish the same sort of goals as individual stocks, it's a better use of your time to first become acquainted with mutual funds. Over the long haul, they're your best bet.

↗ Useful Web Sites

John Hancock has a nice little Webpage that offers an overview of mutual fund advantages (http://www.jhancock.com/basics/principles/eight.html). The page also offers links to sites that provide further information on things like diversification and can hook you up with similar pages that detail other important elements of successful investing.

The Case for Long-Term Investing

Speaking of the long haul, there are several compelling reasons why investing should always be looked at as a long-term proposition. The first is sheer practicality. Few of us have either the time or the knowledge to be truly active traders—if you don't have the necessary expertise or the time to steer the ship, your Titanic is headed straight for an iceberg (what a night to remember that would be). The second is cost. One thing that *Wall Street* and other "real-life" movies that address the world of investing (there's today's oxymoron) tend to gloss over is that every time you buy or sell something, you pay a commission to someone, somewhere (a commission is essentially a fee you pay to have your investment decision carried out and can run the gamut from dirt cheap to the out-and-out exorbitant). Granted, trading on the Internet has slashed commission costs drastically, but you're still paying, nonetheless. And, remember, if you're using a broker to get advice, the commissions can eat into your money stash big time.

The final and most persuasive argument for long-term investing is that, historically speaking, it reduces the risk of what you're trying to do. Never lose sight of the fact that, with apologies to those who would have you believe otherwise—the "wealth without volatility" crowd that, to me, makes as much as sense as, say, "seeing without eyes"—successful investing and money growth by definition have to involve risk. To achieve the results that will allow you to reach your goals, you have to acknowledge that things can turn against you. That's not to say it's an out-and-out crap shoot, but there is a potential downside to investing—you can lose money, often a great deal of it.

The plus side to all of this is that time is your biggest ally in offsetting the risks of investing. The rationale is simple. If you own an investment that drops in value, historical data show that it will recover and actually grow in value, given enough time. For instance, as we pointed out earlier, since 1926 small stocks have increased in value more than 12.5% a year. That's taking into account several huge one-day stock market drops, one lengthy worldwide depression, several wars, a period when people actually bought rocks as pets, and every other aspect of idiocy the human race saw fit to wallow in. Skeptics will argue that this 72-year period isn't an ironclad guarantee of what might happen in the future, and they're right. But it's a powerful argument in favor of investing for the long haul.

Even a shorter-term perspective shows how time can keep the ups and downs of investing in check. Statistics suggest that, in any given year, mutual funds have a one-third to one-fourth chance of losing money. But if you leave the money in for five years, the chance of losing money drops to 4%; over 10 years, the likelihood of taking a net loss is even less than that. So you can make a fair argument that you're likely to come out on top even if you don't leave your money in a fund for a lifetime.

Not only does time tend to smooth out the bumps and bruises investors can experience over the short term, but it also allows compounding to kick in. For those who have heard this term and aren't really sure what it means, here's an example. Start with $5 earning 10% a year. At the end of the year, you have $5.50 (your original five, plus 50¢ interest.) The next year, you also earn 10%, but your investment grows by 55¢. That's because the initial investment, combined with the interest you earned the first year, has grown, so the interest is figured on a larger amount. And this steamrolls on. The longer you let it sit, the more your money earns, the bigger the amount the interest is figured on becomes, and the bigger the return it produces. It's a marvelous no-brainer. (In fact, there's a great *Seinfeld* episode that illustrates this very principle. George tells Jerry about a savings account that he put money into as a kid, then forgot. Turns out, with interest, the account is now worth $1,900, which leads George to declare: "Interest! It's an amazing thing. You make money by doing nothing!")

The joys of compounding don't end there, George. For one thing, if you have a certain goal in mind (say, you plan to buy a house in 10 years and figure you'll need $20,000 for the down payment), compounding lets you figure out how much you'll need to set aside on a regular basis and what sort of return you'll need to reach your goal. In the preceding example, if you've got 10 years to invest and assume that you can earn 10% a year (not an unreasonable assumption), then all you need to do is set aside about $96 a month to achieve your targeted down payment goal.

What can be an even more entertaining and compelling illustration of long-term compounding, particularly for someone young with a long-term investment horizon, is playing around with some numbers to see what they can become, given enough time. For instance, since small stocks have returned 12.5% since Calvin Coolidge was in the White House, assume for a second that, in 1926, your great-grandfather put $100 into a stock that, ultimately, returned that very same 12.5%. From there, he did nothing (oh, maybe he mowed the lawn and took in Coney Island a couple of times), but he just left that money alone. By 1998, that initial $100 would have grown to more than three-quarters of a million dollars, thanks to time and compounding, without a single penny being added to it. Granted, very few of us are looking at a 72-year investment time frame, but this does illustrate how powerful a catalyst time can be when it comes to making your money grow.

↗ Useful Web Sites

> Want to see for yourself how compounding works and why it's such a powerful financial weapon? Check out the Power of Compounding Calculator at http://www.strong-funds.com/strong/LearningCenter/compound.htm. The calculator lets you play with various rates of return, time frames, and investment amounts so that you can see how much a certain amount of money, invested over a period of time, can grow, often substantially.

If you're sold on the value of investing over the long-term (and if the example of Gramps doesn't win you over, I'm hard pressed to think of what will), let's turn to the various ways that you can invest and, with any good fortune, reap the long-term rewards.

A Mutually Beneficial Approach

Discussing mutual funds as an adult is a lot like whispering about sex in junior high—some of us think we understand everything, most of us grasp precious little, and, above all else, no one ever, ever lets on about what they don't know. So if you fall into the massive and ever-growing army of the mutual fund–challenged, don't despair—you aren't alone. Not long ago, *Money Magazine* offered a group of investors a 20-question exercise designed to test their knowledge of mutual funds and investing. The questions weren't designed for Wall Street pros, mind you, just some basic nuts-and-bolts fundamentals about mutual funds and how they work. The result: The average score of all test participants was a bleak 51 out of a possible 100.

That doesn't mean that building a solid mutual fund portfolio boils down to a bona fide act of God. It merely illustrates an important truth—like many things in life, we all take part in things without really knowing what we're getting into. That may not mean much if you check out a show on TV that puts you to sleep in three minutes flat, but it can mean a great deal if you're talking about building your financial future. And when it comes to mutual funds, that means it's essential to learn at least a few basic ideas, principles, and guidelines. What's more, along the way, you may also unearth a few things about yourself as well.

Step one is simply understanding what mutual funds are—they're investment companies that take your money and pool it with others', investing it in stocks, bonds, and other assets. The principle at its heart is basic. Rather than your wading through the thousands of investment options for your money, well-paid money management professionals do the searching on your behalf. When you put money into a mutual fund, the fund's managers then distribute it, along with funds from thousands of other like investors, among the fund's investment choices. Those can include stocks, bonds, and Treasury bills, with a good chunk usually held in reserve as cash. The price per share of the fund—the dollar figure that you see listed in the newspaper stock pages and elsewhere—represents a composite of all those various investments.

One of the most immediate advantages to mutual fund investing is diversification. As we noted earlier, while, acting alone, you could buy only a few stocks with $500, a similar stake in a mutual fund spreads your investment over dozens of stocks, all chosen and monitored by professional money managers.

And, as we also discussed, diversification pays off, both in return and in risk reduction. While small stocks have performed exceedingly well since the Great Depression, shorter-term results are even more impressive. Over the past 20 years, growth mutual funds (funds investing in companies experiencing steady growth) have enjoyed an average annual return of 14.96%, while small-company growth funds (a slightly more aggressive type of fund) have notched a 15.74% annual return. Compare that with the return on less risky investments such as certificates of deposit (in 1998 a one-year CD paid a whopping 5% or so), and you see how the inherent risk of mutual funds can reap greater rewards.

↗ *Useful Web Sites*

A nice summary on mutual fund basics is available at <u>http://www.investaq.</u> <u>com/articles/mfund-a-basics.html</u>. The piece hits on a number of salient points we mention in the text and also goes into additional issues we'll discuss later, such as expenses, specific types of funds, and turnover rates. It also provides a great linkup to other sources of information on mutual funds, investing, and other financial topics.

Choosing a Mutual Fund

Finding a mutual fund that's a good fit for you can seem a daunting process. After all, there are literally thousands of these things floating around. And if you pick up a financial magazine in hopes of sorting through this mess, you're bombarded by a ton of fund advertisements, all touting that particular fund family's great returns and often including pictures of the fund managers, arms crossed and looking fiercely insightful. (Why fund companies think how their managers look is somehow enticing to investors remains a mystery to me.)

Instead of picking a fund by all the fabulous numbers being thrown at you, turn the process around. Start by assessing where you are and what you want to achieve with the money you're investing. Here, an old maxim of money remains partially true. As we discussed earlier, the younger you are and the longer you have to invest, the more aggressive you can afford to be with your decision; again, the power of time to smooth out volatility is that much more in your favor. So if you're single and just turned 20, you can look at funds that are a good deal more aggressive than can, say, a 35-year-old who's married with three kids.

But don't lose sight of your goals, something that may have little to do with your age. Simply put, what do you want to do with the money once you need it? Buy a house? Use it for retirement? Take a once-in-a-lifetime vacation? Each of these targets has a decidedly different time frame, which, in turn, dictates what sort of investment best fits. Again, the further away the goal, the more aggressive you can afford to be.

Equally important is your own psychology. You can hear every argument about diversification, time frame, and volatility until your head is ready to explode, but the fact remains that you have to be comfortable with the decisions that you make. Never, ever make any sort of financial decision that rubs you the wrong way. First off, it's impractical. If you're not brutally honest about what sort of fund you'll be comfortable with, you may be working against your best interests. To illustrate: In the early 1970s, investing $10,000 in an aggressive growth fund may have seemed a horrific choice. Chances are you would have lost half that money during that decade. But that same $10,000, if you had allowed it to stay in the fund, would probably be worth more than $150,000 today. The question is, would you have been able to stick with the fund long enough to ride out the rough spots? If your answer is no, that's a pretty good argument for looking at funds that are not as prone to those sorts of ups and downs—you're more likely to stand by them.

The second reason not to choose a fund that doesn't match your emotional makeup is that the stress simply isn't worth it. If there's anything I'd like to get across with this book, it's this: However important informed and sensible money habits can be, they are not the end-all to life. Handling money is a tough enough job sometimes without losing sleep because you're investing in a fund whose highs and lows are driving you nuts. An extra point or two of return is too costly when it comes at the expense of worry. Go with a more stable choice and chill out.

That being said, here's a rundown of the some major types of stock mutual funds from which you'll be able to choose, along with a few suggestions of which ones fit various sorts of situations. Bear in mind, however, that mutual fund names are rather mercurial. Fund families can slap almost any sort of name on a fund, whether or not it accurately reflects how the fund works. Although we'll be discussing various categories of funds, it's essential that you go beyond mere names to investigate a fund before investing, as its name may be misleading. More on this later:

▶ *Aggressive Growth Funds.* If you liken mutual funds to cars, these would be the Formula One models. They're high-powered and can achieve great results but are also the most prone to breakdowns. Aggressive growth funds generally invest in stocks from companies that really have a chance to take off, such as small companies that are developing products and services that, the management hopes, will be in great demand in the future. The downside, not surprisingly, is that aggressive growth funds are generally the most volatile of all types of funds. Since they're putting their money into companies that may succeed big-time or fail just as spectacularly, they tend to rise and fall in price with just as much bravado.

Good Fit: Investors who are taking a long-term perspective with their money. While these funds take a sort of "come home with your shield or on it" approach, they can be the biggest winners, provided you're willing to stick with them over the long haul. They make a great choice for young investors for something such as an IRA or other retirement account.

Bad Fit: Investors with a shorter time frame—say, someone trying to piece together a house down payment in the next five years—should steer clear of these. That amount of time simply isn't long enough to smooth out the bumps. Likewise for investors who don't have the stomach for what can prove a rough ride—again, if things get too crazy and you sell out, all you're doing is working against yourself.

▶ *Growth Funds.* These are like aggressive growth funds but with a bit less adrenaline pumping through their veins. Like aggressive funds, these funds are looking for growth opportunities, but they tend to go with more stable, established companies that, while showing plenty of potential for further growth, have more of a track record in place. Growth funds' returns may not be as high as those achieved by some aggressive funds, but the fall off the cliff isn't so steep if things go sour.

Good Fit: These funds are a solid choice for long-term growth, even with their slightly more conservative bent. They're particularly suited to investors who want long-term growth potential but haven't the stomach for the wild ride proffered by more aggressive funds.

Bad Fit: More stable they may be, but growth funds do carry a fair degree of risk. So these aren't the gig of choice for investors who are skittish about any sort of risk.

▶ Index Funds. This is an interesting type of fund that has attracted a good deal of attention of late, positive as well as critical. You may see them as stable, long-term winners or as underachievers by design, depending on your perspective. Index funds try to match the rate of return of major indices, such as the Dow Jones Industrials. So, for instance, if the Dow is earning 10% a year, an index fund manager will select a portfolio of Dow Jones stocks designed to match that return.

Good Fit: This is a great choice if you'd be satisfied with matching how major barometers of the market are doing (in addition to the Dow Jones, there are a number of other index funds which track and mirror other indices). There are certainly worse places to put your money, what with the way major indices have performed in 1998 and 1999. In fact, in recent years, index funds as a group have outperformed other types of funds, which argues for going with the flow rather than buying and selling a great deal in hopes of beating the rest of the market. Another plus—since index funds tend to buy and hold more than other funds, they also have lower operating expenses, which puts more of their returns in your pocket.

Bad Fit: Many investors and financial pros argue that it's absurd to just match what the overall market is doing—why not try doing better? There are plenty of funds that are doing just that. So if you fall into that category or are simply more aggressive by nature, an index fund may drive you up a wall. And, in down markets, index funds will likely follow the tide and drop as well. By contrast, other sorts of mutual funds may be able to buck the downward trend.

▶ *International Funds.* These funds, like index funds, have gotten a lot of attention of late, primarily because, as the U.S. stock markets continue to hit dizzying heights, investors are looking to other places to invest where a lot of upside potential exists. Basically, international funds invest in companies that are located outside the United States. Some funds may pay attention to companies in so-called emerging growth areas (countries that, while historically underdeveloped, are beginning to advance economically), while others may also mix in bonds from overseas companies and governments.

Good Fit: International funds may well be an aggressive investor's Mecca. Many are highly speculative and promise substantial returns, given that many such developing companies and regions are forecast to experience remarkable growth. Best if used for long-term holding in hopes of riding out volatility, particularly when balanced with more stable funds.

Bad Fit: The conservative investor's nightmare. While the return potential may be super, so are the risks. For instance, political instability such as the potential overthrow of the ruling government isn't exactly a day-to-day concern for most U.S. companies. In contrast, for many foreign companies, who happens to be running the political show on that particular day is a very real issue. Add economic uncertainty to political, and your international fund may offer you one wild ride. Not for the timid.

▶ *Growth and Income Funds.* These are something of a hybrid. On the one hand, such funds usually invest in growth companies, mirroring the aggressive philosophy of the first four funds we've discussed. However, growth and income funds also put a portion of their money into more stable investments, such as established stocks that pay a large dividend (these are income paid by investments, which investors can reinvest or take from a fund in the form of cash). In that sense, the funds can also be a more conservative source of regular income.

Good Fit: G and I funds are, overall, definitely more conservative than the other funds we've covered. In that sense, they're suitable for investors who worry about losing money and prefer to avoid taking extreme risks in hopes of landing a big return. These funds can also provide a nice balance when mixed with more aggressive types of funds.

Bad Fit: Not for the investor who's willing to risk some volatility. And a mix solely of growth and income funds may be simply too conservative for the investor with a long-term outlook. With a big chunk of time, many investors can afford to be more risky.

▶ *Sector Funds.* These funds invest in stocks within a particular industry or economic sector, such as high technology, health care, or utilities. By concentrating their stock purchases, sector-fund managers hope to score big if the industry as a whole does well. But the opposite side of the coin is equally true. Should an industry fare poorly or be out of favor with the investment community, sector funds can take a big hit.

Good Fit: Sector funds are akin to hopping a ride on a bucking bronco. If you stay aboard, you can score big points, but there's an equal chance of your being tossed off and landing on your butt. Sector funds are suited to investors who are willing to ride out the ups and downs, particularly if they offset sector funds' risk with more stable types of funds.

Bad Fit: Just about everybody else. Many financial pros argue that sector funds contradict the basic principle of diversification by sticking to one industry. Others contend that the only investors who belong in sector funds are people with a firsthand knowledge of the sector the fund is investing in, such as a banker who invests in a financial services fund. If you don't know an industry backward and forward, some say, investing in a sector fund is little more than a crapshoot

Needless to say, there are many more types of mutual funds, but this gives you a basic overview of some of the major players. Most of the other mutual funds you'll encounter will likely be some sort of subsection of these broad categories.

Going Green

One last mutual fund category that's worth a word or two is known as socially responsible mutual funds. This is a rather mercurial term that, in general terms, means that such funds invest in socially responsible companies while avoiding others with activities in nuclear power, tobacco, liquor, gambling, defense-related operations, and other controversial areas. For those who like to see their values reflected in their choice of investments, socially responsible funds can be a suitable match.

Needless to say, while you can select a fund according to the types of investments it chooses as well as the ones it avoids, it also pays to look at overall performance. Like any other type of fund, socially responsible funds have their solid performers as well as their dogs (in fact, the line for years has been that so-called green funds can't possibly perform as well as conventional funds, given that they avoid "bad" companies that are top performers, although this thinking has softened of late). Moreover, pay attention to the stocks a fund selects, as one person's view of socially responsible will differ from another's. Finally, bear in mind that, since these funds remain relatively small, it's likely they will cost you more to invest in than other types of funds.

A great place on the Web to familiarize yourself with socially responsible investing is The Green Money On-Line Guide (http://www.green-money.com/index.htm). There, you can browse through articles published in the Green Money Journal, a quarterly magazine promoting socially responsible investing; a green money bookstore, and a list of green fund families. The site also provides a chart detailing performance, expenses, and other data from major socially responsible mutual funds.

Choose!

Now that you're acquainted with some of the major types of funds and have an idea of what sorts of funds match certain kinds of situations, we can now look at strategies for selecting particular funds. This involves several steps, all of which should be taken into consideration when choosing a fund or funds.

To get your feet wet, start by picking up a mutual fund guide that's published on a regular basis by any number of financial publications (*Money Magazine,* for instance, regularly publishes an exhaustive overview of mutual funds). Such guides often offer tables providing detailed information on thousands of mutual funds. In particular, mutual fund guides usually offer results of top performers in various types of mutual funds. Look at how the best in the bunch have done, particularly over at least a 10-year period (by comparison, don't pay a whole lot of attention to the high flyers that have scored best over the past year, let alone last month, as some pubs also list. That's much too short a time frame to be indicative of anything.) If the guide assigns some sort of risk rating to a fund (or shows how the fund performs in down markets), note those as well. Acquaint yourself with the names of funds that, on the surface, seem attractive, bearing in mind what sort of investments goals you have, what sort of comfort level you have, and other factors we talked about earlier in this chapter.

From there, you can take one of two steps. One choice is calling the company that manages a fund that seems interesting (many fund guides provide an 800 number for this purpose. If they don't, call 800 information at 1-800-555-1212. Almost all fund families have 800 numbers that you can call to request information.) Ask them to mail you a prospectus. These are documents that all funds, by law, are required to compile and make available to anyone who asks for them. They provide information such as the fund's investment goals, performance track record, operating expenses, and a description of what sort of investments the fund is putting its money into.

↗ Useful Web Sites

Don't overlook the Internet if you want a prospectus on a particular mutual fund. For instance, you can download any number of the hundreds of Fidelity funds at the company's Web site (http://www.fidelity.com). Likewise, the fund family T. Rowe Price (www.troweprice.com) has a handy selection page that lists all the company's funds. From there, you can either download the prospectuses directly or complete an online form to have them mailed to you.

Many investment guides say it's an absolute must to read a prospectus. I agree, but only to a point. For one thing, many are as boring as the day is long—lots of details about how the fund is run and other bits of information presented in a bone-dry format that will likely cure the most diehard insomniac. However, there are some things in a prospectus that are worth paying attention to, such as the fund's performance. Look hard at these numbers, particularly the long-term stats. Have a look at what the fund is investing in. If you're like many investors, there are certain types of companies you'd rather not invest in, whether for philosophical reasons or because you have firsthand knowledge that the company's products are awful. (If this is of particular concern to you, ask for an annual or semiannual report when you request the prospectus. These will give you a more current list of where the fund is putting its money.)

Then check the expense table, which details how much it will cost to invest in the fund. Watch for sales loads (how much it costs to buy shares), redemption fees (what it costs to get your money out), management costs, and other expenses. Once you've reviewed the costs individually, see what they add up to, then subtract that from those marvelous performance numbers to see what you really earn (this figure is known as return net of fees). As a general rule, bypass funds whose overall expenses exceed 1% (a fund's expenses are expressed as a percentage of your investment)—there are plenty of top-performing funds whose expenses are a good deal lower than that.

There are four other areas in a prospectus that are also worth at least a glance:

▶ Check the portfolio turnover rate, which is also included on the financial highlights table. Expressed as a percentage of the overall portfolio, this shows how much trading has occurred in the fund. A high figure—some funds' turnover can run 200% and even higher—shows that the fund manager is busy moving things around. Not only can that increase the fund's volatility, but high turnover means greater operating expenses and tax liability.

▶ Give the investment objectives section a read. This outlines how the fund operates. Some funds may be growth oriented, while others focus on protecting current value. Be sure the fund's objectives match your own. A companion section, known as investment policies, shows how the fund tries to reach its goals. This section identifies what sorts of stocks, bonds, and fixed-income securities the fund buys and what percentage of the portfolio is allocated to various sectors. This section offers further insight on how appropriate a fund may be to your investment goals. If, for instance, you want conservative growth and the fund is buying every international stock in sight, you're better off looking for another fund.

▶ Finally, check out the investment risks section. This provides greater detail on what the fund is trying to achieve and the risks those investment choices can encounter. Again, read this with your investment goals and timeframe in mind.

There are other (and for many folks, far better) places to research mutual funds. One name you should familiarize yourself with is Morningstar, a Chicago-based research and publication organization that tracks thousands of mutual funds. In the old days, if you wanted to see a Morningstar report on a particular fund, you had to subscribe to the service or know a friendly stockbroker or planner who could pass along the report to you. Now, all you need to do is visit the company's Internet Web site (www. morningstar. net) to gain firsthand access to precisely the same sort of critical information and analysis.

In particular, pay attention to Morningstar's "Quicktake" reports (these are touted prominently on the main page). These address many of the criteria that any prudent investor should take into account when considering a mutual fund. For an extra charge, you can also buy "on demand" reports that offer additional detail and analysis. Search out the following information whether using Morningstar or any other information source:

> *Performance.* Again, look at the numbers on how the fund has done. Compare them with other similar funds. See how the fund stacks up against a major index (QuickTake does this as part of its performance overview.) One last time: Look at long-term performance, not just how the fund has done over the past year or two. The way the market has soared over the past several years, you'd have to have a state-of-the-art nincompoop running the fund not to rack up some pretty impressive numbers.

> *Fund management.* See who's running the fund and what the manager's investment philosophy is. How long has the manager been there? If he or she is new, all those hot performance numbers may not mean boo, since they were earned by another manager. Check to see if the fund is managed by one manager or a team. If it's just one person, that's fine, but what happens to the fund if that manager leaves?

> *Costs.* This is something that many investors overlook, and, not surprisingly, costs are also ignored in all those flashy

ads that tout a fund's fantastic performance. But cost is a critical consideration, because this is what you'll be paying to invest in the fund. And those costs are subtracted from whatever the fund earns on your behalf.

Morningstar's research section also lets you screen funds automatically by choosing the kind of fund you're interested in, then selecting the criterion you're looking for (total return over various periods of time, volatility, and inclusion among Morningstar's top-rated funds). The site then shows those funds that match your search guidelines. (A more involved search engine that allows you to be much more specific is available for Morningstar members. This costs $9.95 a month or $99 a year).

⤴ *Useful Web Site*

For all the data it has, one drawback to Morningstar is that its fund search engines are rather limited (unless, of course, you're willing to pay extra). As an alternative that provides a cost-free way to track down the mutual fund that best meets your needs, have a look at The Ultimate Guide to Mutual Funds (http://pathfinder.com/money/funds/). The brainchild of *Money Magazine*, this site has a search engine through which users can screen funds using up to five different selection criterion (there's also a fee-for-service arrangement that lets you track down funds using as many as 28 parameters). Type in your criterion and the system comes back with funds that match what you're looking for. The site also offers news, a handy glossary, and that infamous mutual fund quiz we talked about earlier.

Likewise, the Web site for Charles Schwab and Co. (www.schwab.com) offers One Source, an online search tool that lets you sort through hundreds of mutual funds according to the parameters you establish. You can look for funds by the types of stocks they invest in, the size of the fund, performance (you can even see performance records dating back as much as 10 years), and how much they charge. Once you've typed in what you're looking for, the system pops back with the funds that meet your specifications.

Other Fund Considerations

The next pertinent topic with mutual funds may be the financial correlative to the "heat versus humidity" debate. Basically, there are two sorts of mutual funds—loads and no-loads. A load fund levies a sales commission that is paid to a broker, financial planner, or someone else who sells you the fund. Loads can be as low as 3% but can jump all the way up to 8% and even higher. Not only can that prove a substantial expense in and of itself, but bear in mind too that there are additional fund expenses that must also be taken into account. By comparison, a no-load fund levies no sales charge for buying shares in the fund.

NOTE: Don't confuse loads with operating expenses. Every fund, whether a load fund or not, has annual expenses that you must pay to invest in the fund. Loads, by comparison, are costs that you pay every time you buy shares in a fund (or, in some cases, when you sell you shares. This is known as a "back load".)

Some financial pros argue that, should a load fund outperform its no-load brethren, the additional charge is worth it. However, from my perspective, it's better to stick with the no-loads. For one thing, with a load, that's merely a hole you have to dig your way out of the minute you buy into the fund. Moreover, several studies have shown that loads as a group don't outperform no-loads. Finally, there's the issue of objectivity. If a broker or planner has the choice of recommending two funds—one from which he'll get a commission, the other commission-free—it would be awfully tempting to push the load fund, human nature being what it is. Put another way, someone hawking load funds may be recommending something that's in his or her best interest, not yours—something that's rendered moot if you go with no-load funds.

⬈ Useful Web Sites

For more on the no-load versus load debate, check out the article at (http://www.investorama.com/features/piazza1.shtml). The piece, along with supplemental charts and statistics, makes a convincing case for the wisdom of sticking with no-load funds whenever possible.

Another stumbling block for many would-be investors, particularly younger ones without a whole lot of up-front cash to get started investing, is the minimum investment. Again, a glance through any one of the readily available mutual funds guides reveals some substantial minimum investments. The lowest minimum required by most funds is $500, and it's not out of the ordinary to see minimums of $10,000 and even greater.

Most fund families, however, provide a way around these minimums. Names vary from fund family to fund family, but ask about programs that allow you to get started with a minuscule starting investment. Some funds require $25 or $50, while others actually require no up-front money at all. The catch is that you have to set up an automatic withdrawal program through which the fund family withdraws a regular amount from checking, savings, or some similar type of account every month. The monthly amount can be as modest as $25.

Actually, in fairness, that's not much of a catch. One of the biggest problems all investors face once they've opened up mutual fund accounts is maintaining a steady stream of deposits into their funds; for many of us, there always seems to be some other place the money has to go. An automatic withdrawal program takes this worry out of the mix, since it keeps a regular flow of money going into a fund without your having to give it a single thought. On top of that, since you don't actually have to cut a check to make the investment, you're less likely to think it some sort of deprivation.

Not only is an automatic investment plan an easy form of financial discipline, but it also lets you take advantage of a time-tested investment principle called dollar-cost averaging. This involves systematically investing a specified amount on a regular basis. The thinking is that if you put a certain amount of money into a mutual fund and the price drops, you'll be able to buy more shares at a lower price come your next investment. If, however, you had dumped a lump sum into the fund and the price slipped, all you'd have to show for it is lower overall value. Of course, if you'd opted for a huge investment all at once and the price then shot up, you'd have made far more money than you would have through dollar-cost averaging, but this possibility strikes me as a relatively small price to pay for the added security of dollar-cost averaging.

One final consideration—while automatic programs open up investing to many people who otherwise could not come up with a sufficient starting sum, don't neglect to screen such funds as you would any other. It makes no sense to get into an inferior fund just because it has a cheap enough program. Better instead to save your money until you have enough to start with a fund that you genuinely like.

↗ Useful Web Sites

A great source of information on mutual funds is available at Mutual Funds Interactive (http://www.fundsinteractive.com/), a site run by Marla Brill, a mutual funds columnist for *The Boston Globe*. Although you can't access any tools to screen funds as you can at other sites, the site is particularly useful for the mutual fund novice, as its "Mutual Funds 101" section walks you through a number of basics. There are also columns on mutual funds (no surprise there) and a question-and-answer feature where experts help you unravel your mutual fund confusion.

Invest Wisely: An Introduction to Mutual Funds (http://www.sec.gov/consumer/inwsmf.htm) is a simple, easy-to-follow primer on what mutual funds are, what they aren't, and the varied risks they can pose. Put out by the United States Securities and Exchange Commission, the federal agency that regulates stock trading, the site gives you a very handy checklist of mutual funds dos and don'ts. It's also a great starting point to other links of interest.

Fund Spot (http://www.fundspot.com/) places particular emphasis on links to up-to-date mutual fund news and information. The site does have a modest but useful section on investing tips for mutual fund newcomers. Also handy is a message board to chat with other investors.

Another good site for mutual fund newbies is Mutual Funds Made Simple (http://members.aol.com/plweiss1/mfunds.htm). This site offers an elementary breakdown of mutual funds, including how they work, major types of funds, and how to start figuring out which fund may be right for you. Some may find this site unduly basic, while others may feel comfortable with the simple, nuts-and-bolts focus.

> To find out more about all types of mutual funds, go to http://www.mfea.com/educidx.html. Not only does the site address almost any mutual fund available, but it's a handy link to other sources of information on topics related to mutual fund investing, including how to read a prospectus, what tax implications to consider, and even how to make heads or tails of fund listings in the business section of your newspaper.

Supplemental Real-Life Interlude

I hear you: "All this stuff about investing sounds great, but where am I supposed to find the money to do it?" If investing does intrigue you but you doubt you have sufficient funds, here are a few ideas that may help you free up some extra cash to start your investment program:

▶ *Pay yourself first.* This is a financial maxim you may have heard before, but it bears repeating. Simply put, put yourself at the top of the list when you're planning on paying bills. If you want to earmark $25 a month to start with a mutual fund, try paying that before you get to the phone or cable television bill. Not only does that put your investment program at the top of your priorities, but it also instills a sense of discipline with your other payments—if you have only so much money to go around, you'd be surprised how often you make ends meet. And, if you come up short, consider some other ideas to save even more money, such as:

▶ *Brown bag it.* Say you eat lunch out an average of eight times a month at an average cost of, say, seven bucks a pop. Add to that four dinners out at $20 a go. Between the two, that comes to $136. I'm not suggesting that you become a hermit, huddled at home every day and night poking a fork into a cold can of Spaghettios, but consider cutting your eating out by half. Not only does that keep your social activity at a reasonable level, but it also frees up nearly $70 that you could be investing. Not a bad compromise.

▶ *Empty your pockets.* Laugh if you will, but this is something I've done for years. At the end of the day, I have a large glass jar where, as a matter of thoughtless habit, I empty whatever change I have in my pockets. It may seem a matter of nickels and dimes, but you'd be amazed how fast your change can add up once you starting dropping it in the same place. For instance, last time I emptied the jar I use, the total came to nearly $80 after only a couple of months. That, too, can be money you can designate for investing.

▶ *Cut your credit card costs.* As we talked about in the preceding chapter, carrying a card with an 18% interest rate (even a really "cool" one that tosses 3% cash back at you) can drain you. Try to find the lowest interest card you can find, and do your utmost to pay the balance down as fast as possible. That could save you hundreds a year in interest costs.

▶ *Cut your housing costs.* We'll go into this more in Chapter 6, but, if you live in an area where rents are high, consider bringing in a roommate to cut your housing costs. You may sacrifice some privacy, but you can easily pocket thousands in savings every year.

▶ Remember that it doesn't take much to get started. Investing is not just for Daddy Warbucks and the fat little man on the Monopoly cards. Put another way, you don't have to be rich to invest. As we discussed in this chapter, you can get started with next to nothing. So every little bit of extra savings that you can piece together can make a very big difference in the long run.

↗ *Useful Web Sites*

WFLA television in Tampa, Florida, has posted a great list of 101 often overlooked ways to save money. Some are a little obvious, some a bit quirky, but the list is certainly worth a peek at http://www.wfla.com/indepth/5.htm.

Now That You're Up and Running...

How many funds should a good portfolio contain? Here, the pros part ways. Some believe it's virtually impossible to overdiversify, while others argue that even a single fund by its very makeup can provide adequate diversity. For me, something of a middle course seems the best choice for newcomers. Two or three funds are probably a reasonable starting point—if you can't swing that, at least get started with one. Again, craft your portfolio to reflect what investment goal or goals you may have—if your target is retirement or some other long-term objective, maybe a growth or aggressive growth fund offset by a more conservative choice such as an index fund. If you expect to be getting into several different funds over the course of time, look at funds that are in the same company; that way, should you decide to move your money later, you can usually switch between funds for free.

Now that your money is in one or more funds, here's a tip that may save your sanity: As tempting as it may be, don't obsess over your funds' performance. Try not to look at the stock pages every day and, if you can't resist, don't hyperventilate if your funds drop in value—remember, you're in this for the long haul. And, don't necessarily dump a fund whose performance seems consistently disappointing; instead, find out why a fund is doing poorly. If, on one hand, the market has turned against the kinds of stocks the fund owns and other similar funds are also lagging, that may not be cause for panic. However, should the fund underperform its peers or you discover a key manager has jumped ship, that may warrant some changes.

↗ Useful Web Sites

Now that we've gone through some basics about mutual funds and ways to get started with investing, here's a sampling of some more Web sites that provide news, information, research, and a host of other goodies for the informed investor. As time permits, give each one a look:

Combining ongoing business and financial news with a variety of timely features and functions, Money.Com (www.money.com), the online counterpart of *Money Magazine,* offers an extensive array of information and assistance to consumers and investors. While the Web site's heart may be its news service, offering up-to-date stock market information, a financial feature story that's updated daily, and recent *Money* articles, the site augments the print magazine by providing tools and features for various types of financial planning, such as saving for retirement or college, and information on the best savings and borrowing deals. There are even online calculators that let users figure out what works best for them. Money.com also provides visitors with bulletin boards for questions on specific financial topics.

—Wait. Don't assume the *Wall Street Journal*'s interactive edition (www.wsj.com) is some stuffy financial fish wrap read only by corporate raiders and old men half-asleep in leather chairs. The fact is that the *Journal* is a fantastic source of news, analysis, and information for the investment new-comer, as there are a lot of nuts-and-bolts stories on the basics of money management and investing. The site also lets you search through back issues on topics that interest you. Cost is $49 a year ($29 if you already subscribe to the print edition), which also lets you access *Barron's* and *Smart Money*'s online editions. Finally, don't overlook the *Journal* as a superb general news source, covering national and international goings-on, sports, and the arts. In fact, some of the very best feature stories—many of which don't have the slightest connection to money or investing—appear every day in the *Journal*.

It may sound like a kid's show, but Invest-O-Rama (www. investorama.com) may well be the single best jumping-off point for all sorts of financial information available on the Web. Run by Douglas Ger-lach, the site puts you in touch with news, tools, analysis, reports, chats—you name it, it's likely there, more than 7,000 links in total. If you're inter-ested in tracking down a site that addresses a particular question or con-cern, there's no better place to start your expedition.

From there, investors searching for a jumping off point for a variety of research services need look no further than Wall Street Research Net (www.wsrn.com). The site has thousands of links to help investors perform fun-damental research on actively traded companies and mutual funds. The site offers easy access to financial information, including charts and earnings fore-casts. One special feature is QuickSearch, which allows the user to enter various performance criteria; the system then pops up detailed reports on companies that match those parameters. Wall Street Research Net also provides links to press releases, research publications, and a rash of economic news and analysis.

Yahoo's Financial Center (www.quote.yahoo.com) offers an array of links to news, research, and reference sources. You can get news head-lines, chat rooms, and free quotes for stock and mutual funds. In partic-ular, the site also provides links to more information- and education-related sites, such as a number of areas that address common questions and issues about choosing the mutual fund that's right for you. Again, a great starting-off point that can put you in touch with a variety of infor-mation sources, provided you're willing to take some time and explore.

CHAPTER 4

Other Ways to Invest

Now that you've got a working knowledge of stock mutual funds and how they can get you started with investing, we can shift gears to look at other places to put your money and when it makes sense to do so.

However, bear in mind a significant prejudice of mine as we proceed. I am a firm believer in the idea that young investors (that takes in a broad spectrum of people, by the way) should put the lion's share of their available investment dollars into stock mutual funds. The reason, as we've said previously, is that stock funds offer the best chance for the best possible return, hands down—particularly if you're looking at an investment timeline that spans decades. They may go down for a time, but over the long haul they tend to go up, much more so than any other investment around. There just isn't a better spot to stash your long-term bucks, and statistics bear this out.

But there are other types of investments that meet particular needs that stock mutual funds can't address. Moreover, as we've repeated ad nauseam, there's a decided advantage to spreading out your investments, even if that sphere extends beyond the stock market. And there are many of us who just aren't comfortable with the volatility of the stock market. So, having been up front about my little monetary bigotry, let's get to some other types of investments.

Government Securities

This category takes in various forms of investments offered by the federal government. They include one thing you may already know—the good old U.S. savings bond. Others include such investments as Treasury bills and Treasury notes, all of which offer various types of returns. In so many words, government securities are IOUs to the federal government—you lend it some money for a period of time, and it repays you with interest.

The nice thing about this arrangement is that it offers a great deal of flexibility. For instance, you can buy a Treasury bill that you can cash in as fast as three months; by the same token, there are Treasury bonds that you can hold onto for as long as 30 years. Another thing—unlike most other types of investments, government securities are guaranteed by the federal government, so there's virtually no chance whatsoever of your losing money.

Unfortunately, there is the inevitable downside. Returns from government securities are rather, shall we say, diminutive. For instance, as of this writing, a one-year Treasury bill is paying roughly 4.5%. A 30-year Treasury bond isn't faring much better at about 5%. (These returns, by the way, are free of state and local taxes but not federal.)

There are potential headaches even with savings bonds, long the gift of choice for graduates. The most commonly known savings bond is the Series EE, which you buy at half the "face value" (for instance, you pay $50 for a $100 bond). You can hang onto these for up to 30 years, and they accrue interest (as of this writing, a bit more than 5%—again, not absolutely dreadful, but nothing to write home about, either).

Although savings bonds can be effective for long-term savings, just how much you get out of them is predicated on how long you hang onto them. For instance, you can cash in a savings bond after only six months, but you'll get only half the face value, plus any interest. Things don't get a whole lot better if you wait a bit longer—as an example, a $100 bond bought in January 1996 would bring you only $57 if you cashed it in three years later. In fact, to have a $100 EE bond reach face value in February 1999, you would have had to buy it back in February 1987—a full 12 years' wait.

My feeling about these kinds of investments is that they can be a good place for your savings—they certainly beat savings account returns hands down. And they're certainly a suitable choice for an ultraconservative investor who doesn't want to run the least bit of risk. Moreover, particularly with savings bonds, they can be convenient to buy (if you're working, there's a chance your employer may offer an automatic payroll deduction plan to buy savings bonds). And for a short-term place to park money that you plan to invest somewhere else, Treasury bills are a nice choice.

But bear in mind that all these investments pay out rather modest returns (all the more so if you factor in inflation). And, with savings bonds, you can end up in the tank if you're not prepared to stick with them for a good long while. So, even though they may have a place as an adjunct spot for a portion of your money, there are better places to put the lion's share of your bucks, particularly if you're young with a long investment horizon.

➚ Useful Web Sites

Bonds Online (www.bondsonline.com) is a great one-stop place to learn about all types of bonds, including Treasuries and savings bonds. You can get information on how much these investments are currently paying and how to go about buying them.

If your particular interest runs to U.S. savings bonds, check out U.S. Savings Bonds Online at http://www.publicdebt.treas.gov/sav/sav.htm. The site also has information on the new Series I savings bond, whose interest is adjusted to compensate for inflation.

Have a savings bond stashed away somewhere and want to know how much it's worth? Go to http://www.ny.frb.org/pihome/svg_bnds/sb_val.html, an online calculator that lets you figure the value of U.S. savings bonds. Just enter the type of bond, the amount, and when you bought it, and the calculator gives you the cash-in value for the next six months.

Municipal and Corporate Bonds

Remember when as a kid you borrowed a quarter from your brother, and, on penalty of death, he made you scribble out an IOU just to make sure you didn't conveniently forget the debt? Well, as we mentioned earlier in the portion on government securities, that's what a bond is (short of the death threat, of course). Companies and government agencies issue bonds as a means of borrowing money. The bonds specify a certain interest rate and maturity (this is the time when the loan comes due and the money you gave the borrower is returned to you.) The general rule of thumb is, the longer the maturity, the more the bond will pay you.

↗ Useful Web Sites

The Vanguard fund family has put together a nice tutorial on bonds, covering basic definitions, the various types of bonds, and the varied risks and rewards that come from investing in them. The starting point for the bond section is at http://www.vanguard.com/educ/module1/m1_3_2.html.

Not surprisingly, there are all types of bonds. As we noted in the preceding section, the government has been issuing savings bonds for years. Another sort of bond put out by the feds is known as zero coupon treasuries or STRIPS, which you buy at a deep discount, receiving their full value (plus interest) only when you cash them in at maturity. Yet a third government-issued type of bond is called a municipal bond. Issued by states and local governments, often to finance projects such as road repair and bridge building, the big plus to municipal bonds is that all your earnings are free from federal taxes.

↗ Useful Web Sites

Here are a couple additional Web sites that go into various types of bonds: The Vanguard site listed above (http://www.vanguard.com/educ/module1/m1_3_2.html) offers a nice primer into zero coupon bonds, doing a particularly good job of explaining how they work and, as we'll discuss later, how interest rates can hurt their returns.

T. Rowe Price provides a handy introduction to municipal bonds at http://www.troweprice.com/mutual/insights/. In fact, the site's creators are to be applauded; even though the purpose of many such sites is to entice your interest in a particular kind of investment, this site is objective enough to mention (as we will later in the chapter) that munis are generally not a good idea for investors in lower tax brackets.

Then there are bonds issued by companies. Known as corporate bonds, these range from very secure bonds offered by stable conglomerates to so-called junk bonds (remember the name Mike Milken? Junk bonds were his stock in trade, pardon the pun). Unlike stable bonds, junk bonds have a high risk of default; that means that the company that issued the bond has gone into the tank, taking with it its ability to pay on the bond you own. Not a pleasant picture by any means.

One way to gauge the risk of corporate and municipal bonds is to find out the issuer's credit rating. This, represented by a letter grade and/or a number, represents an evaluation of the security of the business or government agency issuing the bond. The general rule is, the higher the rating, the greater the likelihood that the issuer of your bond is going to be around to pay you back. For instance, the highest rated bonds—hence, the safest—are given at least an A rating (even safer bonds earn ratings of AA and even higher). The next ranking is B or a combination of multiple Bs; bonds so rated are a bit more speculative. From there, the ranking drops into the Cs, made up of bonds with the greatest likelihood of default. As a rule, bonds with more speculative rankings can offer greater paybacks to investors than more secure bonds. The downside is that there's a greater chance that the issuer may default, taking your investment with it.

↗ Useful Web Sites

If you're interested in looking up the rating of a particular bond—or just want to find out more about bonds in general—two excellent Web sites are Moodys (www.moodys.com) and Standard and Poors (www.standard poor.com). These are the two largest and best-known companies that assign bond credit ratings.

Another risk you take with bonds involves interest rates. Simply put, if interest rates go up (meaning the cost of borrowing becomes more expensive), existing bonds are worth less. Why? Because, if you're holding a bond paying 8% and interest rates jump, creating new bonds that pay 9%, your old bond is worth less because it pays a lower rate of return. That means that, should you try to sell the bond, you'll get less than what you expected. However, the good news is the reverse—should interest rates go down while you own a bond, its value will increase, since the new ones coming out can't match the interest yours is paying.

↗ *Useful Web Sites*

A somewhat academic—but comprehensive and easy-to-follow—explanation of how interest rates affect bonds can be found at http://www.cis.ohio state.edu/hypertext/faq/usenet/investment-faq/general/part3/faq-doc-5.html. The page even offers a mathematical formula—for those who are interested— that walks you through the impact of changing interest rates.

A final aspect to consider when looking at bonds is how long they have until they mature, which means when you get your money back. Basically, bonds that have a short-term maturity (say, up to 10 years) will not drop in value as much if interest rates go up than will those with longer terms, up to 30 years. The reason is simple. If interest rates go up, their effect on short-term bonds will not be as great because you're not going to hold them for that long. That also means interest rate fluctuations are much more destructive to the value of long-term bonds (that's one reason why long-term bonds pay more than short term—you're taking a bigger risk with interest rates).

Stocks and Bonds—Different Investment, Same Caveat

Before we tackle where, if anywhere, bonds may fit into your financial plan, know up front that I treat bonds as I do individual stocks. I believe that, with very few exceptions, most investors (particularly newcomers) are far better off in mutual funds. Like stocks, bonds come in a variety of mutual funds, offering many of the same advantages that stock funds provide—professional management, diversification (unlike many individuals, bond funds have the wherewithal to invest in all types of bonds simultaneously, including corporate, government, and even junk bonds), and research and analysis far beyond the reach of most mortal investors, among other pluses. So, when we're talking bonds, we're talking bond funds.

↗ Useful Web Sites

For more information on the mechanics and advantages of various types of bond funds, have a look at Templeton's Web site (http://www.franklin-templeton.com/public/education/bond_mutual/bond_mutual.htm.)

Just Where Do They Fit?

Just where a bond fund might work in your own financial picture depends, as does just about everything else, on you and on what you hope to achieve. Remember, historically speaking, bonds just don't provide the same kinds of returns as stocks do, so if you're talking about money that's going to be invested for a long period of time, a stock mutual fund offers you the best opportunity for the biggest payback.

That being said, however, there are some instances where a bond fund works. For instance, if you're somewhat conservative, you may want to earmark a certain portion of your investment dollars for a bond fund. Not only are they, as a group, less volatile than stocks, but bonds tend to move in the opposite direction of stocks—when stocks go down, bonds tend to move up, and vice versa. (Needless to say, this isn't always the case, but it does happen). So, in that sense, a bond fund can augment stock mutual funds nicely by providing some diversification.

There are also other scenarios where a bond fund fits the bill. For instance, if you're planning on buying a house or car in, say, three years, you may want to stash the money in a short-term bond fund. It may not pay as well as a stock fund, but it will be less vulnerable to losses (not to mention the fact that the return will beat savings accounts hands down). For myself, since I'm self-employed and have to set aside a certain portion of my income for taxes, I use a short-term bond fund—again, it fluctuates a little, but, overall, the return is better than what I can get elsewhere. Finally, since bond funds pay dividends monthly, they can also be useful if, for whatever reason, you need a regular flow of money to supplement your regular income.

Just how much of your portfolio should be in bonds is also a matter of personal preference. Forget those formulas that say you should allocate so much of your money to bonds depending on your age, and instead look at what you have and what you want to achieve. If you have a couple of solid stock mutual funds in place and think it's time to diversify a bit to lower your risk, it's perfectly fine to look into a bond fund. And, as we mentioned earlier, if you have a short-term goal that's not suited to the ups and downs of a stock fund, that, too, can argue for a bond fund.

➚ Useful Web Sites

A nice primer on bonds and how they can fit into your overall portfolio is available at http://www.prusec.com/whyfi.htm.

How to Bond with a Bond Fund

Selecting the proper bond fund is, in many ways, very similar to choosing the right stock mutual fund. You can obtain a prospectus and an annual report; you can also access such services as Morningstar to get the lowdown on bond funds. However you go about it, here are some shopping tips to bear in mind:

> ▶ *Stick with no-loads.* Like stock funds, bond funds come in two types—those sold by someone who gets a commission for the sale and no-load funds that don't cost you a dime up front. Go with the no-loads; you'll save money right off the bat.

▶ *Look at long-term performance.* Again, as with stock funds, check out fund guides like *Money Magazine's* fund roundup to see which funds are the best performers. If you're looking to sink your money into a fund for at least a few years, pay particular attention to the fund's long-term return record—no shorter than, say, five years.

If you want to look at performance in greater detail, look at the fund's yield as well as its total return. Yield is the amount of compounded monthly dividends that the fund pays out to its investors; couple that with price movement (whether the fund's price went up or down in reaction to interest rates) and you get the fund's total return.

▶ *Check out expenses.* As you did with stock mutual funds, look at how much you'll be paying for the privilege of giving the fund your business. As a general rule, it's hard to justify investing in a bond fund that charges more than 1% of your investment.

▶ *Review the maturities of the bonds in the fund.* Knowing the maturities gives you an excellent idea of just how the fund will react to interest rate movements. If, for instance, the fund has lots of bonds that have a short-term maturity (say, in the neighborhood of five to ten years), the fund will not react as badly to interest rate increases as will a fund that's heavy in long-term maturity. For a quick take on the overall maturity of bonds in a fund, keep an eye peeled for weighted average maturity—this stat is the average of all the bonds in the fund.

▶ *Look at the minimum investment.* Again, as with a stock mutual fund, different sorts of bond funds require different minimums to get started. Some require as little as $100, while others mandate a whopping $25,000. But, like stock mutual funds, bond funds are available via automatic investment programs. At the Putnam family of funds, for instance, you can invest in any of their bond funds with $25 up front and as little as $25 a month withdrawn automatically from a checking or savings account. So, if a bond fund or family interests you, call its 800 number and see what it offers to help you get started on the cheap.

One Mistake Never to Make with Bonds

One final word about bonds. Although bond funds do serve a useful purpose for many investors, there's one type of bond that, almost without exception, younger investors should avoid: municipal bonds and funds that invest heavily in them. As we discussed earlier, muni bonds are issued by the government to finance things such as road construction, bridge building, and other similar projects. And, since you're doing your civic duty by dropping your hard-earned dollars into them, munis are freed from federal and, depending on where you live, state and local taxes.

Although the notion of a completely tax-free investment may set your eyes spinning like pinwheels, think again. Chances are, there are much, much better places to put your money. The reason is that many of us simply don't have a large enough income to make the tax-free return from munis worthwhile.

The way to tell that involves a simple equation. Take the tax-free yield of a municipal bond or fund and divide it by one minus your tax bracket. For instance, for a muni fund yielding 7%, the taxable equivalent yield for someone in the 15% tax bracket would be 8.23% (7 divided by .85). The message is simple: Find something that can beat 8.23%, and you're better off in the long run, regardless of the fact that the investment is taxed. And, given the way the stock market has performed over, say, the past 70 years or so, that shouldn't be too darned hard to find.

The short message: Unless you're already making scads of money or have inherited a goodly enough pile to push you into the stratosphere of tax brackets, tax-free municipal bonds really don't pay off. Find something like a good stock fund, take the tax hit, and you'll likely come out ahead in the long run.

Real-Life Interlude

Lest you think I, your beloved money mentor, am bereft of financial miscues, ponder this:

When I first began investing (the result of a small inheritance from my parents), a financial planner convinced me to sink $10,000 into a municipal bond fund. The carrot was its tax-free status—every penny I earned was mine, all mine. For a couple of years, I would eagerly read the monthly statement I got from the fund, tallying up the dividend I got every month that the feds could never get their mitts on. And the longer I held the fund, the bigger the payout got, however modestly.

Several years later, I hooked up with another financial planner, who promptly pointed out the muni fund.

"What are you doing in this?" he asked.

"Isn't that great?" I bleated with pride. "All that—not a penny in tax!"

Not so great. Since, at the time I was single and earning, shall we say, a modest income as a writer, I was happily ensconced in the 15% tax bracket. That, my new planner pointed out with all the delicacy he could muster, amounted to something less than common sense. Working out the formula, he showed me that the 7% or so I was earning tax-free was equal to about 8.2% fully taxed. Put another way, all I had to do was find something paying 8.2% or better and I would come out ahead (which, given that this was in the days when "bad" stock mutual funds routinely turned in 15% a year or more, wasn't the equivalent of building the pyramids in terms of difficulty).

In short, my little foray in munis probably cost me thousands of dollars I could have earned elsewhere. So don't be blinded by the lure of tax-free—sometimes, a little whap from the tax paddle may actually be a good thing.

↗ Useful Web Sites

Okay, okay, there may be some of you out there who, my diatribe notwithstanding, would like to find out more about municipal bonds. Have a look at An Investor's Guide To Municipal Bonds (http://www.investinginbonds.com/info/igmunis/what.htm), which offers a nice, comprehensive overview of what munis are, their risks, and the advantages of tax-free investing (note, however, that the example the site gives in the tax pluses of muni bonds cites a couple in the 36% tax bracket pulling down $150,000 a year. We should all be in that sort of predicament).

Money Market Mutual Funds

As we mentioned in our section on Basics in Chapter 1, money market funds have it all over bank savings accounts and interest-bearing checking accounts when it comes to being a good place to stash your savings. Money market funds are, in fact, a type of mutual fund, the difference being that the price per "share" sticks at $1 and never changes. That, from a purely technical standpoint, makes money markets riskier than checking and savings accounts. For one thing, unlike checking and savings accounts, money market accounts are not guaranteed by the federal government. In addition, it's theoretically possible for a money market fund to fluctuate and, perhaps, lose some of its value.

If that worries you, relax. First off, particularly if you buy a money market from a large mutual fund company, there's virtually no chance that the fund is going to go into the tank (larger fund families have the financial wherewithal to cover any sort of shortfalls). And, while there have been instances of money markets dropping a bit in value, the fund companies have always been there to make up the difference to ensure that the $1 per share price held.

A few random calls bear out just how better off you can be with a money market. For instance, a money market fund at a large, well-known mutual fund company was paying about 5% when I happened to phone them up. By comparison, savings returns at one local bank checked in at an anemic 2.42%, with the bank's interest-bearing checking account even worse—1%, the equivalent of throwing your money into the air and hoping that it will somehow reproduce itself on the way down.

Note that with money markets (and, for that matter, certificates of deposit), you'll see a term we mentioned in the section on bonds: yield. You'll note that this number usually differs from the quoted "rate" that a fund or CD is paying. All this means is that the fund or CD is paying dividends on the money you have in it, which in turn also earns money (we touched on this in Chapter 1 in the section on compounding). Pay attention to yield when shopping for a money market fund or a CD, since it tells you what your money will actually earn in a particular investment.

As we mentioned earlier, higher overall returns make a money market fund the ideal spot to build up a reserve of emergency cash. Money market funds are also useful as a short-term layover spot for money that you intend to invest—again, that keeps your money in the highest-yielding spot for the longest amount of time while limiting what you have in checking and savings, where it's doing you no good whatsoever.

Bear in mind a few shopping tips when looking around for a money market fund. Some money markets require that any amount withdrawn from the account be of a certain minimum, often $250 or so. Other money market funds, which function more like a bank account (some, in fact, offer check-writing privileges) let you withdraw whatever amount your little heart desires. So choose a money market fund depending on what you want to use it for; if, for instance, you're going to be paying monthly bills from it, go for the no-minimum money market fund.

Like other sorts of financial products, there's also the issue of the minimum you have to put up to open up a money market account. Some fund families require you to deposit as much as several thousand dollars to get into a money market fund. However, as is the case with their other products, fund families also let you set up an automatic withdrawal program that can get you into a money market fund with nothing down and $50 or so taken automatically from an account you designate.

↗ *Useful Web Sites*

Most large mutual fund companies include information on money market mutual funds on their Web sites. Vanguard, for instance, has a handy chart comparing returns for all five of its money market funds at http://www.vanguard.com/daily/pricesyields.html#30. For a great link that can put you in touch with the Web pages of any number of funds families, point your browser to http://www.investorama.com/funds.html.

As is the case with other money topics, Vanguard has a nice tutorial on money market funds at http://www.vanguard.com/educ/module1/m1_2_0.html.

Certificates of Deposit

Maybe ten years back, there was a great ad on television that featured several types of people—a young married couple, a recently retired gentleman, and a family with about six kids—all going into a bank seeking financial advice. Naturally, each was different; one wanted retirement income, another wanted a good place to put long-term savings, and the third wanted a spot for the kids' college stash. In every instance, this gravel-voiced banker pushed a certificate across his desk toward the customer, announcing, "What you need is our supersaver CD!" I don't recall precisely what the ad was for (which, I guess, makes it not all that effective an ad) but it nonetheless has stuck with me to this day, maybe because a different version of that same mentality can be seen almost any day in the newspaper, where ad after ad touts "super" CD returns of 5% or so, as if that were some sort of financial panacea.

To be blunt, I'm not the biggest fan of certificates of deposit. Basically, all they are is a savings contract: You give us your money for a certain amount of time, and, if you don't touch it until that time is up, we'll give you back your money, plus interest. On the one hand, that may not seem all that bad—if you don't need your money for a while and want to put it into something that beats interest-bearing checking and savings accounts, CDs may, in fact, seem somewhat attractive.

Unfortunately, they're just not all that hot a spot for your money in most cases. For one thing, although CDs offer better interest rates than savings and checking-with-interest accounts, their rate of return is still nothing to write home about. In fact, it becomes even worse when you take inflation into account. For instance, if you've got money tied up in a CD paying 5% and the going rate of inflation is 3%, all you're effectively getting is a bit over 2% on your money.

On top of that, unlike money market funds, where you can withdraw money when you please, CDs obligate you to keep your money tied up for a specified amount of time (this can range from a few months up to 10 years or so.) That carries a double whammy. Should you pull your money out before time's up, you can be hit with a nasty penalty, reducing what little pay-off you may have gotten in interest in the first place. And you may be stuck with a low-paying CD if interest rates go up. For instance, if you buy a 5% CD and interest rates go up to 6, you've effectively cheated yourself out of an additional 1% interest. And, unless you're willing to pull your money out and take the penalty hit, you're stuck. Moreover, unlike money market funds, CDs often require a goodly sum for an initial investment, $500 and even more; in fact, some of the "super" returns CDs tout (which at 5% or so aren't my idea of super) mandate at least $50,000.

Don't misunderstand—all this does not make CDs the Evil Empire of the financial world. If, for instance, you know you won't need a certain amount of money for a specified amount of time and the thought of putting it into something that could drop in value makes you jumpy, there are certainly worse choices than a CD. But, for my money, it's better to go with a money market fund. The interest rates are comparable, they're easier to get into, and your money isn't held captive.

↗ Useful Web Sites

As is the case with other savings-type vehicles, the Bank Rate Monitor is an absolutely killer source for information about the best CD deals around. Just go to http://www.bankrate.com/brm/rate/high_ratehome.asp, where you can select from more than a dozen different types of CDs. The system then shows you the name of the bank or other institution offering the CD, what it's paying, minimum deposits, and even a contact telephone number.

The Better Business Bureau has a brief online primer on CDs that offers a handy review of some of the basics of CD shopping and buying. It's at http://www.bbb.org/library/cds.html.

CHAPTER 5

Who Is This Guy Ira Roth, and What Does He Want with Me?

W hile it may seem a bit outlandish to someone still in school or not very far removed, it's never too early to start thinking about your retirement. Why? Because, no matter whether you see yourself sunning on the Riviera, bouncing countless grandkids on your knee, or wearing tasteless clothes careening after a little white ball in a golf cart, your retirement is going to take money. Lots of it. And that means starting early.

To illustrate, if you're 22 years old now and living on a monthly budget of $1,600, you're going to need $893,353 in savings by the time you retire at age 65 to provide you with a comparable lifestyle. That assumes a 10% annual return on your investments. (The monthly amount needed at retirement, by the way, works out to $5,703 per month). If that strikes you as outrageous, you can thank inflation, which, as we discussed in Chapter 1, is increasing costs that erode the purchasing power of your money. And this example assumes an inflation rate of only 3% a year. Should inflation come in higher, say, 4%, you're going to need to save even more—a remarkable $1.491 million—to live the way you do now (under that scenario, you'll need $8,641 every month). On top of that, if you come from a long line of long-lived folk, you'll require even more money, since every year you live means—in pure financial terms, of course—another year whose expenses have to be met.

Real-Life Interlude

Want to see how inflation can take the wind out of your financial sails over time? Consider the lifelong house-buying predicament of one Average Joe. In 1950, A.J. decides he wants to buy a house that, at that time, costs $8,500. For the 20% down payment, he needs $1,700, but he has only $850. No problem, A.J. decides. He puts his money into a bank savings account paying 4% and bides his time.

By 1965, A.J.'s bank account has grown to $1,547, and he can throw an additional $500 into the down payment. Back to the real estate office he goes. Unfortunately, inflation has outpaced the growth in his savings. The average home price has jumped to $16,000, meaning that he now needs $3,200 to make his 20% down. Undaunted, A.J. tosses the extra $500 into the bank account still paying 4% and decides to wait things out.

Ten years pass. A. J.'s bank stash is now at $3,051, so he figures his down payment is in the bag. But more grim news awaits. Houses are now at $27,000, so A.J. is more than a couple of thousand bucks shy of the $5,400 he needs to get into that house he's coveted for a quarter century. Starting to get a bit discouraged, A.J. adds another $1,000 to his savings account and hopes for the best.

Unfortunately, the best never arrives. By 1998, at the 4% he has been getting from the bank, A.J.'s account is now worth $10,149. But the going price for homes has exploded to more than $130,000, requiring a $26,000 down payment. Thanks to the ravages of inflation—and A.J.'s unwillingness to choose a savings vehicle that stood a better chance of keeping pace—his dream of home ownership has to remain just that—a dream. So, as we pointed out in Chapter 1, bear the effects of inflation in mind when choosing where to put your money, particularly for the long term. All those wonderful "conservative, safe" places may prove to be anything but, at least in terms of reaching the goal you're trying to save for.

↗ Useful Web Sites

Money Online has a nice, easy-to–follow, yet comprehensive online calculator that lets you plug in where you are now financially and what you'll need come retirement. Even better, it also shows what elements of your overall financial plan need revamping to reach your goals. Check it out at http://cgi.pathfinder.com/cgi-bin/Money/retire.cgi.

Now that I may well have succeeded in scaring the bejeebers out of you, remember that you have a few powerful allies on your side. First is time. Again, the magic of saving over the long term, coupled with the power of compounding, can work to offset the ravages of inflation. Your other influential friends are several types of retirement savings programs that not only provide effective ways to save for your golden years but kick in some tax advantages along the way as well. (We cover employer-funded plans such as 401ks and 403-bs in Chapter 11).

IRA and You

Individual retirement accounts (IRAs) have been around for a good long while. Approved by Congress in 1981, the original version of the IRA let you contribute as much as $2,000 a year toward your retirement in a specially designated account. The original IRA also offered two sweet tax benefits—first off, everyone could deduct their IRA contributions from their taxes in the year they made the contribution, whether or not they had some sort of retirement program where they worked. And the money grew tax-deferred, meaning that contributors paid no taxes on anything their IRA accounts earned until they actually withdrew the money, which they could do penalty-free starting at age 59½. The thinking was that by the time people retired and started withdrawing the money from an IRA, their tax bite would be low, since they were no longer working and generating a taxable income.

Sound too good to be true? Well, our duly elected representatives apparently thought so. Under the guise of "tax reform"— sweeping change in the tax code that many liken to Armageddon in terms of disasters of note—Congress in 1986 repealed the original IRA in favor of a new version that imposed strict limits on tax deductibility. With Son of IRA, gone were the days when everyone could take the deduction; now, for instance, if you were single and covered by a retirement program at work, you could take the full deduction only if you made $25,000 or less. For those earning between $25,000 and $35,000 the deduction was phased out, and, if you pulled down more than $35,000, you could no longer deduct a single penny. Even though lawmakers in their insight—or oversight, depending on how you look at things—kept the full deduction for anyone who was not covered by an employer-sponsored retirement plan, the results were predictable: IRA contributions plummeted, simply because fewer people could get the tax break that formerly made IRAs such a great benefit.

Ultimately, however, Congress recognized this financial faux pas and, in 1997, took steps to correct it. For starters, they upped the income limits for deductibility, allowing the full deduction for singles making $30,000 a year or less, increasing every year until it hits $50,000 in the year 2005, even if their employer offers a retirement plan. With a comparable liberalization for married couples, estimates suggest that the new legislation opens up deductible IRAs to nearly nine out of 10 working Americans. The following chart summarizes the 1998 IRA deductibility rules for singles as well as married couples:

Income for Singles	Eligible IRA Deduction
$30,000.00	$2,000.00
31,000.00	1,800.00
32,000.00	1,600.00
33,000.00	1,400.00
34,000.00	1,200.00
35,000.00	1,000.00
36,000.00	800.00
37,000.00	600.00
38,000.00	400.00
39,000.00	200.00
40,000.00 and higher	0.00

Joint Income for Married People	Eligible IRA Deduction
$50,000.00	$2,000.00
51,000.00	1,800.00
52,000.00	1,600.00
53,000.00	1,400.00
54,000.00	1,200.00
55,000.00	1,000.00
56,000.00	800.00

57,000.00	600.00
58,000.00	400.00
59,000.00	200.00
60,000.00 and higher	0.00

↗ Useful Web Sites

> Vanguard has a great page discussing various elements of IRAs, including deductibility questions. Have a look at http://www.vanguard.com/educ/lib/retire/faqira.html.

In its largesse, your Congress didn't stop there. It also unveiled a new IRA known as an IRA Plus—or, more commonly, the Roth IRA, after Senator William Roth of Delaware, chairman of the Senate Finance Committee that oversaw the new set of tax laws. The Roth IRA offers enticing wrinkles to retirement savings. For one thing, singles making up to $95,000 a year (couples as much as $150,000) are eligible to contribute as much as $2,000 a year, even if they're taking part in a retirement program at work. Although Roth IRAs don't let you deduct the contribution from your taxes under any circumstances, it's a free ride from there on—your money grows tax-deferred, and you can withdraw the money tax-free once you retire.

↗ Useful Web Sites

> While many debate the pluses and minuses of Roth IRAs compared to traditional IRAs, one thing certainly isn't up for discussion—the fact that Roths have spawned a good deal of confusion among investors. A couple of Web sites that do a decent job of trying to separate Roth fact from fiction are http://www.nbfunds.com and http://www.datachimp.com/articles/rothira/rothintro.htm.

So, unlike the good old days when IRAs were available to all and the tax break was universal, we are now faced with what amounts to three different choices among IRAs—the old-fashioned IRA whose contributions you can deduct, the old-fashioned IRA that you can contribute to but cannot deduct because of your income (refer to the preceding charts to see what, if any, deduction, your income qualifies you for), and the new Roth IRA. While that may seem a bit bewildering, it actually offers a nice range of opportunity and choices, once you've sorted through the particulars of each option.

Should I Contribute?

The most basic question that we need to tackle first is: Are IRAs as a whole a good thing and should you open one and contribute to it? The answer is yes, with only minor qualifications. The reason is that, no matter which IRA you qualify for and whether or not your contribution is tax-deductible, all three let your money grow tax-free. And that's nothing to sneeze at, even if you don't get nickel one in deductions.

Let's illustrate the point: Assume you're investing $2,000 for 10 years with an average return of 10% a year. At the end of 10 years, if you're in the 15% tax bracket, you come out with $29,670, having paid taxes on your investment every year. If, however, that money is in an IRA where everything is tax-deferred, that same $2,000 nest egg grows to $31,874. The difference becomes more striking once you up your tax bracket, the time frame, and the amount you're investing. For instance, if you're socking away $2,000 every year for 20 years with a 10% return and are in the 28% tax bracket, you've got $83,803 at the other end. Not bad, but it pales next to the $114,500 you would have gotten if the money were in a tax-deferred IRA. Admittedly, you'll have to pay taxes once you start withdrawing the money (if you're not in a Roth IRA), but you're bound to come out way ahead if you take full advantage of tax deferral.

↗ Useful Web Sites

Interested in seeing how much you can rack up in an IRA—whether you can deduct the contribution or not—thanks to the power of tax deferral? The Prudential has a handy online calculator that lets you plug in any number of variables (including how much you invest, tax bracket, various types of returns), then displays how far ahead you come out by not having to pay taxes. Have a look at http://www.prudential.com/retirement/rpzzz1009.html.

Nor do the pluses of IRAs end there. Current law lets you withdraw up to $10,000 from an IRA without penalty if you're using the money to buy your first house (the usual early withdrawal penalty is 10% of whatever you're taking out—more about the first house perk in Chapter 7). You can also withdraw IRA money penalty-free to pay for college expenses for yourself, a spouse, your children, or your grandchildren. IRA proceeds are also available penalty-free to pay for medical expenses that exceed 7.5% of your adjusted gross income (adjusted gross income is what you make from salary and investments before you pay any taxes, minus things such as IRA contributions and other deductible expenses).

That being said, there's only one instance where opening and funding an IRA doesn't make overwhelming financial sense, and that is if you're in a tax-deferred retirement plan at work, such as a 401k or 403b. In that case, it behooves you to fund that plan to the max before turning your attention to an IRA of any kind. The reason, as we'll go over in greater detail in Chapter 11, is that employer-sponsored retirement plans always offer an immediate tax break, not to mention tax-deferred growth. Add to that your employer's matching contribution, and 401ks and 403bs turn into out-and-out slam dunks that literally scream for your participation. In short, don't fund an IRA at the expense of your employer's retirement plan—despite all the pluses of an IRA, you'll be selling yourself short.

Whither IRA?

If you're not covered by a retirement plan at work or—crafty you— you are taking full part in your company's 401k or 403b, the question then becomes: Which IRA to choose? Not surprisingly, the answer has its share of if-and-only-if scenarios but, as a general rule, here are some guidelines to keep in mind when shopping around:

▶ If you're eligible to get the tax deduction offered by the good old IRA, the question of choosing between that and a Roth IRA can be a bit dicey. On the one hand, it makes perfect sense to choose the old IRA and grab the tax break up front. Since you can't ever be certain what situation you'll be in come retirement—and whether the tax-free provisions of the Roth IRA would be better for you than getting hit by taxes—it never hurts to get what you can while you can.

However, the Roth's tax-free withdrawal provision also makes a good case for a younger investor planning for his or her retirement. Here you have to consider just where you expect you'll be when you retire. Since the issue is when you can take the most advantage of the tax break—now or when you withdraw the money in retirement—the question boils down to whether you think you'll be in a higher bracket when you retire or during your earning years. So, if you're already in the 28% tax bracket, conventional IRA wisdom would argue for the old IRA since—so traditional thinking goes—you'll likely take less of a tax hit in retirement than when you're working. If, on the other hand, it's possible that you'll be in a higher bracket come retirement—say, for instance, you have held down a relatively modestly paying job for years but are stashing away lots for your retirement—a Roth would be a better choice, since the money can be withdrawn without tax consequences.

▶ If, on the other hand, you don't qualify for an up-front deduction on a regular IRA, the decision is more clear-cut: Opt for the Roth. The reasoning is easy. With a nondeductible IRA, although your earnings are tax-deferred, not only do you not get any sort of tax break on the contribution but you're taxed when you start withdrawing the money on the other end. With Roth, you get the benefits of tax-deferred earnings plus tax-free withdrawals.

▶ Two last wrinkles to weigh. If you plan on living a long time, consider the Roth alternative. That's because conventional IRAs require you to start making withdrawals at age 70½, while the Roth version lets you keep the money in your IRA until the cows come home, metaphorically speaking. However far-fetched that may seem, it can make a difference—if you come from a family noted for longevity, and have put away ample retirement savings in places other than an IRA, being forced to withdraw money when you may not really need it can only increase your tax bill. On the other hand, if you're opening an IRA knowing that you may take some of the money out in five years or less for something like your first home, you may want to skirt the Roth—you're hit with taxes as well as a 10% penalty on any earnings that are withdrawn.

↗ Useful Web Sites

An interesting article that goes into a good deal of detail comparing Roth IRAs with traditional IRAs is available at http://www.invest-faq.com/articles/ret-plan-roth-ira.html.

To Convert or Not to Convert?

If, by chance, you already have a conventional IRA in place, that begs the question whether you should convert it to a Roth. In most cases, the answer is no—if nothing else, you'll owe taxes on every deductible contribution you made (as well as taxes on every penny of earnings, whether in a deductible account or not). For example, say you've made a $2,000 contribution to an old-fashioned IRA every year for 10 years and that each contribution has been fully deductible. If you're in the 15% tax bracket, that spells a $3,000 penalty if you roll the IRA over into a Roth ($20,000 times .15). That's no one's idea of fun, and it doesn't even take into account the taxes you would owe for any earnings the IRA generated. On top of that, you'll pay an even bigger penalty if you are in a higher tax bracket.

However, one scenario where it does make sense to convert is if you have a nondeductible IRA that hasn't done much of anything in terms of growth. For instance, if you started a nondeductible IRA a couple of years back that has stayed pretty much the same in value, shoot it on over to a Roth. Your taxes to convert will be light, and you'll be able to enjoy all the benefits of the Roth.

↗ Useful Web Sites

A handy calculator to help you determine whether you should move your existing IRA into a Roth is available at Microsoft Money Central (http://moneycentral.msn.com).

If a discussion on the pluses and minuses of Roths and conventional IRAs is more to your interest, an informative article at http://www. slfcu.org/slfcu_financial_life/roth_convert.html may help shed some light on your quandary.

Choosing How to Invest Your IRA

Like any other investment you can buy, you're the one who decides how to invest the money you deposit in your IRA—stocks, bonds, mutual funds, money markets, CDs, pretty much the whole gamut of investment vehicles is there for the choosing. And, in that sense, you should approach your IRA investment as you would any other investment. For the most part, it's best to stick with a mutual fund or funds whose risk level is comfortable for you and whose long-term performance suggests continued success. Again, keep an eye on expenses and give some attention to the large mutual fund families, which will let you move from one fund to another at no cost should you become dissatisfied with a fund's performance.

However, bear one additional consideration in mind. For the most part, an IRA is as long-term an investment as you will likely have—remember, unlike taxed investments and with only a few exceptions, it's for retirement and nothing else. Given that, you're definitely looking at the long haul, which, in turn, suggests that you give growth and aggressive growth funds careful consideration; since you've got years before you touch the money, you've plenty of time to ride out the rough spots and cash in on the type of returns those funds can offer. So that may argue for a bit more aggressiveness than you might otherwise be comfortable in taking on. But, once more, never get into an investment that makes you antsy. If a more conservative fund seems a better match for your personality, pass up the potential for better returns, go with the less volatile choice and congratulate yourself on being mature enough not to put yourself through a lot of nonsense just to make a few extra bucks.

CHAPTER 6

Smart Spending

T he next time you happen to be watching an old television show rerun—say, *The Andy Griffith Show* or something else from the early to mid-60s—pay particular attention when the action takes someone past the grocery store, a restaurant or some other sort of retail outlet. Check out the prices: hamburgers for a quarter; haircuts for a buck; houses in perfect shape for a couple of thousand dollars. Barney Fife never knew just how good he had it.

This, I think, illustrates a powerful reality far more effectively than any sort of dry comparison chart. The fact is that the price of just about everything has skyrocketed and will likely continue to do so in the future. That, unlike other aspects of our financial life, is something over which we have no control whatsoever; it's happened and will probably continue to happen, whether we like it or not.

That hasn't made us anything less of a consumption-oriented society. In fact, just the opposite has happened. Older people are out there buying stuff because they feel that they've earned it, baby boomers are dropping money on toys because they feel they deserve it, and generation Xers are spending money out of fear that whatever they want now simply will be out of reach financially tomorrow. Go to a mall any weekend, then stop by the local art museum—sad as it may be to many, the crowds are gawking at Segas, not Cezanne.

Nonetheless, that seemingly thoughtless consumer blitzkrieg does not make the title of this chapter a contradiction in terms—in fact, just the opposite, because intelligent money management means having the financial wherewithal to pay for the things we both require and enjoy, not squirreling away every penny in a masochistic exercise in self-denial. But there's a decided difference between using effective shopping strategies to spend your money thoughtfully and dropping money on something just because you can. Therefore, with an eye on both major and minor purchases you may make over the next several years, here are a few ideas and suggestions to help you make smart shopping decisions.

NOTE: Given the financial commitment and import of buying your own home, that topic is covered separately in Chapter 7.

Renting Without Ranting

While many other topics discussed in this chapter may apply only to certain people, renting a home or apartment is an issue of broad interest. That's because, whether you're still in school or not long removed, chances are fairly good that you're renting, are thinking about renting, or, at the very least, are giving some thought to changing a renting arrangement. Obviously, this section can't go into the particulars of all sorts of rental situations—if nothing else, market conditions are drastically different across the country—but we can touch on some major points to help ensure that you spend your rent money wisely, protect your interests as a tenant, and, equally important, look to the future when, someday, the only landlord you'll have will be yourself.

↗ Useful Web Sites

Relocating to a new city? Looking for a new place where you already live? All Apartments (http://www.springstreet.com) offers detailed information on more than 5 million apartments in more than 5,000 cities. Students can check out A Break For Students (http://www.abreak4students.com/), which has listings sorted by region and, occasionally, by individual college or university.

Perhaps the most important bit of advice about renting a home or apartment is always to try to rent less than you can afford. Unfortunately, this can go against human nature; after all, if you can afford a $1,000-a-month apartment in the chic part of town, why spend less on a place that may not be nearly as nice or in as good a location? There's a powerful reason: If you spend less on your rent, you can start pocketing the difference and saving it for something else. Remember, unlike other types of purchases discussed in this chapter, renting doesn't actually buy you anything you can call your own, except for a place to crash for 30 more days. Unlike home ownership, renting an apartment doesn't take anything off your taxes and, unlike buying a car, renting doesn't confer ownership, payment by payment. In terms of what the money is really doing for you, renting is akin to setting a match to it.

That's why it behooves you to save on how much you spend on rent. Start by going back to what we discussed about setting up a budget in Chapter 1. On the basis of what you're spending, figure out how much you can afford on rent, and then try to trim that figure back some. Stash what you save in a money market fund or, if you're looking at building up for a long-term goal, a mutual fund. This doesn't mean you should have to live in some rat trap to save a few hundred dollars every month, but give some thought to going with less than you can actually spend. If you live in a metro area where rentals are exorbitant, consider a roommate or two so that you can share housing costs and other expenses. Ultimately, the money you save can go toward something a bit more permanent, such as a car, furniture, or even a place of your own.

Once you've found a place you like, be prepared to convince your would-be landlord that you're the ideal tenant. Have ready materials to document that you're financially able to pay the rent you agree on (these can include such things as bank statements and pay stubs). Moreover, have current references—both on paper and via phone—ready if the landlord asks for them. A lot of landlords ask for references and never bother to follow up on them, but most do to get a feel for the sort of person (and tenant) you're likely to be.

Give careful thought to the length of the lease you agree to. Many renters think that a long-term lease provides security—and it can, to some degree—but particularly lengthy leases can work against you if you have to move before the lease expires. In many cases, even if you move out of a house or an apartment, you could still be liable for paying the remainder of the lease if the landlord can't find a replacement tenant. By the same token, a month-to-month lease offers renters the most freedom in leaving a place (you usually have to give only one month's notice) but also gives the landlord the greatest leeway to terminate a lease (or, for that matter, hike the rent). So try to gauge realistically how long you will likely want to stay in your rental—don't make it so short that your month-to-month situation becomes tenuous but also don't make it so lengthy that you're compelled to gut it out in a place you would otherwise gladly have left long ago.

Make certain you read your lease agreement carefully before you sign it. As with other parts of our financial lives, we'd all be horrified to admit just how often we sign off on something of significance without first giving it careful consideration, but don't make that mistake with your lease. Needless to say, it covers the provisions you're going to have to live with as long as the lease is in force. In addition to the monthly rent, watch for issues such as repairs (in some cases, renters assume a portion of financial responsibility for fixing anything that breaks in the rental, whether or not the problem was their fault), size of your security deposit (obviously, less is better), how soon your landlord has to return the deposit after you vacate (depending on where you live, this can range all over the place), the acceptability of pets (some landlords require an additional security deposit if you want one), and the various reasons that a lease can be terminated.

In particular, lease agreements generally stipulate that you as the tenant have examined the premises and found them to be in good condition. Well, that may be so, but go through the apartment or house with a magnifying glass before you sign on to rent it. Check all the light switches, make sure the stove works and the toilets flush, and point out every little ding that you can to your landlord. That way, when the time comes for you to leave, you won't have to lay out cash for problems that weren't of your doing. Likewise, walk through with your landlord after you've packed up and left. Although laws differ, in many cases the landlord has to document in writing those problems that compelled him or her to withhold part or all of your security deposit. So trail along with the landlord so that you know precisely what he or she is talking about.

Don't be afraid to negotiate some of the terms of your lease. Whether you can do this is largely a question of supply and demand. If you live in an area where decent apartments are had only by the swift, you probably can't dicker all that much about what's in the lease—if you don't want it as is, there's going to be somebody else who does. However, if your apartment rental market is a bit slower—for instance, you visit an apartment you like whose want ad has been in the paper a couple of weeks—the landlord may be open to revamping some of the provisions of the lease just to get a warm body in there. And don't just focus on the monthly rent; if the security deposit seems prohibitive, ask your landlord to trim it. By the same token, if the landlord asks for a couple of months' notice before you leave, see if he or she could see their way to making that one month instead.

Know your rights as a tenant. Although there are some federal fair housing laws in place, most statutes relating to tenants and renting are more localized. If you're having a problem with your landlord or would just like to know what protections are in place, contact a local housing authority to see if it can fill you in on local rent laws. In some larger metro areas, there are also renters' rights and advocacy groups around; these can prove an excellent source of legal ammunition should you need it.

↗ Useful Web Sites

The Cornell University Law School has posted an overview of landlord-tenant law at http://www.law.cornell.edu/topics/landlord_tenant.html.

Finding a central source of tenant information and associations isn't easy, but your best bet may be at Tenant Net (http://tenant.net/main.html). While the site focuses primarily on New York City and State, it also provides some tenant information on other states.

Last, if you deal fairly with your landlord, you're likely to get the same treatment in return. For the most part, landlords want to rent their property out without any hassles or headaches; so if you treat the place and your landlord with a certain amount of dignity, you'll likely get along famously. That can come in pretty handy if you need to have your landlord cut you some slack. For instance, a landlord and tenant who get along well will agree on an early out from a lease a whole lot easier than two who are at each other's throats. And, if nothing else, trying to get along with your landlord can take a good deal of stress out of your day-to-day life (one source interviewed for this book knew of a tenant-landlord relationship that was so horrific that, every time the landlord tried to show the apartment in hopes of forcing the tenant to leave, the tenant would cook fish so that the place would stink to high heaven. Needless to say, those sorts of annoying histrionics are usually unnecessary.)

↗ *Useful Web Sites*

One excellent source for renters' information of all sorts is located at http://www.bostonapartments.com/rentips.htm. Although it's a Boston-based site, it nonetheless provides valuable information to renters everywhere, addressing such topics as renters' rights, handicap accessibility, and even a mortgage calculator to help you figure out whether it might not be less expensive to buy a place of your own.

Of particular interest to college students is a University of Massachusetts apartment hunters' questionnaire at http://home.oit.umass.edu/~cshrc/housing/questions.html. The site is a handy checklist of must-ask questions about any home or apartment.

Fuel for Thought

Let's drive home a basic fact of life—short of the occasional hermit, monks chanting away in some far-flung monastery, or the most dedicated of urbanites who hasn't seen an open parking space since Eisenhower was president, almost everyone needs a car. That truth takes on an even greater scope in the United States, where car ownership supersedes necessity to blossom into an absolute God-given right. Buying a car—particularly your first brand-spanking-new model—is as much a rite of passage as moving out of your parents' house into your first apartment.

But, like many first apartments—where sweet independence can quickly give way to leaky pipes, insects the size of briefcases, and neighbors who insist on watching "Hee Haw" at deafening levels—your foray into the world of automobile ownership can prove less than idyllic. The trick is to know how to shop intelligently and to use every tool at your disposal to make your money go as far as it possibly can.

The first step is to back up and decide whether leasing may be a better option that buying. The distinction is simple. When you buy a car you're taking actual ownership of it, while leasing is a form of rent. When the lease is up, you simply return the car to a dealer or other leasing agent. Buying makes the most sense if you're genuinely interested in a low-cost, long-term means of transportation. No matter how much you spend, sooner or later you will own the car if you make the payments and keep it long enough. Buying also works if you know you'll be driving a lot; leases levy a mileage cap, beyond which you're obligated to pay a penalty upward of 15¢ per mile. On the other hand, leasing can work if you plan to trade in your car every few years. Leasing also makes sense if you lack a sufficient down payment or if you want to check out a car before actually buying it.

Let's tackle the first scenario and assume you've decided to buy a car outright. The choice comes down to new versus used. Admittedly, there's a lot to be said for the sexiness of a brand-new ride, not to mention that incredible new car smell. But do think long and hard about opting for a used car. The primary reason is that a new car's value plummets quickly, starting the second that you tool off the lot. In fact, the Kelly Blue Book estimates that a car's trade-in value drops as much as 40% in its first two years. That may not mean all that much if you intend to drive that new car until the day it up and dies, but it carries a lot of weight if you expect to trade it in in a few years. One additional caveat, especially if you want to get the most when you resell: Keep an eye peeled for significant changes in body styling in newer versions of your car. Historically, depreciation in used models is particularly sharp after the "new version" is released.

↗ Useful Web Sites

It never hurts to consult the Bible of new and used car prices when making a car buying decision. So, don't overlook the Kelly Blue Book on-line (http://www.kbb.com). Another source for new and used car price data can be found at Auto Pricing. Com (http://www.autopricing.com).

If you think a used car might be the better choice—if the price of a new car is sufficiently outlandish to put it out of your price range or if you won't be driving it forever—that doesn't necessarily mean you have to settle for some rattling old clunker. One good strategy is to keep your eyes open for a car that's coming off a two- or three-year lease—not only is it likely to be in good shape and available at a good price, but it may also have some of its new car warranty in place. Estimates hold that between two and three million cars come off short-term leases every year, so be sure to ask your dealer if there are any for sale. That gives you the best of both worlds—a cut-rate used-car price, but with some of the new car pluses intact. When haggling over a used car, be aware that, for the most part, auto dealers' profit margins—the difference between what the dealer pays for the car and the price you pay the dealer—are usually considerably higher than those for new cars (profit margins for used cars can range upward of 25%, as opposed to 10 to 12% for new cars.) One good rule of thumb for used cars is to try offering 80 to 85% of the asking price and never to pay more than 90%. That way, you get a car at a reasonable price while the seller also makes a decent profit.

↗ Useful Web Sites

America's Auto Mall (http://www.aautomall.com) has a nice search engine that lets you search either by the kind of used car you're looking for or the location where you'd like to buy it.

Auto Site (http://www.autosite.com/) is an automotive buyer's guide offering information on new and used car pricing, specs, rebates, book values, troubleshooting, recalls, and more.

Don't trust anyone who tells you that a used car was driven only twice a month to the 4-H Club meetings. To get the real skinny on where a used car has really been, check out Carfax (www.carfax.com), which lets you order detailed histories on any used car you're considering. Just provide the service with the 17-character vehicle identification number and you'll get back a report that details ownership history, mileage, and, most important, details on problems such as odometer rollbacks, accidents, and cars that may have been repurchased by dealerships because they were lemons. Cost is $19.50 per report.

If your heart is set on a new car from the outset, don't assume a nightmarish trip to a local dealership is your only option. Nowadays, there are smarter and infinitely more pleasant ways to shop, starting with the Internet. For instance, AutoVantage (www.eauto.com/carbuyingsvc) is a free shopping service that lets buyers specify the make and model of car they want to buy; the service then e-mails back the name of a nearby dealership that has that car in stock, along with a price quote. Other Web-based car shopping services include Microsoft's Car-Point (www.carpoint.com) and IntelliChoice (www.intellichoice.com). Know, too, that services such as CarPoint also provide leasing information if you're shopping around for the best lease deal available. Bear in mind, however, that online quotes may be best used for comparison shopping; since, in many cases, you may get only one bid, there's no guarantee that you're going to get the very best deal.

↗ Useful Web Sites

No matter how you go about shopping for a new car, one invaluable stopover point on the Internet is Fighting Chance (http://fightingchance.com). The brainchild of W. James Bragg, the site lets car shoppers buy a comprehensive information package featuring information on car pricing, trends in the auto industry, little-known pricing perks, and tips that may save you hundreds or thousands on your next car. Of particular use is Fighting Chance's compilation of actual transaction prices, which give you a real-world feel for what other shoppers have paid for a car that interests you. Cost is $24.95 for an information package on one car and $8 for every additional car's report. The Web site lets you order online.

Nor is the World Wide Web the only means of taking the headache out of car shopping. Auto buying services can also work to your advantage, since you usually pay a few hundred dollars to get dealers' absolute rock-bottom prices. One such service, Car Bargains, in Washington, D.C. (202-347-7283), charges $165, for which you receive the best prices from five dealers so that you can comparison shop even further. In fact, although services such as Car Bargains cost more than some of the free services, they may be worth the money, since the competitive nature of the bids you get may get you a much lower purchase price in the long run.

If you're set on doing the shopping yourself, look into services that help ensure you're getting the best deal possible. For instance, Nationwide Auto Brokers (800-521-7257) gives shoppers an item-by-item breakdown of what a particular car cost a dealer (lovingly known as a "cheat sheet.") That way, you know precisely what the dealer paid so that you can dicker from a realistic perspective. In other words, if you want to add air conditioning and the dealer says it cost him $500 but your sheet says he laid out only $300, you can correct his "honesty" with whatever level of decorum you choose. Cost of one report is $11.95, and additional reports are $9.95 each.

↗ Useful Web Sites

For a great central linkup to any number of automotive buying and shopping services, point your browser to http://www.handilinks.com/cat1/a/a1684.htm.

Also be on the lookout for additional discount programs that many car manufacturers offer to recent college grads. Ford, for instance, dangles an additional $400 discount to recent college graduates who purchase a new car, over and above whatever other incentives might be available (for further information on this program, go to Ford's special programs Web page at http://www.ford.com/us/collegegrad/. Be sure to check out the particulars, since each manufacturer defines "recent" differently. To find out more, call the manufacturer's toll-free 800 number or check out its Internet Web site (usually the name of the company, followed by .com).

No-haggle buying has become increasingly popular of late. Dealers give you the price of a particular car, and you can choose to take it or leave it. However tempting it might be to take price dickering out of the car buying process, it's generally a good idea to bypass no-haggle dealerships. You may avoid the mind games and other baloney of trying to talk a dealer into the best price, but you're also unlikely to get a particularly good deal, since the price will certainly include a substantial profit margin. So, unless the thought of wrangling with a salesperson absolutely makes your skin crawl, it's best to haggle, since you're likely to benefit in the long run.

Additionally, if you're considering a new car that you'll keep for awhile, give some thought to extended warranty coverage, which can often save you big-time on repairs and maintenance. However, consider the price quoted by the dealer for extended warranty coverage as open to negotiation, just like the price of the car itself. Ask for the dealer's best price on extended warranties; then offer to pay half. And never pay more than two-thirds of what the dealer quoted.

There are alternatives to extended warranties. For instance, many credit unions offer mechanical breakdown insurance policies that offer bumper-to-bumper coverage at a price that can be considerably cheaper than dealer-provided coverage. Additionally, some insurance companies such as Geico offer mechanical breakdown insurance to their auto insurance policyholders. So shop around.

One rather Byzantine addendum—women shopping for a car still may encounter more headaches than their male counterparts, such as condescending salespeople or an insulting emphasis on cosmetic issues such as color and vanity mirrors. The best advice—do your homework and be assertive about what you want. Have a price list at the ready, and insist on being treated as a serious customer. If you don't like the attitude at a particular dealership, look around until you find one that treats you with respect. Finally, if all else fails, look into one of the Web-based networks or a car-buying service— that may well save you some money as well as a good deal of need- less aggravation.

One final tip: Think female salespeople necessarily treat women car buyers any better or negotiate better deals? Unfortu- nately not. A study published in the early 1990s in the *Harvard Law Review* showed that women shoppers, systematically steered to a female salesperson, in fact let their guard down and actually end up paying more for a car than if they had worked with a salesman. (Sad to say, the study also showed the same relationship with per- sons of color assuming they'd get better treatment from a sales- person from a similar ethnic background). So not only should women shoppers never assume they'll receive more empathetic treatment from another woman, it hammers home the importance of doing your homework and never tipping your hand, regardless of the salesperson with whom you're dealing.

Real-Life Interlude

However hands-off and even impersonal the Internet and other car-buying ser- vices have made the process of choosing and buying a car, one very old- fashioned element lives on—the test drive. Here are a few tips from W. James Bragg, head of the automotive information service "Fighting Chance," that can help make that as well as other steps in the car buying process less harrowing:

First, don't call a dealership once you have a car in mind. Instead, check out inventories to see how well your model is selling. Stop by a deal- ership early on a weekday morning and have a look around. If you see scads of the model you like, you know you'll be in a better position to bargain, since the dealer will likely be eager to move them. If, however, there's only one or two around, you may want to hold off for a bit—the model may be popular, which means dealers may not be as open to bargaining.

When you go in for a test drive, be as businesslike as possible. Simply tell the salesperson that you'd like to drive a particular model. Moreover, remember that car salespeople are in the "today business"—they'll pull out every stop to get you to buy the car right then and there. If the salesperson tries to pressure you into making a decision right away, say that you can't because you have another appointment in an hour to test-drive another car. In short, make it clear that you're not going to be bullied into a decision, and establish a competitive environment with another dealer (even if there is no other dealer—don't be skittish about telling a few white lies to better your bargaining position).

As when making any other major purchase, keep a poker face. Don't let on that you've fallen in love with a car, even though you'd be willing to marry it the minute you drove it off the lot. Instead, remain as cool and detached as possible. As Bragg puts it: "Don't ever get caught doing heavy breathing around a car."

Once you've chosen the model you like, here's another way to go about buying it. Visit the manufacturer's Web site and see if it has information on any dealerships within a reasonable distance of where you live. Get the fleet manager's name and phone and fax numbers. Then, send each manager a fax, saying that you're interested in buying such-and-such a model and asking for his best possible price. Make it clear that it's a competitive process, and instruct the managers to submit their bids via fax. That sets up the best possible chance for you to get the best deal. One final tip: If you're a woman, just use your first initial rather than your full name when you send the fax. That way, you can bypass any nonsense from some chauvinistic dealer who thinks he can bully you into considering a higher bid.

⬈ Useful Web Sites

Sure, getting the most for your buck is an essential element of car shopping. But don't overlook safety, since the best deal in the world may land you in a car that's something less than secure. As a precaution, have a look at these two Web sites:

The National Highway Traffic Safety Administration offers detailed safety and crash test results data at http://www.nhtsa.dot.gov/cars/testing/. There, you can study comparative safety and crash test information on any number of auto makes, models, and years. There's even a survey of tire safety to help you buy the best set of tires possible.

The Insurance Institute for Highway Safety (http://www.hwysafety.org) provides a wealth of safety and crash test information on specific cars. You can get data on low-speed crash tests, airbags, head restraint ratings (that thing behind your head in the car is for safety, not comfort), and, on a more macabre note, driver death rates for specific models. You can also look up information on cars the insurance industry considers the safest, something that may save you some money on auto insurance.

Please Release Me

Now, to the subject of leasing. As we discussed before, leasing can be an attractive choice if you don't have sufficient funds for a down payment to buy a car. And, if it means something to you to be tooling around in a new car every so often, leasing can certainly beat the financial commitment and expense of buying a car and trading it in every few years.

Basically, leasing involves three elements: the transaction price when you first obtain the car, the value when you return it to the dealership, and the cost of financing the difference between the two values. That's it. With that in mind, the first rule of leasing is to negotiate the deal as you would if you were buying the car outright. That means dickering and making it clear to anyone with whom you're dealing that you're not there by a sheer act of the Deity—your approach to leasing is competitive, and, if you don't get the terms you want, you'll keep looking around until someone gives them to you.

The first element is the starting price, known as the "capitalized cost." This is the price you cut with the leasing company at the outset of the lease. The second element is the "residual value," or how much the car is deemed to be worth when you turn it in at the end of the lease (this is based on estimates published every two months by the Automotive Lease Guide's Residual Percentage Guide and, unfortunately, is typically nonnegotiable). The third factor is the interest rate or "money factor," which is how much the leasing company will charge you to drive the car around during the lease. Subtract the residual value from the capitalized cost, divide by the number of months the lease covers, add on the interest charges, and you've got your deal.

Looking at leasing from this rather simple perspective shows why it pays to negotiate. The lower the difference between your capitalized cost and the residual value and the lower the interest rate, the less the car will end up costing you over the life of the lease. And all those values can add up; for example, if you agree to a capitalized cost of $22,000 and a residual value of $12,000, you'll end up paying about $60 a month more on a 7% lease than you would if you set the capitalized cost at $20,000 and used the same residual value. So, when shopping around for a lease, try calling finance managers at several dealerships to get competitive quotes. Again, make it clear that you're shopping around and that there are other dealerships who are bidding for your business. Moreover, stress that you're interested in negotiating as if you were buying the car (remember, just as a lower purchase price means lower costs when buying, so does a lower capitalized cost at the beginning of a lease spell lower costs). Additionally, as we pointed out earlier, some of the online car shopping networks also let you go into cyberspace to roust out competitive lease arrangements.

Unfortunately, there's no law requiring leasing companies to tell you the interest rate they're charging for leases; in many cases, all they'll quote you is the capitalized cost, residual value, and monthly lease payment. But there is a way to figure out just how much interest a leasing company is charging, an essential element in your leasing decision. Just follow the following formula:

First, subtract the residual value from the capitalized cost. For example, a $12,000 residual value from a $20,000 capitalized cost leaves $8,000 in depreciation. Divide that by the number of months the lease is in effect and you've got your depreciation charge. In the example just given, a 36-month lease would result in a charge of $222.22 a month.

Now calculate the monthly finance charge. First, total the residual value and the capitalized cost ($32,000 in our example). Then, take a reasonable guess what the dealer might be charging in interest—let's say 7%. Now, convert that into a money factor by dividing seven by 24 (believe it or not, the 24 figure is a mathematical constant unrelated to the length of the lease). For 7%, that comes out to .0029166. Multiply that number by the $32,000 figure we got earlier, and you arrive at a monthly finance charge of $93.33. Add that to the monthly depreciation ($222.22) and you come out with a total monthly payment of $315.55 (plus sales tax in many states).

Now, match that to what the leasing company is quoting you. If the quote is higher, you're getting hit with an interest rate higher than 7% (you'll then probably want to refigure the lease based on a higher percentage so that you can see exactly what interest rate is in play.) If it's lower, do the same thing. Either way, this formula lets you calculate what a leasing company is offering you in terms of interest—add that on to depreciation, and you've got a clear view of the total lease package.

Two last thoughts. First, never sign off on anything until you understand clearly every charge and penalty that's part of the lease. As we talked about earlier, leases levy penalties if you exceed a certain amount of mileage. Have your leasing company give you a printed list of every charge that's part of the lease; don't get caught by some "special fee" or some such nonsense after you've signed the lease. If the leasing company balks, walk out the door.

Also, check to make sure that your auto insurance has "gap insurance." Should the car be stolen or totaled during the lease, insurers will pay you the market value for the car. Unfortunately, that may be less than what you owe on the lease. Gap insurance covers the difference and is often included in many policies at no extra cost. If it's not already on your policy, have it added; it should run you no more than a few extra dollars a month and can conceivably save you thousands.

↗ Useful Web Sites

The Connecticut Attorney General's Office has compiled a handy checklist of warning signs for any consumer considering leasing a car. Have a look at http://www.cslnet.ctstateu.edu/attygenl/reality1.htm. If you're interested in getting an insider view of the perils of leasing, check out consumer advocate Mark Eskeldson's Web site at http://www.carinfo.com/. There, a detailed article points out the various ways you can be overcharged on a lease and what you can do about it.

There's a handy online calculator to help you figure out whether leasing or buying may be a better options for you at http://www. leasesource.com/workshop/leasewizard_jr.htm. The site http://www. financenter.com/autos.htm also has an array of calculators that let you tackle the question of whether it's better to lease or buy.

Shop 'Til You CyberDrop

It's a cocooner's dream. You can now shop around and buy anything from a leather bomber jacket to a bottle of Bordeaux without ever once stepping outside the confines of your home. While somewhat slow to take off, the Internet is fast transforming the nature of shopping as more and more retailers set up shop on the World Wide Web. Some advantages are readily evident—round-the-clock access, virtually unlimited shelf space, and the sheer convenience of being able to select and order an item with a few clicks of a mouse are transforming the Internet into a veritable shopper's Mecca.

But what makes the Internet a genuinely valuable tool for consumers really has nothing to do with those elements of buying and selling we would normally identify as advantages. For instance, the most immediate question one might ask is whether it's really cheaper to buy something on the Internet. Well, that depends— there are some instances (such as airline tickets, as we'll discuss later) where the Web's capacity to let shoppers compare and shop around can, in fact, mean lower prices.

But there are also scads of items that cost you just as much— and, in fact, likely even a bit more—than they would have had you gone to the mall to purchase them yourself. Take, for instance, a book you order online. The price may be a dollar or so less than what they're charging at your neighborhood bookstore. But add on a couple of bucks for shipping and handling charges, and that purported bargain is so much dust in the wind.

Therein lies the first rule of cybershopping: When comparing items, particularly with goods that you can go out and buy on your own, be sure to add on every pertinent charge so that you have a clear picture of what all this wonderful convenience is going to cost you. Here, online shopping outlets differ considerably. Some are very forthcoming about shipping and handling charges and even include an online chart to let you figure those expenses to the penny. Others, however, are something less than up front, even going so far as to add on taxes, shipping, and handling after you've placed your order and logged off. So check around a merchant's Website to determine the true overall cost of what you're buying; if you have any doubts, you may do well to look somewhere else to get what you need.

↗ Useful Web Sites

If you're interested in the very best online deals for books and computer equipment, be sure to have a look at PriceScan (http://www.pricescan.com/). There, you can roust out the cheapest prices for books and a variety of computer gear, often with links that let you jump right over to the vendor with the best deal. Of particular value is PriceScan's capacity to add on pertinent shipping charges, which allows for genuine comparison between vendors. As of this writing, PriceScan is soliciting feedback from users as to what sorts of other goodies should be added to the service.

Microsoft Money Central has a great archive of columns that deal exclusively with the advantages and drawbacks of shopping on the Internet. Go to http://moneycentral.msn.com/home.asp, then look for the "net sales" feature in the "Living Well" section. From shopping for food to clothes to the question of whether the Internet is, in fact, less expensive than conventional methods of shopping, these columns can be rather eye-opening to the would-be Web consumer.

So, while the Internet isn't necessarily any cheaper than more traditional means of shopping, it does offer an unparalleled source of consumer information and guidance to help you make intelligent shopping choices, no matter how you eventually lay out your money. As we pointed out earlier in this chapter, buying or leasing a car through an Internet-based service lets you establish a competitive environment in your favor that would have taken hours or days of legwork if you pursued it the old-fashioned way.

The same can be said for shopping for airline tickets online. Not too long ago, travelers had to choose between working through a travel agent and buying the tickets directly from the airline. In either case, important information, such as seat availability and surcharges—not to mention alternate flights and routes that were less expensive—were kept from the traveler. Now, there are a number of online sites where ticket shoppers can go to research and book airline reservations. While details vary from one service to another, it's simple to get comparative data on any number of flights, and not just on fare alone; for example, with one service you type in where you're traveling to and from and when, and the system presents you with every conceivable carrier and itinerary that matches your plans. Departure times, type of plane, meals, estimated travel time, the applicability of any sort of prepurchase plan, and even the likelihood that the flight will arrive on time are all there for comparison—details and nuggets that can all enter into your eventual choice of carrier and flight.

↗ Useful Web Sites

Looking for a particular airline that offers online pricing and reservations? Go to http://www.airlines.thelinks.com/, which provides a guide to all online airline sites, listed alphabetically.

Now that you've got your plane reservations all socked away, check out All Hotels on The Web (http://www.all-hotels.com/), which provides links to more than 10,000 hotels on the Web, listed by country and continent. Also a great source for discount packages and other perks.

Of course, you've got to get to your hotel from the airport. So have a look at Guide to Airport Rental Cars http://www.bnm.com/, offering information and reservations for more than 70 rental car companies.

Finally, students looking for travel packages and deals should get on over to STA Travel http://www.sta-travel.com/. There, you can arrange airfare, rail travel passes and check out various perks and travel discounts.

Naturally, that doesn't mean that the fares and prices these systems give you are necessarily the cheapest to be found; there are any number of other services that probably stand at least a chance of offering you a better deal. But what it does illustrate is the investigatory muscle of the Internet—the World Wide Web is giving consumers the opportunity to research and analyze almost any purchase they make more comprehensively than our predecessors could ever have imagined. Whether you explore the intricate details of competing airline fares or simply compare prices of pullover jackets, the Web is a limitless source of consumer information, comparison, and, ultimately, power. And whether or not you decide that actually buying something on the Web makes better financial sense than going down to the corner store, that kind of information can only help make your hard-earned shopping dollars stretch that much further.

➚ Useful Web Sites

Surf before you fly. That may well by the credo of Best Fares (www.best fares.com), the online companion to the popular Best Fares Discount Travel Magazine. While the magazine has a well-deserved reputation for clueing its readers into little-known airfare, hotel, and other travel-related discount deals, the Web site goes the printed version one better through a feature called "Today's Hot Deals," breaking specials that miss the magazine's deadline and will expire before the next issue comes out. Web site visitors can also access a travel news desk, insider travel secrets, and a directory of hotels offering 50% discounts. As an added service, visitors can enter their e-mail addresses so that Best Fares can automatically alert them to breaking travel deals.

Cheaper by the Dozen(s)

What about shopping at warehouse clubs like Costco and Sam's Club, where things, taken individually, are dirt cheap but you have to buy enough to fill a gymnasium? The bottom line: On the whole, you're likely to do better at such places than you would buying comparable items elsewhere. The reason is twofold—not only do such clubs buy in huge quantities, which allows them to sell many items for less, but the prices always remain the same. By contrast, supermarkets employ a "high-low" principle—most of their everyday items are priced more expensively than similar items at Costco and other warehouse clubs, but occasionally they'll put something on sale at a price lower than that charged at the warehouses. The idea is to rid their shelves of a particular item while getting you into the store to buy other, more expensive items—that's how supermarkets make their bucks. So you can occasionally get a better deal at supermarkets if you're obsessive enough to keep an eye out for sales, but, day in and out, the prices are better at the warehouse clubs.

As for other items, warehouse clubs can be substantially less expensive than other retail outlets; computers, exercise equipment, electronics, and other household goods are consistently cheaper. (The one occasional exception is camera equipment—that can often be bought less expensively via mail order.) However, for most items, particularly expensive ones, it's easy to make back your annual membership fee (which usually runs about $20 to $30), occasionally with just a single purchase.

There are, however, some caveats to warehouse clubs:

▶ *Keep an eye out for unusual brands.* Shoppers often won't find mainstream electronic products in warehouse clubs, such as products that are rated in publications like *Consumer Reports*. Instead, since they can buy in such bulk, clubs often have manufacturers produce items specifically for them (this avoids antagonizing conventional retailers). While that makes for cheap prices, it also makes genuine head-to-head shopping comparisons impossible.

▶ *Don't shop at a discount club as you would a grocery store.* It simply doesn't make sense to stop at Costco for one item. Rather, it seems better to augment your usual grocery shopping by stocking up on those items that are available at a warehouse club, particularly nonperishables.

▶ *If service is important, bypass the warehouse clubs.* The clubs are not the place to shop if you need expert advice on choosing the item that's right for you. Instead, do your research beforehand, choose the item that you want, then see if the warehouse club happens to stock it.

▶ *Think about your storage capacity.* While it isn't as bad as it used to be, many items available at warehouse clubs still are sold in large, bulk quantities (the proverbial bale of toilet paper, for instance). Large families, groups, or shoppers with a good deal of storage space are best suited to these sorts of bulk purchases. If all you have is a small apartment with little in the way of storage, you might find yourself lining the walls with shrink-wrapped multi-packs of Kleenex and telephone-booth-size Cheerios boxes. One way around this is to split up warehouse orders with friends or relatives.

▶ *As is the case with shopping anywhere, be particularly leery of impulse buying at warehouses.* Since items are proportionately a good deal cheaper than you can find them elsewhere, it's easy to talk yourself into buying something, not because you genuinely need it but because the price makes it irresistible. Well, do your best to resist, because the consequences can be nasty, since you're convincing yourself to buy things that add up fast. For instance, an impulse decision to buy a bottle of spring water at the grocery store may cost you a dollar, but making the same choice with a case of water can cost you ten. A few like decisions, and it's awfully easy to walk out of a warehouse having spent a hundred dollars, mostly on items that would be surprisingly unappealing elsewhere.

↗ Useful Web Sites

Ranging from the general to the somewhat eccentric, Consumer World (www.consumerworld.org) offers more than 1,400 consumer-related resources. As at other sites, you can check credit card and mortgage rates and tap into discount travel deals. But Consumer World also provides specific information and guidance, including product reviews, comparison pricing services, and direct links to the Better Business Bureau and companies' customer service departments. Web site visitors can examine prepaid phone card deals, explore a database comparing the fat, calories, and salt content of foods at popular fast food outlets, and "clip" electronic coupons. The site also offers a daily "scam alert" to warn consumers about the latest in snake oil skulduggery.

CHAPTER 7

Mi Casa, Su Casa?

For our parents, owning their own home was a realistic, even expected element of the American Dream, much like buying a new car every couple of years and holding a lifelong job culminating in a gold watch and a comfortable pension. If one recalls days not that long ago when a decent home in a nice neighborhood with good schools cost only a few thousand bucks, it's not surprising that people treated home ownership as a fait accompli.

Now, unfortunately, the prospect of home ownership seems more remote for many, particularly young, first-time buyers. For one thing, the cost of home ownership has exploded. As of mid-1998, according to the National Association of Realtors, the median price of a single-family home in the United States had topped $132,000 (for those who aren't clear on the term "median," it's simple—in this case, it means half of all homes sold for more than $132,000, half for less). And that stat is misleading, as it doesn't begin to approach the average price in any number of large metropolitan areas; San Francisco, by comparison, had exceeded $329,000 in median price by the same time, while Boston had topped $206,000.

If those numbers are completely discouraging, they needn't be, because, however horrific the comparison might be between what we might have to pay for a home and what our parents might have forked over only a couple of decades ago, other conditions are sufficiently different to put home ownership in an entirely different perspective. The first, and by far most important, consideration for people who are giving some thought to buying their first home is whether home ownership is a good idea in the first place. Consider: When many of our parents started work, they probably went with a company where they expected to remain for most, if not all, of their working careers. That meant a great deal more predictability, particularly when it came to how long they would stay in one place. In turn, that made home ownership that much more attractive and desirable; if you were putting down roots, it only made sense to buy.

But things today are not so stable (some might argue stagnant). People right out of college move around quite a bit, not only from place to place but from employer to employer. And that makes home ownership less practical from any number of perspectives. First, there's the financial. What with the expense of getting a mortgage, putting money down on a home, and other related expenses of home buying and ownership, you're looking at a fair chunk of up-front change that you have to recoup. Equally important is the emotional strain—buying or selling a home has often been likened to root canal work in terms of pleasurable experiences. There are any number of books on the market that promise to make buying or selling a home carefree and painless, but take my word for it—it can be a physically and emotionally draining process in which, as often as not, things go wrong more frequently than they go as they should. In a few words, home buying is not something that should be entered into frivolously.

The general rule of thumb: Experts say don't even think about buying a home unless you're certain you'll be staying put in the same general vicinity for at least three years. As we discuss later in this chapter, the combined expense of getting a loan and other upfront costs (let alone what incidental expenses such as moving might run you) makes this three-year breakpoint the bare minimum for you to recover those initial expenses. So, if you think you'll be relocating soon or just aren't sure where the future will find you, it's probably the better part of valor to hold off on buying a home. Instead, keep saving for the day when you will know that home ownership makes a good deal more sense than it may now.

If, however, you find yourself in a different situation—say, you've been out of school for a few years, you've changed jobs a bit but now have settled on a community and employer that you like—it may be time to start giving some thought to investing in your own place. And, with that goal in mind, the first point is not to be intimidated; however daunting the expense and process can seem, buying your first home is not the intellectual equivalent of sending an astronaut to Mars. It is very doable, provided that you take the time to absorb some ideas, techniques, and suggestions.

↗ Useful Web Sites

Here are a few great Web sites that offer comprehensive information on selecting and buying a home. They're good supplements to the material we'll be talking about in this chapter:

Want a look at more than a million homes for sale? Want helpful advice on the mechanics of buying a home? Http://www.realtor.com/ offers that and more, as well as links to help you shop for a real estate broker in your area. The site also provides up-to-date stats on mortgage rates of all types.

Similarly, Real Times (http://www.realtimes.com/) offers data and articles of interest to prospective homebuyers. For instance, when I stopped by the site, articles included a step-by-step guide for first-time buyers, features on various communities throughout the country, and a piece warning consumers not to overpay for homes just because interest rates are low. A very handy, useful site, particularly for the home-buying newcomer.

Another great Web site for information on various topics connected with home buying is the OurBroker Consumer Real Estate Center (http://www.ourbroker.com/). The brainchild of real estate author Peter Miller, the site offers a comprehensive array of news, information, calculators, and links to other sites that will prove helpful to the home shopper. There's even a handy online dictionary that can help you fathom baffling real estate terminology.

HomeStarterPath, a service of Fannie Mae (a source of home loans we'll discuss later), has a nice article that walks you through the process of deciding whether home ownership is right for you. It's at http://www.homepath.com/hsp2.html. There's even a quiz at http://www.homepath.com/hsp3.html that takes you through some (not all) of the factors involved in that decision.

Mi Casa? Porque?

As we discussed above, home ownership, like other elements of your financial life, is not something you should get into without a good deal of emotional and intellectual self-examination. When weighing the pluses and minuses of becoming a person of property, be sure to give just due to your emotional readiness as well as to the fundamentals of your finances. Are you emotionally ready to settle down? Are you prepared for the commitment home ownership entails (for instance, unlike renting, when you can scream for the landlord or super every time the sink shoots a leak, home ownership puts the wrench in your hands.) If you have any genuine doubts that you're prepared emotionally to accept the responsibility of home ownership, by all means hold off. It's infinitely better to wait a bit longer than to get into something sooner than you should and regret it after the fact.

However, there are any number of advantages to home ownership, provided your situation warrants its consideration. First, as we touched on in the chapter on renting, owning a home is an investment, whereas renting is an expense that merely gets you temporary occupancy under a roof. When you take out a mortgage, the payment—with additional wrinkles we'll touch on later—is essentially divvied up into two elements, interest and principal. Interest—surprise, surprise—is the charge you're paying to the bank or organization that gave you the money to buy your house. In no way does your ownership of the home increase with the more interest you pay. Principal, however, does just that—that's the portion of your mortgage payment that goes directly toward the value of your home. And, with every payment you make, you increase your stake in the home (this is known as equity).

Principal doesn't just buy you a bigger and bigger chunk of ownership; it also pays off nicely if your home increases in value. This is how a home can also become an investment. Although increasing property values are by no means a sure thing (and never, ever buy a home just because you want to invest in one), all you have to do is look at the trend in home prices over the past decade or so to conclude that it's a reasonable bet that the home you buy will likely go up in value. For example: say you buy a home for $100,000 and the home increases 4% a year in value (not an unreasonable guesstimate). In five years' time, that home you bought for one hundred grand will be worth about $122,000. That, and with every payment you make, that portion going to the principal means you own more and more of that wonderful thing that keeps getting more and more valuable.

Even that part of your mortgage payment that goes toward interest has its advantages. Every penny you pay in interest is tax-deductible (the only time when mortgage interest may not pay off is with very small mortgages. Under those circumstances, you may be better off with the tax breaks offered with what's known as a "standard deduction" instead of your mortgage interest. More on this in Chapter 12, which covers taxes.) Since your interest payments are reducing what you pay out in taxes, the "return" on your investment begins to look even better. Add to that the tax deductibility of property taxes—these, either added to your monthly payment or paid in a lump sum, go to local government to fund schools and other municipal expenses—and the cost of home ownership becomes all the more attractive.

While there are other upsides to home ownership, the last ones I'll go into are the personal satisfaction and sense of autonomy you can enjoy by buying your own place. Consider this: Just how wonderful do you think it would be to go ahead and turn your garage into a workshop or redo the landscaping without having to call your landlord to ask permission? The freedom to do what you want with the space you live in, particularly if it's something that makes the place more valuable or just better looking or more comfortable, offers an exhilarating rush of independence that many other experiences cannot approach. In that sense, while some may argue that home ownership just ties you down, I would also point out that it also provides a form of independence and self-sufficiency on its own terms. And that's something that may, in fact, supersede simple monetary value.

Getting Started

If the preceding discussion has, at the very least, whetted your appetite some about buying a home, let's get into some of the nuts and bolts of how to get started doing just that. One thing I will not go into in much detail is the mechanics of finding the home you want—that's much too personal a consideration to warrant a whole lot of attention. Suffice it to say to go with what's comfortable when it comes to seeking out a home. For some of us, that means cruising the want ads and checking out those that seem interesting. Others may want to drive around and stop in at open houses (occasions when home sellers make their property available for inspection to whomever wants to drop by and look around). Still others may focus on a particular neighborhood and just keep their eyes peeled for homes that come up for sale in that particular part of town.

But before you go and flip head over heels over a home, get a genuine sense of what you'll be able to afford. The easiest and most reliable way to do that is to go to a mortgage lender and become what's known as prequalified, which means that the lender has examined your financial particulars and has determined just how much you can pay for a home (or, looked at another way, how large a mortgage you can afford to obtain). While determining how much you may be qualified to buy is a complicated and often convoluted process, the system effectively boils down to two different ratios, the front and the back. Here's an overview of how they work:

The front involves a breakdown of everything that can go into the monthly payment for a home and your corresponding ability to meet those expenses. For instance, if you want to get a $90,000 30-year mortgage at an interest rate of 8%, your monthly payment of principal and interest will be $660.39. Add to that the cost of property taxes and homeowners' insurance (this protects your property and is absolutely required), and you've got your final monthly housing expense. In this example, let's add on $150 a month for property taxes and an extra $30 a month for insurance. Total it up, and you've got $840.39 for overall monthly home ownership costs.

Then, to determine the front ratio, the lender will want to see how your income stacks up against that debt. Let's say you now earn $40,000 a year or $3,333 a month. In this case, the projected monthly payment of $840.39 represents just a bit more than 25% of your monthly income; that 25 becomes the front-end ratio.

The back ratio is your projected monthly housing costs plus any other debt you may have, including student loans, credit card debt (taking into account minimum monthly payments, if any), car loans, and other expenses. For the preceding example, let's say the back end adds another $400 a month. Add that to the $840.39 housing costs and divide it by your income, and you get a back-end ratio of just a bit more than 37%.

This leaves us with a front ratio of 25 and a back of 37. Simply put, the lower the numbers, the better, since that means that what you're spending on your housing and other debt make up a relatively small cut of your income. Moreover, how those front and back ratios are interpreted depends on the lender; some will let you carry more debt, some less. Although numbers will vary, most lenders won't want to see a front ratio that's greater than 28 and a back ratio that exceeds 36.

Bear in mind, however, that prequalification doesn't mean you'll actually get a loan. It's merely an educated estimate of just how large a loan you will likely be able to obtain. Final loan approval depends on other factors, including the home's appraised value and the results of a final credit check. So, if you prequalify for a good-size mortgage, congratulations, but don't assume the money's already in your pocket just yet.

↗ Useful Web Sites

The Loan Tutor (http://www.loanlocator.com/tutor/tutor.vlc) has an array of online calculators to help you figure out home affordability. The site is great for home-buying newbies, with a "loan ABCs" feature, a question-and-answer function, and a handy glossary.

There are also several other elements that lenders will examine when considering whether to fork over a mortgage. One is the down payment. With very few exceptions, you're not going to find a lender who's willing to finance the entire cost of a home. As a rule, lenders will want anywhere from 3 to 20% as a down payment. In the case of a $100,000 home, that means anywhere from $3,000 up to $20,000 in cash up front. On top of that, you can also expect to pay, on average, 5% or so in closing costs at the time you actually buy a house. These cover expenses such as the cost of obtaining a mortgage, property inspection, and other costs related to just getting into the house.

Not surprisingly, this makes the up-front expenses—down payment and closing costs—the biggest hurdle to home ownership, particularly for first-time buyers. Even a dirt-cheap down payment of 3% and a relatively chintzy 4% in closing costs translates to $7,000 on the barrelhead for a $100,000 home, cash that many prospective buyers simply don't have lying around. (Don't get all bent out of shape just yet—there are some ways to tackle this headache, which we'll discuss a bit later in this chapter. But it's best to know just how sizable the more immediate costs of home buying can be.)

Lenders will also look at your history of meeting your financial obligations. To do that, they'll go over a copy of your credit report in painstaking detail. Your credit report, which is a composite of financial information compiled from any of several agencies, offers an exhaustive (and, for many, unnerving) financial and personal profile. It's very much an X-ray; in addition to things such as your social security number and employment history, credit reports contain data on every time you've taken out some sort of debt or credit, such as loans, credit cards, and lines of credit, and your payment history in making good on them. Credit reports can also contain information on late payments and, even worse, on any failure on your part to pay back a loan and on any declared bankruptcy. Needless to say, the fewer the black marks and the more impressive the documentation of responsible debt management, the better you will appear to the lender.

Finally, lenders will also have a look at your employment history. While that may not carry as much weight as, say, your income or payment history, lenders never mind seeing a stable employment pattern where, for instance, you've held your current job for a couple of years or so. In particular, lenders like to see a history of employment within the same field; ex-lawyers who become pearl divers, then later move on to the sanitation and removal engineering industry will be studied with an especially keen eye.

↗ Useful Web Sites

Want to know if your credit history may cause you home-buying problems? Keystroke Financial has an online questionnaire at http://www.snws.com/loan-bin/credit/ that addresses the major questions that a lender will likely address. Answer them accurately, and you'll know just how well your past financial dealings may affect your chances of buying that home of your dreams.

The nuts and bolts of a good credit report—and ways to repair reports that are less than perfect—are addressed on a number of Web sites, including Consumer Credit Counseling (http://www.cccsdc.org/credit-road.html), Experian (http://www.experian.com/personal/repair.html), and http://www.start-smart.com/creditrepairfaq.html. These sites also offer step-by step guidelines on how to erase bad credit as well as information on new legislation that affects credit reporting.

Now That My Head Is Ready to Implode, How Can I Get Past Some of These Home Ownership Migraines?

Having possibly discouraged you about home ownership to no end, I think it's now time to deliver some good news. First of all, since most people reading this material will be first-time home buyers, be sure to check out what your state or local municipality has in the way of special programs for first-time buyers. These often overlooked programs can be a veritable godsend for someone who wants to buy a house but may for some reason lack the money to pursue it through more conventional means. For one thing, first-time-buyer programs frequently levy interest rates that are a good deal lower than the going average, which can mean hundreds less in monthly mortgage payments. On top of that, first-time-buyer programs have greatly liberalized down payment requirements, frequently requiring as little as 5% down or even less (some don't require any down payment at all). That removes the biggest stumbling block most prospective first-timers face—ponying up enough to meet down payment requirements. Some programs, in fact, are generous enough to include people who have owned property in the past but who haven't owned a home for the past several years.

The wrinkle—yes, there are always those to be had—is that many such programs have income caps that limit how much money you can make to qualify. Additionally, some programs, with an eye toward steering first-time buyers to property overlooked by conventional buyers, limit the value of the home. But bear in mind that requirements vary according to the state or local agency that's overseeing the programs and that most places have a variety of first-time-buyer incentives from which to choose. Start by contacting your state housing office to find out all that may be available in your area.

↗ Useful Web Sites

The National Council of State Housing Agencies has an online interactive map that gives you contact telephone numbers for state housing finance agencies. Have a look at http://www.ncsha.org/.

If, by chance, you make too much money to fall within the confines of a first-time-buyer's arrangement—or the homes within those programs don't appeal to you—try looking into Fannie Mae or Freddie Mac loans. These agencies (which are shortened nicknames for the Federal National Mortgage Association and the Federal Home Loan Mortgage Corporation) also offer attractive packages for first-time buyers. These private companies, which don't actually sell any mortgages but buy them from banks, credit unions, and other lenders, were created by the federal government to, among other things, make first-time home ownership more viable for more people.

Fannie Mae and Freddie Mac have any number of provisions that make home ownership more affordable. For one thing, down payment requirements are a good deal lower than those for conventional loans (as skimpy as 3% down). Income-to-debt ratios are also more forgiving than many run-of-the-mill mortgages. On top of all that, unlike other types of first-time buyer programs, these usually involve no income restrictions. So, if you're shopping for a first-time-buyer deal, be sure to ask any lender you talk to about what sorts of Fannie Mae and Freddie Mac programs it may offer; lenders usually package such programs under some sort of cutesy name of their own concoction, so just be sure to ask for Fannie Mae or Freddie Mac.

⬈ Useful Web Sites

For more information on Fannie Mae and its array of home-buying programs, pay a visit to its Web site at http://www.fanniemae.com/. Likewise, have a look at the Freddie Mac Web site at http://www.freddiemac.com/. Both sites are packed with information for people new to the home-buying and financing process.

Finally, don't overlook Federal Housing Administration or FHA loans. These loans, again provided to local lenders, let you get into a home with a fraction of the usual down payment. The system involves a sliding scale based on the size of the mortgage. For instance, lenders require 3% down on the first $25,000, 5% on the next $100,000 loaned, and 10% on anything beyond that. It works out a good deal cheaper than the 20% down most lenders require. For a $100,000 loan, for instance, an FHA down payment would come to only $3,750, compared to the $10,000 to $20,000 a regular loan would mandate. And, since these loans are insured by the feds, lenders offer more leeway as to how much money you make and the amount of debt they will let you carry.

⬈ Useful Web Sites

For more details on FHA loans and how to go about getting them, go to a handy question and answer page posted by East West Mortgage at http://www.ewmortgage.com/scheng/fhaloans.htm.

Ways to Beat Those Down Payment Blues

If by chance you don't qualify for any of the special programs we talked about earlier or if you prefer to seek more conventional financing, you may well be staring at a hefty down payment—maybe upward of 20% or so. Substantial as this is, it's not necessarily insurmountable, as there are a few strategies you can pursue to either get enough money for a down payment or at least reduce it.

The first option is rather obvious: Ask family members if they'd be willing to help you out. Don't be embarrassed by this—since the greatest hurdle most first-time buyers face is the down payment, this is an exceedingly common way to piece together enough up-front money. There are essentially two ways to do this: through an outright gift or through a loan. With a gift, if you have a family member sufficiently generous to give you enough to cover a 20% down payment, it's a very good idea to draw up a gift letter explaining who's giving what to whom for what purpose and that repayment isn't expected.

If you don't happen to have anyone in your family with piles of cash lying around, the next consideration is a loan. While this may sound appealing to you because you don't have to accept someone's blind generosity—and, by the same token, may be more acceptable to a family member who's skittish about simply handing the money over without any prospect of repayment—the downside to loans is that they have to be repaid. Therefore, anyone looking at your mortgage application will add the loan your debt ratio, which, in turn, could kill your entire application if it pushes your debt load too high. So, approach a loan carefully, as it might effectively backfire against you.

↗ Useful Web Sites

Getting married? Have enough woks to open your own Chinese restaurant? Request wedding gifts in the form of a contribution to your home down payment. Go to http://www.interest.com/sa961029.htm to get the shimmy on ways to do this, including opening up a down payment bridal registry at a bank.

Another option that lets you get into a home with less than 20% down is called private mortgage insurance or PMI. This is an invention by the private sector to basically "protect" themselves from buyers who put down less than 20% (which, according to lenders' infinite wisdom and statistical wherewithal, makes you a greater risk than someone who can come up with 20% down). Since, so the thinking goes, buyers who put less than 20% down are more likely to default on their mortgages, PMI protects the lenders in the event you do default. In this sense, PMI is a very weird anomaly in the financial world—you as the buyer pay the premiums, but it's your lender, not you, who is protected against loss.

⤴ Useful Web Sites

For a brief overview of PMI, along with a listing of major companies that sell it, go to http://www.loanpage.com/morpmi.htm.

A more detailed view of PMI that examines various aspects of its use is available at http://www.amo-mortgage.com/library/mortgageinsurance.html.

Weird or not, PMI has opened up home ownership for many who could never have come up with the usual 20% down. How PMI works and how much you end up paying and when will differ depending on the provider. For instance, the size of the PMI payment is based on how large your loan is, the amount required by the particular lender, and the type of loan the insurance will cover (adjustable rate loans, for instance, are considered more risky than fixed rate and therefore usually lead to larger PMI payments). The bigger the loan, the greater the PMI. To give you an idea, I once owned a house where I could put down only 10% and carried a loan of about $140,000. To that I added a monthly PMI payment of about $75. While many PMI programs just tack on an extra amount to your monthly payment, there are also PMI setups where you can pay the entire premium up front when you close on the house.

While PMI does nothing more than get you into a home with less than 20% down—unlike your mortgage interest, for example, you can't deduct PMI from your taxes—it need not be a lifelong commitment. Federal legislation passed in 1998 allows you to cancel PMI if your equity in your home reaches 20%, there's no other loan attached to the house, and you've made your mortgage payments on time for the prior two years. Even better, should your equity climb to 22%, the new law stipulates that cancellation occurs automatically.

There are, however, some drawbacks to the new legislation. The law doesn't apply to any mortgage that's taken out prior to July 1999. And, to make matters worse, the law requires lenders to include only the principle from mortgage payments when figuring equity (that eliminates property value appreciation, which often gives equity a huge boost). Because of these limitations, getting to 20% may still take a long time, since, as it's defined by the new law, equity is purely a matter of mortgage paydown.

That said, it pays to know precisely how your lender will handle your PMI and what you'll need to do to eliminate it. Be sure to ask at the outset what the requirements are for cancellation of PMI coverage; if you can, get the answer in writing. In many cases, lenders will require an appraisal (which can cost you several hundred bucks) and extensive documentation to prove that, in fact, you now own 20% of your home. So, be aware of PMI and try to keep track of your equity on your own so that you know exactly where you stand (there have been some horror stories about buyers who unknowingly paid PMI year after year, unaware that they had long passed the 20% equity mark and could get rid of their PMI. In one shocking example, an elderly woman in Texas was found to still be paying PMI, even though she nearly owned her house free and clear.)

➚ *Useful Web Sites*

If you find you need PMI, don't make the mistake of paying it forever. To track down strategies and other ideas to cancel PMI, have a look at http://www.pmirescue.com/index.html (a Web site that takes a rather militant view of PMI and the need to remove such a scourge from the landscape.) For a bit less acidic view of getting rid of PMI, have a look at http://www.ahahome.com/topics/finance/pmi.html.

Finally, as you would for a mortgage or any other sort of financial deal, shop aggressively for a down payment. Again, money is a very competitive game, and lenders are eager to entice your business. A 20% down payment is by no means cast in stone for some lenders; some may, in fact, be willing to consider regular financing with less up front. So it never hurts to ask—the worst they'll say is no.

Adding Muscle to Your Monthly Money

If by chance, your problem isn't the down payment—say Gramps left you a pile or you've been a world-class saver—but your income is, there are ways to correct that situation as well. Once again, try looking to your family and see if someone might be willing to cosign your mortgage. Under this arrangement, although you as the buyer may be paying every penny of the mortgage, a cosigner legally acknowledges a responsibility in making sure that the mortgage is paid. In effect, when someone cosigns with you, he or she agrees to make the mortgage payments in the event that you can't. That's why, during the loan application process, lenders will want to see as much financial information from cosigners as they will from the borrowers themselves.

There's no denying it—when someone cosigns a loan, that person is sticking his or her neck out for you, since he or she is agreeing to cover the payments if you cannot. But cosigning also helps buyers who are short on income get into homes, because most lenders will loosen up their lending and debt requirements if someone else is making a financial commitment to the loan. In fact, some lenders have been known to increase their accepted level of debt by as much as 7% if a qualified cosigner has also signed on for the mortgage. However, it goes without saying that you have to approach cosigning carefully. If, on the off chance you as the borrower fail to make your mortgage payments, the lender will come after your cosigner for the money. Sad to say, but that has caused many a rift within families and between well-intentioned friends.

A wrinkle on the notion of cosigning is called equity sharing. Unlike cosigning, in which a family member becomes involved in paying for a house only if things head south, equity sharing lets family members purchase an ownership interest in the property—for instance, a family member may agree to pay a third of the monthly mortgage payment in return for part ownership. Not only can this arrangement provide the necessary financial muscle for someone whose income doesn't quite measure up, but equity sharing also creates an investment for the non-occupant owners. When the occupant sells the house, the co-owner gets a portion of the sales proceeds, based on the percentage of the investment he or she has paid. (Not surprisingly, this notion can prove very appealing to parents who provide a very large down payment and wish to exercise continuing control over the money they've sunk into the house.)

Loan Shopping

As we've stressed with other financial services that you're laying out good money to obtain, be certain to shop aggressively for a mortgage loan. It's a good idea to call at least several banks and compare overall loan packages, including interest rates, loan fees, and time required to process the loan application. If you're a member of a credit union, be sure to ask about the union's loan packages, which can often beat those offered by conventional lenders. See if your employer offers any sort of mortgage program (some do, often with very attractive terms). If possible, compare those deals with ones offered by mortgage brokers, loan specialists with access to a great array of mortgage programs and services and who often are exceedingly helpful in tracking down loans for people in unusual circumstances (e.g., someone who can afford to put down only 5%, for example). Finally, don't overlook comparing any offer you may be considering with those provided online by any number of information services and mortgage companies. These can give you information on what the going average is for home loans nationwide and in your part of the country. This information, in turn, can give you a very good feel for whether the deal you're looking at measures up to what else is out there or whether you should keep looking around.

↗ Useful Web Sites

Nowhere may the explosion of online services be more evident than in the hundreds of online services that let you shop for, compare, and apply for a home mortgage. To whet your appetite, punch in "mortgage" in your search engine and watch how many of these goobers show up. However, here are a few to get you started:

There's a great article on the *Detroit News* Web site that helps unravel some of the confusion that can come from choosing an online loan source. It's at http://detnews.com/cyberia/sites/970329/mortgage/mortgage.htm. There's even a listing of links for mortgage lenders, sources of interest rate information, and other useful material.

Mortgage Market Information Services (http://www.interest.com/) is another great starting point for shopping for a loan. In addition to information on interest rates, special mortgages, and other matters of interest, the site lets you track down a lender close to where you live. It even tells you whether or not the lender has a Web site.

The Mortgage Loan Page (http://www.loanpage.com/) lets you search for a mortgage company that meets your needs, be they geographic, a specific type of loan program, or someone who meets some other criterion.

If your interest runs specifically to mortgage rates, check out HSH Associates' Web site (http://www.hsh.com/). There, HSH, the biggest clearinghouse of mortgage information in the country, publishes the mortgage interest rates from more than 2,000 lenders. What's more, the information is updated on a weekly basis. The Web site also offers an easy-to-follow system that tells you how to contact any lender you may be interested in. Rather than running around town talking to every bank in sight, you can use this site to track down the best mortgage available, perhaps in just a few minutes.

Finally, not to beat something to death, but the Bank Rate Monitor has a specific page (http://www.bankrate.com/brm/rate/mtg_home.asp) that lets you find the best mortgage where you live. Type in your state, the city where you want to shop, and the type of mortgage you have in mind, and-presto—you've got the institution making the loan, the date of the interest rate, how long you can "lock" the loan in, and how large a loan you can apply for.

Loans all consist of a number of common features, including the following:

> *Interest rate.* This, like any other sort of loan, is the charge you must pay to the bank or lending institution that's fronting you the money. Within this category are two primary types of interest—fixed rate and adjustable. Fixed rate means what the term implies—the interest rate that you start with stays in place as long as the loan is in place. In that sense, a fixed-rate loan offers predictability and security—come what may, your mortgage payment is always going to be the same, month after month. Fixed mortgages come in two primary forms, 15- and 30-year (15-year fixed mortgages levy a lower interest rate than a 30-year, although you have to pay the money back in half the time, which increases your monthly payments.)
>
> Adjustable mortgages (known in the vernacular as ARMs), on the other hand, also mean what the title says—their interest rate adjusts or changes according to how the loan is set up. For example, a one-year adjustable mortgage's interest rate changes every 12 months—if prevailing interest rates have gone up during that time, an adjustable will likely increase. However, if interest rates have gone down, an adjustable will follow suit. Additionally, there are a number of other adjustable rate mortgages; for example, some adjust every year, some every three years, some every five years, and some according to other time periods.
>
> Which type of mortgage you should choose depends on a number of factors, starting with your own personal makeup. If you like the idea of always knowing what your mortgage payment is going to be, then look long and hard at fixed rate deals—an ARM's uncertainty and volatility may well drive you over the edge. On the other hand, you pay higher interest with a fixed rate than you would with an ARM—as of mid-1998, the average going rate for a 30-year fixed mortgage was hovering around 6.7% or so, while the average one-year ARM was about 5.4%. In that sense, ARMs may be attractive to a buyer who

wants to have lower payments at the beginning of a mortgage (say, someone who expects a steady series of pay raises and, hence, more money that can go toward home payments later on). But bear in mind that while all ARMs have to, by law, stipulate the maximum amount of interest they can adjust up to, things can change quite quickly (for instance, many one-year ARMs can increase by as much as two percentage points in a single year). So, when you're shopping around, be sure you know everything about a loan—and what sort of arrangement you'll be most comfortable with—before you agree to anything. Finally, don't get into an adjustable mortgage if you think—or, even worse, some "expert" has said—that interest rates are going to go down. For the most part, trying to play the interest rate prediction game is a sucker's bet. Choose a mortgage that matches your temperament and what you can afford.

⤤ Useful Web Sites

For a very complete examination of various types of mortgages and ways to evaluate which one may work for you, point your browser to http://www.ces.ncsu.edu/depts/fcs/docs/he437.html.

Points. One element that affects the amount of interest you pay is called points. A point is equivalent to 1% of the amount of the money you're borrowing (one point on a $150,000 loan is worth $1,500, for instance). Points, usually paid up front when you take out a loan, get you lower interest rates. For example, a $100,000 loan with no points may have an interest rate of 8%; paying a point may drop it to 7.7% or so, with two points maybe trimming it to as low as 7.5%.

Deciding between a higher interest rate and paying points up front depends largely on how long you plan to stay in the home. The general rule of thumb is that the longer you'll be there, the more sense it makes to pay the points, since, over time, you can recover their cost and actually save money since you'll be paying a lower interest rate. However, if you suspect you may not be in a home for more than a few years—you expect you'll want to trade up or a job relocation may ultimately be in the works—pocket the money you'd pay for points and pay a slightly larger interest rate. For what it's worth, I've never been that much a fan of paying points (in fact, I've never paid a single point for any of the homes I've bought). Not only do they require you to come up with more cash at the beginning—just when you may be struggling with a down payment and closing costs, plus who knows what else—but the uncertainty of just how long you may own your home makes getting them back an iffy proposition in some cases.

Finally, as it was once explained to me by a knowledgeable real estate broker, both points and interest rates boil down to the same thing—money out of your pocket. In the case of points, the money is taken out in a chunk at the beginning of the loan, while interest is applied in much smaller increments over the life of the loan. Which would you prefer—money pulled from your wallet all at once or money taken bit by bit, thereby freeing up extra cash that you can use for something else? With few exceptions, I'd always go with the latter.

↗ *Useful Web Sites*

For a fast view of whether you're better off paying points or not, plug into the online points calculator at http://www.smartcalc.com/cgi-bin/smart-calcpro/HOM5.cgi/FinanCenter. There, just enter all the particulars, and you'll see in an instant whether points or a slightly higher interest rate is the way to go.

Homeowners Insurance

If home ownership seems in the cards for you—whether round the corner or in the next couple of years or so—be ready to buy homeowner's insurance when you buy your home, because it's essential protection.

Homeowner's insurance covers two protection bases. First, it protects your home and its contents in the event something catastrophic happens, such as a fire or theft. Even more important, it also offers what's known as liability coverage, which protects you should something happen on your property that leads to a lawsuit—say, someone breaks a leg (or even worse, his or her neck) and either the victim or the family decides to sue you for everything you've got, and then some (we'll cover the issue of liability in greater detail in Chapter 8).

A general piece of advice about homeowner's insurance is never, ever to cheap out. With other types of insurance, you can occasionally cut corners and save a few bucks, but don't risk something that you may have worked like the devil to get by pinching pennies. This means a couple of things. First, when discussing how much you may need in "dwelling coverage" (this covers the house itself), be sure you have enough insurance in place to actually rebuild your entire house if need be. Don't base this amount on your property tax valuation or, even worse, on what you may have actually paid for the home. There's a good chance both those figures will fall short of the actual replacement cost. Instead, sit down and figure out how much it would cost if you had to rebuild the entire house, starting tomorrow. While you could do that by taking the square footage and multiplying that by some average per square cost, there's a much easier way—be sure to get guaranteed replacement cost insurance, which means your insurance company guarantees it will pay whatever it costs to rebuild your home, regardless of how much that might come to. It will cost more than regular coverage but, with the spiraling cost of construction, it's money well spent.

One caveat: Make sure you know whether your insurance company sets any maximum to its definition of guaranteed replacement. Some will pay the whole freight no matter how expensive, while others are not so generous. Some, for instance, may say that they'll pay only a certain percentage above what you have in dwelling coverage. Thus, if you have a $100,000 home and your guaranteed replacement coverage is limited to only 25% above that limit, you'll end up making up the $10,000 difference if your house burns to the ground and it actually costs $135,000 to rebuild.

Be sure to get enough liability insurance to cover your assets; for instance, if you guess you're worth $30,000, pay for that much coverage. In fact, if you can afford it, try to get more liability coverage than you're actually worth; these days, with the unpredictability of the court system, this may prove valuable. To hold down the cost of liability coverage—and, for that matter, the cost of dwelling coverage as well—consider raising the deductibles on each type of coverage (this is the amount you have to pay out of your own pocket before your insurance kicks in). You can save some on your premiums if you take higher deductibles.

Know, too, that conventional homeowner's insurance does not cover earthquake and flood damage. As a rule, these two types of additional coverage are worth paying the extra money to get. Don't fool yourself into thinking that an earthquake simply isn't possible where you live—they happen all over the place, and often in areas you would never assume were earthquake vulnerable (for instance, in Maine we've had two quakes in the time I've lived here.) So ask your insurance agent about adding earthquake insurance. The price will be determined by how much your home is worth as well as the earthquake risk in your area.

(In fact, it pays to be proactive if you decide you need earthquake insurance. I bought quake insurance on a home only a year or so before a quake hit the area. While I'd been able to get my earthquake insurance simply by calling my insurance agent and asking that it be added on, after the earthquake hit my insurance company instructed my agent to personally inspect any home whose owner applied for quake coverage. The message was clear: Now that a quake had hit, getting insurance to protect yourself wasn't going to be as easy as it used to be.)

Likewise, unless you live on a mountaintop or a place that hasn't seen a drop of rain in years, look into getting flood insurance. By the government's last count, there are tens of thousands of cities and towns that can be affected by floods—ironically, though, basic homeowner's insurance doesn't mention floods. First investigate whether a flood is of genuine concern. Go to your city or town hall and ask if your community takes part in the federal government's National Flood Insurance system. If your town is included, that means you're at risk, so call the flood insurance program at 800-638-6620 to get information on flood policies offered by private insurers. Another way to see if you're really at risk for floods is to ask your insurance agent to show what's known as a flood insurance rate map. This divides areas according to flood risk—low, medium, and high. If you fall into the high-risk area, by all means get flood insurance. Even if you're in the middle, the couple of hundred dollars a year extra for flood insurance may be a smart buy.

↗ Useful Web Sites

Here are a few Web sites that do a nice job of explaining homeowners' insurance as well as describing ways to obtain it cost-effectively:

The Better Business Bureau offers a great primer on homeowners' insurance at http://www.bosbbb.org/lit/0072.htm.

If getting the most for your homeowners' insurance money is a top priority—and why shouldn't it be?—check out the Insurance Information Institute at http://www.iii.org/individuals/. This is also a great site for other bits of information and insight on homeowners coverage.

The Insurance News Network (http://www.insure.com /home/index.html#basics) has a nice, easy-to-understand explanation about homeowners' insurance, plus a handy link to the 10 largest homeowners insurance companies.

For details on how to go about buying flood insurance, the Federal Emergency Management Agency has a page that addresses that very topic at http://www.fema.gov/home/NFIP/answe2d.htm.

A Few Final Thoughts on Home-Buying

First, treat this chapter as a primer on the subject of buying a home. Any single chapter that claims to tell you everything you could possibly need to know about buying a home is merely fooling both itself and you. Rather, look on what we've covered as a reasonable introduction to the subject. If your interest goes beyond what we've covered, there are any number of additional resources available to help you out (such as the Web sites we've referenced throughout this chapter).

Here are a few final tips that may prove useful if and when you venture forth into the world of property:

▶ *Consider working with a competent real estate agent.* Again, I've had mixed results with real estate salespeople (that's all they are, and never lose sight of that fact). Some have been interested only in making the sale, regardless of whether the home in question matched my family's needs, while others have been genuinely interested and diligent in helping us get into a house we wanted. Suffice it to say, seek out the latter, as they can prove very helpful. For one thing, while you on your own may have access to those homes listed as available for sale in the newspaper and on the occasional sign on the street, real estate agents can tap into the multiple-listing service that lists virtually every home in the area that's for sale. A real estate agent can also help you shop among various neighborhoods and help you focus in on the type of house you want and can afford. My rule of thumb is this: If you find a real estate agent you like, pay particular attention to how well he or she listens when you describe (in great detail) the sort of house you want. Then, see what homes the agent shows you on your first shopping trip. If they generally match the kind of home you described, you've hooked up with someone who's hearing what you're saying, rather than what he or she wants to hear. If, on the other hand, you talk about your desire to live in a classically designed home built in the mid-1930s and all the agent shows you are houses that look like the Brady Bunch is ready to come tripping down the stairs, consider finding another agent.

Again, though, bear in mind that your agent is, at the core, working not for you but for the seller. The agent's commission is usually paid by the person selling the home, so no sale, no commission. Don't lose sight of the fact that not everything your broker tells you may be in your absolute best interest. With that in mind, it's often helpful to have a third party—an attorney, a financial planner, or even someone you know who's been through the house-buying game before—review anything having to do with your house before you sign off on it. That way, you can cover yourself against an agent who, while trying to get you a good deal, may be paying a bit too much attention to simply closing the deal.

↗ Useful Web Sites

If you're interested in working with a Realtor® (these, unlike real estate agents, have passed a series of courses and are members of the National Association of Realtors®), http://www.nnerealestate.com offers a nice checklist of questions and issues to raise before choosing someone to work with.

Likewise, http://www.homespot.com/r4main2w.htm provides an overview of issues to consider when working with a real estate agent, realtor, or buyer's agent.

▶ *Consider using what's called a buyer's broker who works exclusively for you, the buyer, rather than for the seller* (see Web site listed earlier). This can be a particularly good choice if you're looking in an area you don't know a great deal about—unlike a conventional broker, a buyer's broker may be much more up front with you when discussing a home's pluses and drawbacks. The downside is that you have to pay a buyer's broker a fee, which, as of this writing, can range all across the board, so be sure to discuss fees at the outset before working with a buyer's broker (one good tip is to strike a deal wherein your fee is a percentage of your target price range for a home, rather than a simple percentage of the price you actually wind up paying. This gives your broker some negotiating range and can reduce his or her motivation to negotiate a higher price and, as a result, a higher commission). If your broker works hard to get a really low purchase price, that can more than make up for the fee you pay him or her.

▶ *To that end, it's always a very good idea to enlist the help of an attorney who specializes in real estate to review any paperwork you may have before you actually sign it.* Much as some real estate agents and brokers would like to have you believe it, they're not necessarily experts in real estate law. A good lawyer can protect your interests and catch little nuances in contracts and sales agreements that laypeople can overlook. Again, you may end up paying an extra several hundred dollars or more, but the cost is undoubtedly worth it.

▶ *Think about buying a condominium or a townhouse instead of a house.* Going this route, like so much having to do with home buying, may involve something of a tradeoff. While condos and townhomes historically are tougher resells than houses, the lower cost of upkeep required may be particularly appealing to first-time buyers wary of getting themselves involved in something they're not prepared for. And, in many major metro areas, condos and townhomes are often considerably more affordable than single-family homes, particularly for first-time buyers (although, when figuring how much of a condo you may be able to afford, never overlook condominium association dues, which must be included as part of your monthly housing costs).

↗ *Useful Web Sites*

For a brief overview of some issues specific to buying a condo or townhome, check out http://www.bankrate.com/brm/green/mtg/mort7a.asp.

▶ *Additionally, if you're handy with tools, don't bypass a powerful buying principle known as sweat equity.* Here, a buyer purchases a home in need of some fixing up. While the house may need some serious repairs and refurbishing, many sweat equity homes allow buyers to get into a home at a fraction of the cost they might pay for a home in better shape. Moreover, the idea is that the buyer will continue to work on the house until it's transformed into a reasonably attractive, marketable property.

▶ *Finally, whether you're buying a sweat equity property or the Taj Mahal, always, always be sure to get the home inspected before you actually buy it.* A competent inspector will come into a home and examine it in great detail, checking for structural integrity, leaks, problems with termites and other pests, how well the pipes, electrical, and heating systems operate and any number of other critical considerations. Be sure to work with an inspector who's certified by the American Society of Home Inspectors, since this is still an industry where literally anyone can hang out a shingle and call him- or herself an inspector. If possible, tag along with the inspector during the inspection so that you can see firsthand any problems or concerns the inspector may uncover. A good inspection can easily run several hundred dollars, but it's money exceedingly well spent, since it should identify problems that you should know about before you buy any house. If, in fact, the inspector turns up something of concern, you can first try working with the seller to see if he or she might be willing to make some repairs or knock some money off the purchase price. Failing that—or if by chance your inspector finds that your home is located above a major fault line or a decades-old nuclear waste dump—you still have the chance to walk away from the deal free and clear with no harm to you.

↗ Useful Web Sites

For more information on the essentials of home inspection—and ways to find a qualified inspector— have a look at the Home Inspection Supersite (http://www.inspectamerica.com/). The site also offers a checklist of home inspection issues so that you'll know the sorts of things your inspector will be looking for before he or she even sets foot in the door.

Similarly, the American Society of Home Inspectors runs a great Web site that details the ins and outs of home inspection and explains ways to protect yourself during the home-buying process. It's at http://www.ashi.com/.

CHAPTER 8

The Joys of Insurance

For many people, no bigger oxymoron exists than the title of this chapter. For lots of us, there's no faster way to clear a room than to bring up the subject of insurance. Why that is, I've never been sure—maybe it's the stereotype of the pushy insurance salesperson who simply won't take no for an answer (I always think of a scene from an old Woody Allen movie where a political prisoner is tortured by forcing him to spend an entire afternoon with an insurance hawker). Perhaps it's the underlying premise of insurance that puts people off—this is something you have around in case something bad happens (cue *Dragnet* music). Undertakers and actuaries aside, the "if and only if" that insurance can stand for isn't a topic that most of us are particularly keen on discussing.

Admittedly, insurance isn't exactly a crowd pleaser, but knowing the kinds of insurance you need as well as those you can live without can save you a large chunk of money and grief in the long run—particularly if you clue into certain kinds of insurance that, however affordable and essential, are overlooked by many. Here, therefore, is a breakdown of the major forms of insurance available, as well as some ideas on how to sort out the necessary and the merely wasteful.

↗ Useful Web Sites

Here are a couple of useful general insurance Web sites that provide a variety of information and links to various types of insurance and insurance-related topics:

The Insurance News Network (http://www.insure.com) is a nice starting point for research and news on an array of insurance issues and questions. For instance, the site recently rated the best kind of health plans and examined the financial stability of major insurance carriers. A handy glossary of insurance terms and a compendium of frequently asked questions bolster the site's usefulness.

Quicken InsureMarket (http://www.insuremarket.com/) also offers an array of nuts and bolts information on insurance, including an insurance planner to help you figure out your insurance needs. Insure Market also offers direct links to a number of major carriers for policy information and price quotes.

To Your Health

There's no other way to put it: Health insurance is an absolute must. Despite that stark bit of reality, the number of Americans who put their financial lives and futures at risk to illness or injury is staggering. As of January 1998, the American Hospital Association estimated that some 42 million Americans lacked health care coverage.

Admittedly, many people who fall within that 42 million simply can't afford health insurance. Nobody's about to argue that health insurance is cheap, particularly for those living at or below the poverty level or who merely don't have an extra dime to spare. But also included in the ranks of the uninsured are millions of young people, still in college or not long out, who, for one reason or another, don't have health insurance. For some, it's an oversight, while for others, it's pure delusion—I'm young, healthy and I can better spend my money on things other than some insurance I probably won't ever have to use.

Sad to say, all it takes is an auto accident, a prolonged illness, or even something as "simple" as a broken leg to force you to experience the sobering reality of paying for medical care without any sort of insurance to protect you. To illustrate, my young daughter a couple of years ago had to spend one night in the hospital after she contracted pneumonia. Thankfully, she was home the next afternoon, well on her way to recovery. Cost of one night in the hospital and a few tests—more than $2,000. To say that I was thankful not just for her health but for the fact that her treatment didn't put us into hock for months is an understatement.

The bottom line—is this: No matter your circumstances, make sure you have adequate health insurance. If you don't have it, get it. If you have it, try to make time to review it so that you at least have a working knowledge of what your coverage entails (or, if you're already working with an insurance agent, ask him or her to review it with you).

Health Insurance 101

Although it may seem to have more twists and turns than the human intestine, health insurance basically boils down to two types—fee-for-service and what's known as managed care. Fee-for-service is more pricey but also offers more options. Fee-for-service allows you to go to any doctor you choose (which is great if, for instance, you've been seeing the same doctor for years and have no desire to switch). Generally, the policy pays 80% of any costs you rack up, after any deductible, with you as the patient responsible for the remaining 20%. Most fee-for-service programs also set limits on how much you may have to pay in a given year, as well as how much the plan will pay you overall.

Sound good? Well, there are a few catches. For one thing, fee-for-service policies can be costly (prices vary according to where you live, your health, and even your gender (women generally pay more for health coverage than men). And, on top of that, they all set a requisite limit on how much you have to pay out of your own pocket before the policy's 80% share kicks in. That minimum (the deductible, a term we've encountered in prior chapters) can run as high as a couple thousand bucks every year and even higher.

If those numbers make you dizzy (hang on, get your health insurance before you feel like you're going to faint), there's always managed care. These policies are a good deal cheaper than fee-for-service (individual visits to a doctor, for example, often cost you only couple of dollars) and also offer greatly reduced premiums and, with many, no deductible at all. But the wrinkle—yes, yet another—is that you're limited to seeing doctors who are chosen by the insurance provider. Managed care gives you a list of participating doctors who, if you use them, will let you enjoy some of the lower costs we just discussed. Of course, you can always go to any doctor you choose, but with managed care, that will end up costing you. On top of that, some managed care programs are notorious for making you wait days and even weeks before you can get in to see a participating physician.

Managed care offers even bigger headaches if you have to see a specialist. Here, there are two subsections of managed care—health maintenance organizations (commonly known as HMOs) or preferred provider organizations (known by the equally cute PPO). If you belong to an HMO, your regular doctor usually has to clear any visits to specialists before you're covered by insurance. By comparison, PPOs generally don't require your primary-care doctor's okay before you can seek out a specialist.

↗ *Useful Web Sites*

Happily, the Internet offers a number of great Web sites that can help you unravel the confusion surrounding health care coverage and which type might work best for you. Here's a sampling:

The American Medical Association has a comprehensive Web page covering all types of health care coverage and its nuances, both advantages and drawbacks. It's at http://www.ama-assn.org/_insight/gen_hlth/ahcpr/ahcprfin.htm.

If you'd rather use a source other than the AMA, a couple of other sites that go into some detail about choosing a health plan are at http://www.medhelp.org/ccf/insure.htm and http://www.louisville.com/health/insurance.html.

HMOs? PPOs? All the acronyms got your head spinning? Go to http://www.medicalsocieties.org/hmo.htm for a breakdown of what the acronyms all mean and how the various types of insurance differ.

If the question of health insurance boils down to a PPO or an HMO, information at http://www.charm.net/~jmevans/hmo.htm may help make the distinctions between the two a bit clearer.

If You're Still in School

Happily, most of the news in this little section is good. Many, if not most, folks who are enrolled full time as students are covered by their parents' insurance policies, up to age 18 and to 22 if you continue as a full-time student. However, coverage from your parents' policy ends once you leave school or cut back your studies so that you no longer qualify as a full-time student. Even more unfortunate, if you're continuing on to graduate school, you're no longer eligible for coverage from your parents' program once you pass age 22, full-time student or not. An additional wrinkle: Your parents' health insurance may be a form of managed care program that limits the doctors you can see and still be fully covered. Depending on where you attend school, that may make finding a participating doctor or health service difficult to find.

So, if by one of the above wild cards, you no longer qualify for coverage (or if your parents' coverage is severely limited or, even worse, your parents have no health insurance to begin with, a condition that fully justifies a rather ranting lecture on your part), it's essential that you get some. One place to check is the university or college you're attending, since many provide students with low-cost health insurance programs. Obviously, you can also seek out an insurance agent to ask about the sorts of individual policies that may fit your needs, but it behooves you to check with school first. The odds are strong that you'll end up paying less than you will if you have to go out and get a policy on your own. Likewise, if you're in a fraternity or sorority, there's a chance that you can get a similar policy through a deal cut by your national chapter.

On the Job

Here, we also start out with a bit of good news: It's becoming increasingly rare to find a company that doesn't offer its employees some sort of health care coverage. In fact, more and more employers are providing their workers with the choice of either a fee-for-service plan or some sort of managed care arrangement. Usually, with either choice, the cost of the program is split between you and your employer, with regular amounts being withdrawn automatically from your paycheck to cover your share of the expense. At first blush, it may seem like a lot to spend, but bear in mind a similar program would cost one heck of a lot more if you were picking up the entire tab yourself. On top of that, employer-provided coverage is generally easier to get than individual policies, since insurance companies are a good deal more picky when it comes to whom they'll cover on an individual basis.

There are a few issues to bear in mind. While managed care will almost certainly be less expensive than fee-for-service, check to see if the extra money might not be well spent. Ask a few of your fellow employees who are using managed care to see how long it's taken them to get in to see a doctor. Are they happy with the care they're getting, or would they much rather be with a doctor of their own choosing? By the same token, do workers who go with fee-for-service think they're getting a good deal? Is the extra money they're spending worth the freedom of choice and the shorter wait times to see a doctor? Also, be sure to see if you can raise the deductible on the fee-for-service plan your employer offers. This may result in more out-of-pocket expenses if you're sick or injured, but it will also lower the premiums you pay.

Several other considerations: check out how long the waiting period is before your coverage begins. When you start a new job, there usually is a period of time when you're not covered by your new health insurance program. If it's a while, make sure that some sort of short-term coverage is in place, either through an individual policy you buy for only a few months or, if you were covered by insurance at your prior job, by what's known as COBRA coverage (an acronym for the Consolidated Omnibus Budget Reconciliation Act). This coverage, which is available from most employers, allows you to continue to receive health care coverage from your old employer's policy, provided you pay a premium. The monthly cost may seem steep, but it's infinitely better than going without any sort of coverage at all, and, after all, it'll go on for only a short time.

Finally, check out your program's policies regarding preexisting conditions (illnesses or conditions that you had before you signed up for the new health care coverage). Some plans make you wait months before you're covered for these, while others cover you immediately. This is particularly important if you happen to be pregnant. In fact, if you're thinking about having a child, go over your policy's coverage for prenatal and birth expenses. Some are remarkably cheap (the proverbial $2 baby), while others make the patient pay a good deal more. To that end, if you're thinking about starting or adding to your family and your company's health coverage is managed care, it may not be a bad idea to see if you can meet with the doctors who'll be handling your pregnancy and, if possible, tour the facilities covered by your policy. I know of someone whose child cost her a total of a whopping $7; the trouble was that she described the experience of having the baby in the required hospital as giving birth in a barn. A cheap deal, but not one I'm certain I would have been all that happy about.

Health Insurance? Nyet

If, by chance, your employer does not have a health insurance program in place or if you're temporarily unemployed or self-employed, it's incumbent upon you to go out and get coverage on your own. Again, it cannot be emphasized enough how essential this is: Cut corners in other areas of your budget and expenses if you must, but try to find at least something so that an illness or injury doesn't wipe you out completely.

Perhaps the most obvious option here is to seek out an insurance agent who can hook you up with an individual health insurance policy. Obvious it may be, but it may not be the most cost-effective—particularly when compared with group policies, conventional individual health insurance can be exceedingly pricey. Therefore, before you start flipping through the phone book to find an agent, consider a few alternatives:

The first is to look for group coverage through a different medium. Here, professional organizations can be a boon, since many offer members health care coverage at a fraction of the cost of an individual policy. For example, in my field, there are several journalism societies that offer decent health care plans. So, depending on your profession—engineering, legal, medical, what have you—contact one or more professional organizations and price out the policies they offer. Moreover, don't limit your search to just your profession—fraternal and religious organizations, for instance, also offer health care coverage to members.

Another idea is to look for alternative health care coverage that effectively rewards you for staying healthy. These kinds of programs, which are ideal for someone who stays in good shape and doesn't, as a rule, rack up a whole lot of medical costs, aren't particularly comprehensive—for instance, things like checkups, quick doctor visits, and prescriptions will likely come out of your pocket, given that the deductibles are usually pretty high. But the plan premiums are a relative bargain, and the coverage can be pretty good should something occur that results in a hefty bill. To shop for these, look through alternative health magazines and other similar publications (for example, I've seen these sorts of deals advertised in yoga and other sorts of exercise magazines).

Finally, look into what's called temporary coverage. These policies cover you for only a few months and won't help you out if you have any sort of preexisting condition. However, they are inexpensive and are ideal for someone who, say, is temporarily unemployed but who hopes to land a new job that offers a health care plan. These plans can also see you through any waiting period before permanent form of coverage kicks in.

↗ Useful Web Site

For more information on temporary coverage—whether you're in between jobs or just out of school—have a look at http://www.charm.net/~roy/tem.html.

The Tywell Insurance Finder (http://www.tywell.com/tywell01/index.htm) has a handy search system that lets you track down local insurance agents who may meet your needs. You can also use the system to obtain rate quotes via e-mail. Similarly, the AAA National Directory of Insurance Brokers (http://www.dirs.com/insure/) can help you locate a local agent according to a particular insurance specialty.

If, however, your choice is an individual plan bought through your agent, don't be so cost-conscious as to lay out good money for something that borders on worthless. Check the policy's provisions to see how much out-of-pocket expense you'll be expected to pay, as well as the maximum amount of coverage the policy will ultimately afford (the general rule of thumb is to avoid any policy that doesn't offer at least $1million in overall benefits. If you think that's exorbitant, bear in mind that prolonged illnesses requiring hospital stays can pile up expenses in a very big hurry. Remember the example of a one-night hospital stay for my daughter and the four-figure bill that racked up?) Look over the policy to make sure it doesn't have any sort of weird exclusions, such as certain illnesses or injuries that are not covered. Also, make certain the policy has a guaranteed renewal clause; not only does that let you renew the coverage as much as you like, but it means that the insurer can't zap your coverage or raise your premiums if you get sick.

One last rule: When shopping for individual health insurance (or any other insurance, for that matter, that involves your dealing with an insurance salesperson), try using an independent insurance agent rather than one who represents only one company. An independent has programs and policies from a variety of companies, which, in turn, gives you greater shopping muscle and can, perhaps, result in lower costs in the long run.

↗ Useful Web Sites

To track down an independent insurance agent where you live, the Web site of the Independent Insurance Agents of America (http:// www.iiaa.iix.com/) offers an easy-to-use search engine. The site also provides useful information on shopping for insurance and up-to-date news pertaining to insurance issues.

Live-and-Let-Live Insurance

Winston Churchill once described Russia as "a riddle wrapped in a mystery inside an enigma." Today's consumers might well describe life insurance in those very same terms. Life insurance these days comes in a bewildering array of types, payment programs, and coverage options, enough to make the former Soviet Union appear rather straightforward and above board by comparison.

There's a simple maxim that can effectively cut through the confusion enveloping life insurance: Don't buy it if you don't need it. Here, the rule is straightforward—remember, at its most basic level, life insurance is used to replace income in the event of the policyholder's death. If there's no one—a spouse, a child, or someone else—who is depending on your ability to go out and earn a paycheck, then life insurance is a waste. Life insurance is also unnecessary for anyone who simply doesn't generate a substantial percentage of a family's income, such as someone who stays home to help raise children. So, if you're single or not contributing much in the way of financial support, it's difficult to think of many instances when dropping good money on life insurance actually makes sense.

Note: There is, however, one wrinkle worth noting. You may want to consider covering a stay-at-home parent if the other parent works long hours and therefore contributes little to child care and other similar responsibilities. If, by chance, the stay-at-home spouse dies, that means the surviving spouse will have to pay someone to look after the kids, take care of the home, and so on. And that can prove expensive.

If, however, you do have someone who's relying on your income—a spouse, a child, perhaps even a parent for whom your paycheck represents an important form of supplemental income—then you may want to give life insurance a good long look. But before you do that, grind one principle into your brain: No matter how much insurance salespeople will argue to the contrary, never, ever treat life insurance as an investment. Life insurance's primary function derives from its name—to ensure financial safety—so focus on getting the right kind of protection and treat any sort of investment value, purported and otherwise, as an ancillary benefit.

↗ *Useful Web Sites*

For further discussion on what life insurance is and isn't, check out the Insurance FAQ article at http://www.invest-faq.com/articles/ins-life.html.

There's another question that we should tackle before we get into choosing the kind of insurance that fits your needs—how much? Here, start with your living expenses for the number of years the insurance will cover. If you have a toddler at home whom you'd like to send on to higher education, add on college expenses as well as an emergency fund. Then subtract your spouse's income and income from investments, if any. That should give you a fairly good estimate of your insurance needs.

A couple of considerations here. Unfortunately, it's probably prudent not to include Social Security in the equation, the way things are going. Instead, keep that out of the mix, and if by chance it's still around when you hang up your working shoes, treat it as a pleasant surprise. Equally important, while it's always wonderful to economize and save money when you can, don't shortchange yourself when figuring these estimates. However macabre it may seem to look at it in this fashion, remember that dead people don't go back to work. So don't cheap out when you're looking to protect your loved ones. If you're going to spend the money, be ready to spend enough to get decent coverage.

⤴ Useful Web Sites

> For an online calculator that helps you figure out just how much life insurance you may need, have a look at http://www.bygpub.com/finance/LifeInsCalc.htm. Know, too, that many financial software programs also provide similar calculators and can give you a decent idea of just how much coverage you may need.

Now, to the terminology. Term life insurance is the most basic protection. The policyholder pays an annual fee (the premium) and is insured for a specific amount for that year. Term carries no savings component, and the premium usually increases every year. Wrinkles on basic term life include level term insurance, in which the premium holds steady for a specified number of years, and decreasing term, in which the premium stays the same but the policy's death benefit (what the insurance company will pay in the event the Grim Reaper comes calling) goes down.

Term's most appealing element is its simplicity. You pay the money, you get the coverage, and the deal is done, at least for that particular year. Another lure is term's relatively low up-front costs—compared with insurance that's designed to generate some cash value, term's first years are relatively cheap. While rates vary from one company to another, a decent $100,000 term life insurance policy for someone in his or her early 20s and in good health should never run more than a couple of hundred bucks a year. Still another perk is some term policies' "conversion" capability, which allows the policy-holder to convert the term policy (which has no value except for the death benefit) at any time into another kind of insurance that actually has some cash value.

That said, most people do well by choosing term. If nothing else, it's the most affordable form of coverage there is, and that can close the debate for a lot of shoppers. Another way to approach it is to see how long you're going to need the coverage. If you're in your 20s and you're looking to insure yourself for 20 years or less, term insur-ance can be the cheapest way to go. The thinking is that if you're investing during this period in your life, by the time you reach age 50 or thereabouts you may have accumulated sufficient assets to make insurance unnecessary (this state of financial nirvana, by the way, is called self-insurance and means that you have enough money stashed away that you don't need to take out any sort of additional insur-ance—a worthy goal for us all).

↗ Useful Web Sites

To follow up on a Web site mentioned earlier, http://www. quickquote.com/fFaqTermLife.html deals with questions on term life insur-ance.

The other type of life insurance is known as whole life. This type of insurance incorporates a savings mechanism. Whole life premiums are usually set for the life of the policy and invariably start out higher than initial term premiums. A whole life policy for the $100,000 face amount that we mentioned for our hypothetical term policy would likely cost several hundred dollars more a year.

Part of whole life's premiums pay for the actual insurance protection, while the remainder goes into a reserve account. The reserve performs two functions. One is to meet increasing insurance costs as the policyholder gets older. The reserve also builds up cash value through two ways: through a "guaranteed" interest rate and an additional return generated from insurance company investments, usually fairly conservative choices such as low-risk bonds or real estate. Whole life policies these days are paying anywhere from 6 to 7% annually. While that may seem rather paltry, bear in mind that earnings in life insurance policies aren't taxed—still no super return, but at least a bit better than it might seem at first glance. Remember, too, that dying isn't the only way to get money from a policy; should you cash in a whole life policy, you receive the cash value the policy has built up (minus certain surrender charges).

Another supposed advantage to whole life is its potential as a loan source. Policyholders can borrow a portion of the policy's cash value at a relatively low interest rate—currently in the neighborhood of 6 to 7%. Any loan that remains outstanding when the policyholder dies is subtracted from the policy's death benefit or the cash value if the policy is cashed out. (While this may seem like a sweet loan source, bear in mind that you're taking money out of the policy that you're paying into—in other words, you're borrowing from yourself. How generous of you.) A more genuine benefit to whole life is that, unlike term, the premiums don't necessarily go on forever. Many whole life policies can be paid up within a certain amount of time, sometimes as quickly as 10 years. After that, the coverage goes on, the cash value continues to increase, but the policyholder doesn't have to pay another cent in premiums. The downside is that the insurance still has to be paid for, and that comes from the policy itself—with those costs holding down growth, cash values grow more slowly than they would in some other type of investment.

There are several other drawbacks to whole life. Again, whole life costs a good deal more, year in and year out, than term. Moreover, much of these early premiums go toward sales commissions, not to building up cash value—for example, one whole-life policy specifies a cash surrender value of $2,177 if it's cashed out after five years, compared with $3,350 in premiums paid during those five years, a loss of more than one-third of the investment. Critics also discount whole life's tax-deferred earning status, pointing out that money going into such policies could also be placed in tax-deferred IRAs and 401(k) accounts and produce far better returns.

Yet another caveat: when shopping for whole life or any other cash-value product, you need to pay attention to "guaranteed" versus "projected" rates of return. While some companies' cash value projections may appear awfully enticing, make certain you understand the policy's guaranteed return and what may be more speculative. Take a long look at the interest rates used in company illustrations—cash value projections are often based on interest rates that can differ by as many as a couple of points from the policy's guaranteed interest rate. Those couple of points add up to a substantial difference over time.

Bearing all this in mind, the only situation in which whole life might be more useful than term is for someone who's genuinely averse to most kinds of risk—someone, say, who breaks out in a cold sweat at the mere mention of the stock market (as of this writing, given that the market is bounding up and down like a kangaroo with a dozen cappuccinos in him, that description may apply to quite a few of you). For these people, the savings component of whole life may be just the thing. It likely won't pay off as well over the long run as other types of investments, but it's certainly better than nothing at all. But, for most of us, term insurance just makes more sense—it's cheaper and more straightforward, and, as we pointed out earlier, if you keep investing, you may be able to dump it someday.

When shopping around for term insurance, pay attention to several features:

> ► *Check out how often your premium changes.* While many policies simply increase year after year, there are some insurance programs where the same premium holds for several years at a time. Although these premiums may be larger in the earlier

years than those for a policy whose premiums increase every year, at least you have the predictability of knowing how much your insurance is going to cost and can budget accordingly. Policies can now be bought whose premium is fixed for upward of 20 years.

▶ *Make sure that your policy can't be canceled by the insurance company if, for instance, you have a streak of bad health and run up a lot of expenses.* This provision, known as guaranteed renewability, is your insurance (pun once again most definitely intended) that your insurance will be there for you, regardless of your health. Any policy worth its salt will have this feature.

↗ Useful Web Sites

For a nice overview of the pluses and minuses of whole life insurance, go to http://www.e-analytics.com/fp7.htm. Ditto for http://www.insuremarket. com/basics/life/wholelifen.htm.

Needless to say, the terms "whole life" or "cash value" insurance have more than a few offshoots that go by different names, such as "universal life" and "variable life" where the amount you earn on—and pay into—the policy can vary greatly. The reason I didn't discuss them in the main body of the text is that I don't feel they're really suited to most people, let alone young folks with relatively simple coverage needs (that's why I stuck with the white bread whole life discussion). However, if you're interested in finding out more about variants within life insurance offerings, an absolutely great site is located at http://www.safetnet.com/New_Site/www_directory/ life/lifeTypesfrm.html. This page offers more than 30 different articles explaining the workings of virtually every form of life insurance under the sun, describing both their advantages and their drawbacks. Even better, the articles come from a variety of sources, including life insurance companies and consumer groups, so the overall content of the page offers a comprehensive, balanced perspective.

Auto Insurance

All states require that car owners carry some sort of automobile insurance. Even without that legal mandate, it would be foolhardy to drive a single inch without some type of auto insurance in effect. If nothing else, the statistics on the number of accidents, injuries, and resulting fatalities that occur each year should more than convince you of the essential role of auto insurance.

↗ *Useful Web Sites*

> If you're interested in what sort of auto insurance requirements and minimums may be in place where you live, have a look at the handy interactive search vehicle offered by the Insurance News Network at http://www.insure.com/states/index.html.

The largest portion of auto insurance is liability insurance, which covers you in the event you cause an accident and injure someone or something else (the coverage is effectively divided into bodily injury liability and property injury liability). While you'll hear all sorts of theories about how much of this type of coverage you should get, the general rule of thumb is this: The more you can afford, the better, but look for at least $100,000 per person, $100,000 for property, and $300,000 per accident.

The other major component of auto insurance is collision, which covers damage to the car itself as the result of an accident (another wrinkle on collision, known as comprehensive coverage, protects the car from damage in the event of fire or earthquake, or other natural disaster). Neither of these types of coverage is required under most circumstances—(the exception is a used car or a car funded by a bank loan, where collision and comprehensive are often mandated).

A third part of auto insurance is uninsured motorist liability. This can pay for medical costs, lost wages, and other expenses incurred should you have an accident with someone who doesn't have any liability coverage at all. A variant on this type of coverage is known as underinsured motorist liability—(in this case, the guy who slams into you has some liability coverage but not enough to meet all your expenses).

To piece these all together: First, get the most liability coverage you can. Then, if you have to or if, by chance your car is relatively new, check out collision and comprehensive. Finally, if your budget allows it, look into uninsured motorist coverage. One way to make all this more affordable is to take the highest deductibles you can, upwards of $500 and maybe even higher, as these reduce the size of your premiums. Be comfortable with what you choose for a deductible, however, because, after all, that's what's going to come out of your pocket up front in case something happens.

Another way to hold down your auto insurance costs is by eliminating collision coverage. You can do this if your car is several years old and the cost of replacing it wouldn't be as catastrophic if it were new. Alternatively, you can give some thought to dropping collision if the thought of driving a car with a few dings here and there doesn't make your skin crawl. The point is that once a car has aged some and its replacement value has plummeted, it's essentially up to you to decide when you think collision is no longer necessary.

A few other tips to mention that may trim auto insurance costs. First—no shocker here—try to drive safely, since drivers with better records get better rates than drivers who are more at home in a demolition derby. By the same token, don't smoke—statistics show drivers with those wretched things in their hands have more accidents and therefore represent a greater risk to the insurer. Finally, if you're still in school and getting good marks, let your insurance company know that. Many companies reward students with good grades with lower auto insurance premiums.

⤢ Useful Web Sites

Additional information on auto insurance can be found at these Web sites:

A nice primer on auto insurance and ways to cut your costs can be found at http://www.dtonline.com/insur/inauto.htm.

If you've ever wondered why auto insurance seems so reasonable for one driver and so criminally expensive for another, information at http://www.insurance man.com/auto.htm may be able to relieve some of your confusion.

> Last, Infoseek has a comprehensive automobile insurance center where you can research coverage, analyze just how much insurance you need, and get quotes online. Get ready for a mouthful, Web site-wise: http://www. infoseek.com/Topic/Personal_Finance/Insurance/For_individuals/Automotive _Insurance_Center?sv=N6&tid=15376.

"Blink and Miss Them" Types of Insurance

I've titled this section as I have because the next three types of insurance are often overlooked, particularly by people who may have health, life, and auto insurance and feel confident that all their protection bases have been covered. Well, not quite. There are three big holes that need to be filled, and they're essential to your long-term financial well-being.

Disability Insurance

Life insurance you may well be able to do without, health insurance may be relatively cheap if you're covered by your employer, but disability insurance is commonly excluded from many companies' health plans and is even more commonly overlooked by many consumers. And that carries dire possibilities: Statistics show that people in their twenties are far more likely to be disabled than killed.

That's what makes disability insurance costly but critical. Disability insurance protects your income in case you're hurt or sick for a long time and unable to pull down a regular paycheck. A good disability policy will pay anywhere from 60 to 80% of your salary if you become disabled—obviously, that doesn't replace all that you earn, but it's a darn sight better than nothing at all. The thinking behind this partial coverage is that, were disability making up your complete income, your only incentives would be to lay in a large cache of potato chips and a very complete schedule of daytime soaps instead of returning to full-time work.

Given the very real possibility of becoming disabled in some fashion sometime during your lifetime, it's essential that you have some sort of disability coverage. Again, there's a chance that your employer may offer coverage, but it's not a very likely possibility (studies have shown that roughly two out of three employers offer no disability, although, in some states, employers are required to provide disability, albeit for only a fairly short period of time).

A reasonable estimate for disability insurance is about $1,000 a year for roughly $12,000 in annual disability payments. But cheer up—some companies pay for their employees' disability coverage, while others let their employees buy into a plan at relatively inexpensive rates. It's the individual policies that are the most expensive.

One way to hold down the expense of disability insurance is to increase the waiting period (the time between the occurrence of the disability and the date the policy starts paying benefits). Usually, the best kind of disability insurance has a 90-day waiting period, but you may be able to get lower premiums if you increase the amount of time you're willing to go without benefits (to be absolutely specific, the term "waiting period" doesn't mean how long you have to wait to get your first check, as there's a bit of a waiting period after the formal waiting period is up. For instance, with a 90-day waiting period, you can expect to see your first disability check in about 120 days). Upping your waiting period to 180 days may lop off several hundred dollars a year in premium costs. However, if you opt for a longer waiting period, be sure you'll have enough cash in hand from other sources to live on during the extra time. One idea: Take the money you save in premiums and stash it in your emergency fund. That'll go a long way toward making up the difference.

Another element to watch for in a good disability policy is how long it will continue to pay benefits. The best policies will keep paying you until you're able to return to work full-time or, in the case of really severe disability, until you reach age 65, when, so the rationale goes, Social Security will help pick up the slack. By the way, most policies require you to return to full-time work that's suited to your background and experience once you're physically able, not necessarily the job you had prior to the disability. That means that a truck driver who loses his hearing may no longer be able to safely drive a truck but may be fully capable of doing some sort of office administrative work. There is what's known as "own-occupation coverage," which specifies that you can return only to the job you had prior to your disability—in fact, you can keep getting benefits if you're working at some other job, so long as you're under a doctor's care. But own-occupation coverage costs as much as 10% more than conventional disability coverage. Given the expense of disability insurance to begin with, it may not make a whole lot of sense to add to that cost.

↗ *Useful Web Sites*

Here are a few disability insurance Web sites that may be worth a look:

For general further information on disability insurance, have a look at http://www.insweb.com/research/faq/disability-q.htm.

A nice Web site that identifies key points and issues to think about when considering disability insurance is at http://www.alldigins.com/distips.html.

To give you an idea of just how much disability insurance you may need, check out the useful interactive calculator at http://www.life line.org/disability/calc/calcmsg.html, which will give you a ballpark estimate of what you're looking at.

Renter's Insurance

Renter's insurance is yet another form of insurance that is often bypassed, sometimes to the chagrin of the person who overlooked it. Some people think only property owners need insurance, while others assume their landlord has insurance and they, therefore, are in the clear. Allow me to hereby dispel these misconceptions. Admittedly, you don't have to be concerned about insuring the property you're renting, but everything that's inside that rental property, from televisions to computers to clothes, is your responsibility. And you should have insurance to cover any possible losses.

Moreover, while your landlord—unless he's state-of-the-art cheap or absolutely out of his mind—will certainly have insurance to protect the rental property, it's seldom that that insurance covers any tenant's possessions. It behooves you to check this out with your landlord before you sign any sort of lease, but chances are his or her insurance isn't going to extend to any of your stuff.

That makes renter's insurance essential, because it protects in two ways. For one thing, should you lose any of your possessions within the property—there's a fire, for instance, and your stereo's burned up or a burglar makes off with your TV—you're protected. Additionally, renter's insurance offers liability protection, which shields you in the event someone gets hurt or something is damaged in the rental property. That can cover anything from a party guest slipping on a rogue bit of rumaki and deciding to sue you for the resulting broken ankle to a dent you put in the apartment building walls when you're carrying your bed into your new apartment. In fact, liability insurance can also protect you if your landlord accuses you of starting a fire that takes out the entire building.

To track down suitable renter's insurance, start by compiling an inventory of everything you own and what its value might be. To play it particularly safe, keep this printed inventory in a secure place outside your home, such as in a safety deposit box. Another backup measure is to make a videotaped record of all that you own. Then shop around, because renter's insurance can vary widely. For instance, some policies set a minimum protection limit that may be much higher than the value of the items you own. In those instances, you could effectively end up paying for, say, $20,000 in insurance when you have only $4,000 of insurable items. So make sure you don't end up shelling out for an inordinate amount of coverage you don't need. Additionally, check the limitations of policies, since many set coverage limits on things such as jewelry, computers, and other types of valuables. With many policies, you may end up having to take out additional types of insurance, commonly known as "floaters," just to make sure those sorts of things are adequately protected.

Additionally, try to work it out so that you pay a bit extra to get what's known as replacement value coverage. This, as the name suggests, means your policy will pay you whatever it costs to actually replace a certain item, rather than its actual value at the time of the loss. For instance, say you leave the iron on and it tumbles onto your five-year-old sofa, frying it into a rather large briquette. The actual cost of replacing that sofa will likely be a good deal higher than the value of a five-year-old piece of furniture, so without replacement value coverage you'll end up making up the difference between what your insurance pays for your old sofa and the cost of a new one. Replacement value coverage isn't outrageously expensive—on average, it will add about 10% to your premium—but the extra coverage is definitely worth it, particularly if, God forbid, something major occurs and you have to replace a bunch of items.

Finally, bear in mind that renter's insurance remains something of a bargain in the often pricey world of insurance. For example, a policy covering $15,000 of your personal belongings and offering $300,000 in liability coverage should run you anywhere from $95 to $200 a year. Not bad, considering the amount of protection that affords.

One last consideration—if you use a laptop computer, cellular phone, organizer, or other electronic gizmo when you're away from home, chances are good that your renter's policy will offer little, if any protection for it. To insure these often very expensive items, look into separate "floater" policies that are specific to whatever you may be lugging around with you.

↗ Useful Web Sites

The American Renters Association has a great Web page that outlines what renter's insurance covers, why you need it, and what you should expect to pay for various types of coverage. Go to http://www.rentara.com/.

Prudential has put together a nice page covering all aspects of apartment and condo rental coverage. Have a gander at http://www.prudential.com/insurance/home/inhzz1007.html.

Under the Umbrella

Let's face it—we humans (Americans, in particular) are a litigious bunch. We just love to sue one another, often over what, on the surface, appears to be a trifling matter. Even worse, given our propensity to haul each other into court, we're even going so far as to sue under circumstances that many of us would find, well, embarrassing, to say the least (remember the woman a few years ago who sued McDonalds, claiming that she had been injured because their coffee was too hot?) That can make umbrella insurance an essential element of your overall insurance program. Umbrella insurance is liability insurance that adds an extra layer of monetary protection above and beyond that offered by homeowner's, renter's, and automobile insurance. That means that if you have a fender bender where the other driver decides to sue you for physical damage, real or otherwise, umbrella insurance covers you financially if, by chance, he wins a big settlement against you. Moreover, umbrella insurance is cheap—a million-dollar policy costs only a couple of hundred dollars a year.

Some financial pros argue that umbrella insurance is suited only to people with a lot of money to lose. To a certain extent, they're right, so you may be able to bypass umbrella coverage if your assets to date aren't all that substantial. However, if you don't have a lot now but have the potential to amass serious money down the road, umbrella insurance can shield you from any sort of decision that may count against your future earnings. So if you think your income stands to rise substantially in the future, it may well be worth the cost to protect those potential earnings.

↗ Useful Web Sites

Definitions of umbrella insurance, descriptions of the sort of person who may need it, and an idea of what you should expect to pay for a decent policy can be found at http://www.dtonline.com/insur/insurumbrella.htm.

↗ Shopping Online

Inherent in much of the preceding discussion is the idea that scads of information on insurance are available on the Internet, including ways to shop for it online. So here are a few last Web sites that we didn't mention before but that may be helpful as you shop for the best insurance to meet your needs:

One great one-stop shopping spot for auto, health, life, homeowners, and renter's insurance is the Yahoo Insurance Center (http://insurance.yahoo.com/). The site is a fantastic link for news, analysis, quotes, and other money-saving tips on all types of insurance. It's a great place to start research into almost any insurance-related topic or shopping trip.

Another good starting point is 4Insurance.com (http://www.4insurance.com/), which links you automatically to some 500 insurance companies that maintain some sort of Internet site. In some instances, you can get an online quote for coverage immediately, while in others a local agent will contact you. This is also a nice site for general insurance information and includes coverage calculators and tips on ways to save on insurance.

There are also several good online sites for information and quotes for life insurance:

At Quotesmith's online quotes service (www.quotesmith.com), you can instantly view rates and products offered by more than 200 life insurance companies, particularly term life insurance. Just fill in the online questionnaire, and the system provides you with a list of insurance carriers and their best deals. You can even apply for coverage online. The system also provides recent insurance company ratings so that you can be sure that a carrier is financially secure.

Similarly, First Quote (http://www.1stquote.com/front.htm) lets you look up term insurance quotes and apply right there online.

If cash value life insurance has an appeal for you, have a look at Ameritas (http://www.ameritasdirectom/), where the emphasis is on so-called low-load policies—insurance policies whose ongoing charges and fees are lower than those for many conventional policies. Ameritas also provides information and quotes on term life insurance.

Finally, Instaquote (http://www.instaquote.com) lives up to its name by providing quick price quotes online. Just complete an eight-question quiz and you'll know right there what various levels of coverage will cost you.

For online auto insurance, click on InsWeb (http://www.insweb.com/cgi-bin/bozellauto.exe?bid=16203). You complete an online questionnaire and receive quotes from one or more insurance companies. From there, you're given information on how to contact those companies for more information.

CHAPTER 9

Good Help Is So Hard to Find These Days

However condescending and, well, snobby the title of this chapter may seem, it holds a significant truth. When it comes to your money, finding someone to help you manage it isn't easy. Remember when I talked in the Introduction about how there is no shortage of people who think they know a lot about money but who really don't? That problem also exists among so-called financial professionals. The simple truth is that there are tons of money to be made in offering purported financial guidance, which has prompted many—including banks, insurance salespeople, and even writers (gasp!)—to try to cash in while the cashing's good.

Real-Life Interlude

Not too many years ago, the only thing you could "buy" at a bank was a checking or savings account. With the explosion of interest in the stock market and mutual funds in particular, it's hard to find a bank these days where you can't buy a mutual fund or two, not to mention a panoply of other products.

That prompted *Money Magazine* a few years ago to put together a story on the quality of financial advice available at banks. Posing as a customer with investment money aplenty, I was dispatched to a local bank.

The first surprise was that, after I asked to speak to someone about mutual funds, I was referred to a woman who, seemingly only weeks before, had been a fixture behind the teller's window. No matter, I decided, she was to be congratulated for her ambition. I sat down and told her I was interested in mutual funds, whereupon she handed me three brochures, saying they were the bank's top sellers. No questions, mind you, about why I wanted to invest, my goals, my risk tolerance, and all that other peripheral stuff—just what was hot.

Blindly undeterred, I pressed on. "Do these funds have a load?" I asked and promptly received what I refer to as a 'watching-for-ships-on-the-horizon' glaze in the eye. "That's in the brochure."

"Has Morningstar rated these funds?" Here, her eyes again iced over like a freshly frozen pond: "That's in the brochure."

"How have they performed?" Amazingly enough, she had an answer for that one: "Great." I waited for more, but there was none (I probably would still be sitting there if I had just kept twiddling my thumbs, hoping for more information).

Finally came the coup de grace: "What sort of stocks do these funds invest in?" Reply: "You'll have to buy the fund to find that out."

I took my leave shortly thereafter. Luckily, I didn't leave my phone number with the bank rep, because I'm certain she would have followed up, asking me how soon I was going to haul my wheelbarrow full of cash down to the bank. Of course, that would have given me the chance to answer in kind:

"Sorry, that's in the brochure. Once I put one together."

The bottom line here: It's fine to ask about financial products and services at your bank, but it's an awfully good idea to ask about the qualifications of the person you're working with—how long she has been selling these products, her background and training, and so on. Otherwise, you may be looking to brochures for answers that a human being should be giving you.

Get the picture? Just because someone can tell you about money doesn't mean he or she is qualified to do so. So it behooves you to think carefully about whether you need to seek out professional guidance in the first place and, if so, to shop carefully for the right person.

To Seek or Not to Seek

Deciding whether to hook up with a financial pro is pretty subjective, and only you know the answer. As I've tried to impart throughout this book, handling your financial life is definitely a learned skill, but it is one that almost anyone can acquire. In that case, searching for outside help would appear to be a needless chore.

But some circumstances warrant working with someone else. For instance, despite all the knowledge you've undoubtedly gleaned from this book, there are times when you'll be more comfortable discussing prospective financial decisions with a pro. Perfectly sensible: A sounding board can be of great help in making significant financial decisions. Likewise, if your interest runs to investing in individual stocks, a good stockbroker can be invaluable, particularly when you consider all the pitfalls individual stocks can hold for the inexperienced or uninformed. And, as noted later in this chapter, a tax preparer not only can take the headaches out of filing a tax return but may save you money as well.

↗ Useful Web Sites

For an informative and entertaining overview of issues to bear in mind when deciding on using outside financial help and guidance, look at the article "Who Can You Trust?" at http://www.efmoody.com/whouse.html. Going back to the parent page from there (http://www.efmoody.com) also puts you in touch with other useful information about choosing a financial adviser.

Financial Planners

At first blush, using a financial planner to help you sort out your future seems to be a great idea. Trained to examine all facets of a person's financial life, a good planner can help set goals and organize a program to reach them, particularly for younger folks who are interested in establishing a long-term relationship with a financial

adviser. Investments, insurance, how to handle debt—you name it—
a good, well-diversified planner can help with any of those issues.

Unfortunately, like so many things connected with money, the
financial planning world is not as straightforward as it should be.
Planners range all over the board in the type of services they provide, what they charge their clients, and, sad to say, the quality and
integrity of their advice. That makes shopping for a good financial
planner essential.

Here are some steps to follow to help ensure that you receive
cost-effective, competent financial planning:

> ▶ Make certain a financial planner is worth what you spend. If
> you have only a few thousand dollars to invest, paying $100
> an hour—not an exorbitant rate—doesn't make a lot of
> sense. For that matter, many planners will not work with
> someone of limited financial means. It may be wise, however,
> to consult a financial planner when significant life changes
> occur. Events such as marriage, inheritances, job changes—
> anything that complicates your financial situation—are all
> signs that an outside financial opinion may be timely.

> ▶ If you have only a few questions or are just looking for
> feedback, look into buying an hour or two of a planner's
> time. Some planners will do this, and some won't.

↗ Useful Web Sites

Worth Magazine has a handy primer on the various ways you can pay for a
financial planner's services at http://www.worth.com/articles/Z9610F05.html.

The International Association for Financial Planning has a quick
checklist of questions to help you decide whether using a financial planner
is a good idea. That and other handy tools, including a search engine for
planners in your area, are available at http://www.iafp.org.

If you decide that hiring a financial planner is a good idea,
burn the phrase *caveat emptor* into your brain. Many states have

little or nothing in the way of laws establishing training and qualifications guidelines for financial advisers, so anyone can hang out a sign advertising himself as a financial planner. In fact, some say that financial planning is the worst-regulated aspect of the securities industry. The fact that there's no common, legal definition of the term *financial planner* provides a very attractive cover for con artists and those with modest amounts of training and expertise.

To avoid shoddy planners, get referrals from friends or colleagues. Try to interview at least three planners to gauge their qualifications, philosophy, and approach to their clients. Check their records with your state's securities division to see if any clients have filed complaints against them. Ask for references from clients with backgrounds similar to yours.

To expedite many of these questions, be sure to ask any planner for a copy of her Uniform Application for Investment Advisor Registration (ADV). Any planner licensed by the feds to give investment advice must complete this rather voluminous document, which details, among other things, how the planner earns her money, any connections with other companies, the sorts of investments that she recommends, and her education and professional training. By law, planners are obligated to tell the truth in their ADVs. That doesn't mean that they always do, of course, but an ADV will provide a lot of the information you'll need to make an informed decision.

When asking about a planner's experience and any sort of ongoing education credentials, you're likely to encounter a tidal wave of letters representing various titles that planners have earned. Here's a rundown:

▶ *Certified public accountant (CPA).* An accountant who has passed an administered examination that focuses on accounting practices and taxes (not investments). CPAs must also be approved by state boards.

▶ *Certified financial planner (CFP).* A financial planner who has passed exams accredited by the Certified Financial Planner Board of Standards, a regulatory body that sets CFP standards. The tests focus on an applicant's ability to work with clients' estate, insurance, investments, and tax affairs.

▶ *Chartered financial consultant (ChFC).* A designation awarded by the American College, in Bryn Mawr, Pennsylvania, to financial planners who complete ten courses and 20 hours of examinations covering economics, insurance, taxation, estate planning, and other related areas. They must also have at least three years of experience in the field of finance. (This is the insurance-industry equivalent of a CFP.)

▶ *Chartered financial analyst (CFA).* Awarded by the Institute of Chartered Financial Analysts, this designation focuses on portfolio management and securities analysis. It also covers economics, financial accounting, portfolio management, securities analysis, and standards of conduct.

▶ *Registered investment advisor.* Someone who has received approval from the Securities and Exchange Commission to give financial advice to clients for a fee.

▶ *Registered representative.* The official term for a stockbroker or account executive with a brokerage firm. To be registered, a broker must pass licensing exams administered by the National Association of Securities Dealers. Some states require additional testing.

Do these designations automatically mean that the person with whom you're working knows what he or she is doing? Absolutely not, but they can at least verify that a planner has some sort of specialized training in his or her field.

↗ Useful Web Sites

For more on planner designations, as well as links to many useful Web sites that can help with selecting a planner, have a look at http://www. investorhome.com/choosing.htm.

Just what sort of financial planner should you hook up with? Here, I'm going to play devil's advocate a bit. Many financial planning books, guides, and magazines unequivocally urge you to stick with fee-only financial planners who charge either a flat fee or by the hour, rather than earning a commission for selling certain kinds of investments. The major selling point to this sort of arrangement is that their advice isn't be tainted by the influence of commissions—in theory, whatever they recommend to you as a client will be the best investment for your situation, not the one that earns the planner the most money. That may be so, but a fee-only planner may not always be the best choice, particularly with younger investors who don't have a whole lot of money to invest. For instance, a fee-only planner may charge you several hundred dollars to develop a financial plan and a couple of hundred dollars a year thereafter to review it and keep it up to date. By contrast, a commission-based planner may charge less to draw up a plan but make up some of the lost income through commissions. Which works out to be less expensive for you depends on the numbers—for instance, a commission-based planner who charges $400 to develop a plan may pull down a 5% commission every time you buy something. If you invest $100 a month in a mutual fund, that's $60 extra a year ($100 times .05 times 12). Total cost: $460 in the first year, $60 a year thereafter. By contrast, a fee-only planner who charges $600 to draw up a plan and $200 a year after that will be a good deal more expensive.

Don't rule out any planner just because of the way that person sets his or her fees. Instead, do some number crunching to see who actually works out to be most cost-effective. Start by having any planner you consider working with describe clearly how his or her fees are set. A national survey a few years back found that three out of five planners who claimed to be "fee only" actually received commissions as well. Next, have the planner spell out why he or she is recommending particular investments. Do some legwork yourself and look into how those recommendations have performed. That way, you'll have a clear picture of which recommendations are genuinely in your best interests.

Other Shopping Tips

▶ Have planners outline what they'll do for you. Some will claim to offer every financial service imaginable, from investing to insurance to budgeting, while others will be part of a large firm where individual partners tackle specific issues. Make sure to hit your comfort level. If, for instance, you're concerned about objectivity, a do-it-all planner or firm may not work as well for you as several financial professionals without any sort of connection.

▶ On a similar note, ask the planner if you can implement the program that he or she puts together. This can be important, because it's not unheard of for planners to advertise themselves as fee-only, then recommend only commission-based mutual funds. So have your planner make it clear what his or her role will be after your financial plan is assembled—if you can buy what he or she recommends on your own, by all means do it. But if you're crunched for time, or lack the desire, it's not a bad idea to pay your planner a bit extra to make certain the plan actually goes into effect.

▶ Make certain your planner's financial philosophy jibes with yours. Nothing is more harrowing than an investor being force-fed uncomfortable financial choices. If you're looking for solid mutual funds and a planner is talking pork bellies, start feeling around for your car keys. By the same token, make sure that any planner with whom you're considering doing business understands just what you want to achieve and how you'll be most comfortable getting there.

▶ Finally, be aware that many financial planners are also money managers. In effect, you turn your assets over to them and they manage them for you, essentially investing your money in what they deem best. For the most part, steer clear of these guys. For one thing, they stand in direct conflict with the very idea of knowing about and handling your own finances responsibly. If you delegate that duty to someone else, you're taking a chance that the person knows what he or she is doing. On top of that, money managers are more expensive, often charging a few percentage points of your total asset value (ironically enough, many invest in the same no-load funds that you could buy yourself).

In fact, money management may be a moot point for most of us, as most large money-management firms require a minimum investment of $500,000 to $1 million, while smaller firms are willing to accept clients with as little as $25,000. However, there are some money managers who don't require any minimum. The only circumstance where a money manager might be a suitable choice is for someone who has absolutely no time to put into managing his or her own money—mind you, likely a pile of it—or who is petrified about making his or her own financial decisions (for someone matching that description, you've made it a good way into this book). For the vast majority of us, if you decide to work with a planner, find one who's aware of your wants and goals and puts together a program that you can feel comfortable about.

The National Association of Personal Financial Advisors (888-FEE-ONLY) offers a referral service for people looking to hook up with fee-only planners in their area. NAPFA also offers a comprehensive boilerplate list of questions and issues that should be raised with any financial planner you're considering. The Institute of Certified Financial Planners (303-759-4900) offers a similar service exclusively for CFPs.

↗ Useful Web Sites

The National Association of Personal Financial Advisors Web site can be found at http://www.napfa.org. The site has a search engine that lets you find a planner near you. Although much of the site is geared to planners rather than to the investing public, it's still worth a trip to the Institute of Certified Financial Planners Web site at http://www.icfp.org/. Go to "Find a CFP Licensee" for information on tracking down a certified planner, questions you should ask, and a discussion of how planners can be compensated.

> For a checklist of questions to ask any planner you're considering, go to http://www.pueblo.gsa.gov/cic_text/money/financial-planner/10questions.txt.
>
> Investorguide (http://www.investorguide.com/Advisors.htm) has a good article on planner credentials and ways to select one. The site also has links to other Web pages that touch on finding a suitable adviser.

NOTE: For a discussion of financial planning software, check out Chapter 10.

Taking Stock of Brokers

This may seem a somewhat unlikely section to include, given my earlier manifesto about the complicated nature of investing in individual stocks. My feelings about buying stocks haven't changed—it's an exceedingly tricky business and, for the most part, I firmly believe that the vast majority of investors do just as well and even better putting their money into mutual funds. I'm an equally ardent believer in individuals' abilities to make investment decisions on their own, without necessarily involving so-called outside professionals.

But the notion of investing in individual companies remains a powerful lure for many. For one thing, you know precisely where your money is, as opposed to a mutual fund, where your investment is spread out over a number of stocks (many of which you may never have even heard of). And buying individual stocks lets you follow through on one of the most sensible maxims known to the investment community—invest in what you know. In other words, if you know a company's products are consistently high-quality and innovative, you have an idea that that company may be worth some of your investment dollars. By the same token, if you know a company's wares are absolute garbage—say you just bought a software program that practically melts your computer, it's so unusable—you know better than to put dime one into that company's stock.

It therefore behooves us to chat a bit about stockbrokers. An honest, hardworking stockbroker not only can offer you valuable investment ideas—after all, investing is what he or she does for a living—but can also provide useful feedback for investors who approach the broker with investing notions of their own. In that sense, a good broker can fill the void of research, analysis, and information that so many investors face when they're trying to choose individual stocks by themselves. Put another way, if buying individual stocks is too confusing and complicated for many, a worthy stockbroker can bring down the noise level considerably.

However, know up front that brokers have some major drawbacks. For one thing, they're salespeople. Many work purely on commission, so they don't earn a nickel if you don't buy something from them. On top of that, most brokers don't offer the array of services that a financial planner can; their gig is stocks, pure and simple, so don't look for help with your budget or insurance from a broker (by the same coin, however, it can be equally hard to get stock investment advice from a planner, many of whom prefer to work exclusively with mutual funds). On top of that, know too that many stockbrokers are very adept at pushing proprietary products. For example, if a large brokerage house has a vested interest in a particular stock—say the brokerage house helped the company with its public stock offering—don't be surprised if your broker calls you touting the glories of that stock. Whether it may fit your investment needs may be secondary. Additionally, unless you have a dump truck full of money with which to open an account at a brokerage house, don't count on getting one of the house's best brokers. Smaller accounts are usually delegated to new brokers, many of whom haven't much in the way of experience or proven track records.

Finally, a stockbroker can be expensive, especially if he or she works for one of the big brokerage houses. To illustrate: If you go to one national brokerage outfit to buy 500 shares of Microsoft, the commission is a hair-raising $525. That sets up a three-headed problem. First, forking over that amount in commissions is ridiculous for someone who may have only a few thousand dollars to invest, if that. Second, remember that you'll have to pay another commission when you sell the stock. Third, keep in mind that commissions put your investments in a hole from the get-go; to make any profit from your investment, you first have to earn back what you paid out in commissions, both buying and selling.

⤴ *Useful Web Sites*

A fantastic site offering links and articles that address stockbroker issues can be found at http://www.investorhome.com/brokers.htm#info.

If you've ever wondered precisely what a stockbroker is and isn't supposed to do, take time to read the article posted at http://www. securitieslaw.com/main.html. The piece does a nice job outlining stockbroker responsibilities and describes types of securities fraud, and steps to take if you feel you've been wronged.

In the interest of being as complete as possible, I'll also note that the case for full-commission brokers (sympathetically titled "Full Service Brokers— A Misunderstood Lot") is available at http://www.maxinvest.com/html/ full-service_brokers_a_misunderstood_lot.html. The National Association of Securities Dealers has a handy FAQ database on stockbrokers at http://pdpi.nasdr.com/pdpi/helpfiles/faqs_frame.asp.

The Securities and Exchange Commission and Research Magazine have teamed up to present a very useful guide to choosing and using a stockbroker effectively. It's at http://www.researchmag.com/investor/wise.htm.

One alternative way to buy stocks is to go through the growing number of discount brokerage houses. Here, the good news is that you'll pay a fraction of what you fork over in commissions to the full-service guys. A random call to one, for instance, revealed a $100 commission for the same 500-share Microsoft buy that cost $525 with the big boys. In fact, should you be willing to shop around, you can do a good deal better than that, particularly if you're interested in going online to do your trading (see the following chapter for more details). Another plus to going with discount brokers, particularly some of the larger houses, is that you gain access to reams of research reports and other analytic data to help you make investment decisions (granted, these are also available at full-service houses, but you pay a lot less for the privilege at discount houses).

The trouble is that if you're looking for someone to make investment recommendations—as a broker with a full-service house will do—you're pretty much out of luck with discount houses. For example, some of the larger discount houses assign you a "personal broker" when you open an account, someone you can generally reach during business hours. However personal that may seem, that broker is rather limited as to what he or she will do. For instance, the broker will execute any trade you may order and talk about your investments in rather generic terms but will never make any sort of specific stock-buying recommendation—that's your call and your call alone. And, as we've pointed out before, buying individual stocks can be a dicey proposition for anyone, particularly for investment newcomers who have to make those choices pretty much on their own. (In fairness, though, it should be noted that some discount brokers put out newsletters in which they do make recommendations—if that's of interest to you, be sure to ask about it.)

The problem becomes all the more acute with what are known as deep-discount houses. These are the brokerage firms you've probably heard of or read about that charge super-low commissions, often as paltry as a few bucks for any size stock purchase. Cheap they may be, but low price is about all you get. For one thing, since they generally don't have branch offices like some of the larger discounters, your only way of reaching them is via telephone or modem. You can forget the idea of a personal broker—when you call in, you get whom you get (needless to say, that also pretty much negates the idea of personal financial guidance, since you may well speak with a different person every time you call.) On top of that, deep discounters often don't offer customers the types of research reports and other services that bigger houses provide to help their clients make investing decisions. The premise is simple—this is a cheap place to trade, and it assumes you've already done your homework elsewhere.

↗ Useful Web Sites

Perhaps the definitive spot to start any research on discount brokerage houses is On-Line Investment Services at http://www.sonic.net/donaldj/. The main page links you to data rating the best brokerage houses, commission information, and advice on how to go about choosing a house that matches your needs.

> Another great place to start to compare discount brokerage commissions and services is at http://www.angelfire.com/biz/markettiming/discount.html. There you'll find links to dozens of discount brokerage houses, broken down according to the range of commission each charges.
>
> For a good article discussing the pros and cons of discount brokers, point your browser to http://www.invest-faq.com/articles/trade-disc-brok.html.

The bottom line on stockbrokers is this: They can be of great help, but you'll pay dearly for the privilege if you want to work with one who can actually make recommendations. Short of that, it'll be pretty much up to you to do your own legwork. If either of these scenarios fits your situation and mindset, fine. To shop for a stockbroker, employ some of the criteria we mentioned with financial planners—ask about their qualifications, background, and philosophy and find out whether they've worked with clients who are similar to you. Have them spell out in no uncertain terms how they're compensated. If you're talking with someone from a discount house, know precisely what the broker will talk about and where he or she might draw the line. Keep an eye peeled for red flags—for instance, if you're interested in conservative investments and all the broker wants to talk is speculative stocks, look elsewhere. It can get even worse—head for the exit if any broker claims to have access to any sort of inside information about stocks or companies (not only likely a stretch of the truth, but a one-way ticket to the slammer if there's any truth to it.)

If you're hell-bent on investing in individual stocks, a good broker is an essential component. But, for my money, whether you have a modest sum to invest or an out-and-out pile, you're likely far better off with mutual funds. Not only do you get a level of diversification that's just about impossible with individual stocks, but you also receive cost-effective professional management. And that's the smart way to pay a pro to be on your investing team.

Making Taxes Less Taxing

We cover ways to hold down your tax bill in Chapter 12, but here I'd like to raise the issue of using a tax preparer to do your taxes for you. To start with, there are precious few of us who actually enjoy filling out tax returns. Except for those who do so for a living, people who live for doing their taxes probably also get a kick out of nails scraping along a blackboard or pine for the day when Gary Coleman makes his acting comeback (don't ask if the name doesn't ring a bell). Not only are tax forms inherently unpleasant, they're equally bewildering—every tax year dozens of tax laws and regulations are revamped, created, or repealed, which makes keeping current exceedingly difficult even for full-time tax pros. That can make for a fertile breeding ground for mistakes and oversights.

That being said, not everyone needs a tax preparer. If, for instance, your return is relatively simple and straightforward, there's really no need to spend money to have someone else prepare it. Likewise, all sarcasm aside, there are some of us who enjoy the hands-on involvement and/or challenge of preparing their own returns—admittedly, doing your own taxes can often teach you things about your money habits that you might otherwise have overlooked. And, as we'll point out in the next chapter, there are tax preparation software programs that definitely make preparing your return a lot easier than using a number two pencil and a bottomless bottle of aspirin.

But if your return has some complexities to it—say, for instance, you have investment income to report or are self-employed and need to be aware of every break you can find—using a preparer can be an awfully smart and pain-saving decision. Preparers are paid to know what changes have taken place and what strategies can help you save the most on your taxes. In fact, spending the money on a competent tax pro can often save you money in the end, since the preparer may cut your tax bill more than enough to offset his or her fee. If the thought of doing your taxes makes your stomach turn, go ahead and find a good preparer—life's too short to have to put up with aggravation that you can easily solve.

NOTE: Interested in the pluses and drawbacks of tax preparation software? Refer to our discussion in Chapter 12, which also touches on various Internet-based preparation tools.

There are several options among tax preparers. The first, and easily the least expensive, are the tax preparation houses such as

H&R Block (also known as storefront preparers). These preparers are best suited to those with simple or modestly complicated returns. Often, you can simply carry your tax material into the office and meet with a preparer, who may be able to prepare your return on the spot. The cost may be $100 or even less. The downside to storefronts is, first, there's nothing that smacks of tax planning in their services—they do your return for that year and, maybe, go over ways you could have saved some money, but they won't talk about ways to approach next year's tax bill. Likewise, you may not get a whole lot of continuity in your year-to-year tax preparation; many of the people who work for storefronts are part-timers who tend to come and go. There's a decent chance, therefore, that a different preparer will do your taxes every year.

If consistency is important or your return is a bit more complicated—perhaps involving something like a home office deduction or a stock or mutual fund transaction—you may want to take the next step up in tax professionals. Here, the choices boil down to Certified Public Accountants (CPAs) and Enrolled Agents. As we noted earlier in this chapter, CPAs have to pass an exam and also maintain a certain level of ongoing education. By contrast, enrolled agents are former employees of the Internal Revenue Service who have obtained a specific type of license or who have passed an IRS-administered examination.

CPAs and enrolled agents are similar in several ways. Both charge more than a storefront tax preparer (bills can easily range from several hundred dollars and up, depending on the complexity of the return), but both can offer year-round tax guidance and advice, as well as comprehensive tax preparation services. There are, however, differences. First, although there are always exceptions, enrolled agents are likely to charge less than CPAs, particularly if the CPA works for a large firm. Moreover, an enrolled agent's specialty is taxes; by contrast, many CPAs don't specialize in taxes or tax preparation. The first step is to ask any tax pro with whom you're considering working whether, in fact, he or she specializes in tax preparation. Be sure you know what the person's hourly fee is and if there are any other related expenses. Ask for an estimate of how much a return like yours is likely to cost. Get a feel for how aggressive or conservative the person is—as with any other financial pro, it's critical to hook up with someone whose approach is similar to yours. Additionally, if the preparer is part of a large firm or company, ask just how involved he or she will be in the preparation of your return; some preparers do the whole shooting match from start to finish, while others just hand the return off to some underling to prepare and only review the return once it's been completed.

A few final thoughts about tax preparers. First, unless you're going to a storefront, don't start rousting around for a tax preparer when there's only a few weeks to go until April 15—that's akin to trying to find a great Christmas tree on December 24. Instead, start shopping around at the beginning of the year, when competent tax pros will still be able to fit you into their schedules. Then, once you've chosen a tax pro, hold down your bill by doing as much of the work as you can yourself. Organize your receipts, pay stubs, and other material as thoroughly as possible before going in to see your tax pro. That way, the clock isn't ticking away as he or she pores through a pile of papers in a shoebox.

Last, when you get your tax return back from your preparer, go over it thoroughly to check for mistakes and oversights. Try as most do to be as accurate as they can, tax preparers can make mistakes, some of which can yank money from your pocket. Check social security numbers, the spelling of names, and all the numbers you can verify to make sure they're what they're supposed to be. Case in point: One year, my tax return came back with my name misspelled, the wrong social security number, mutual funds that I had sold years before included as still in my portfolio, and a rash of other slip-ups. (In fact, the preparer had even listed one of my mutual funds under my infant son's name, the little capitalist swine).

↗ Useful Web Sites

CPA Link (http://www.cpalink.com/) lets you search for a CPA according to location and area of expertise. The site also offers helpful guidelines for selecting an accountant.

> The National Association of Enrolled Agents' site, which also offers tax information and ways to hook up with an enrolled agent near you, is at http://www.naea.org/.
>
> Http://www.quicken.com/taxes/articles/889832439_2089 offers a fast summary of the three major types of tax preparers.
>
> The veritable king of storefront tax preparation, H & R Block, has a nice Web site at http://hrblock.com/tax/. Lots of information, download-able forms, and, if this sort of tax help seems attractive to you, a search engine to help locate an office near you.

Financial Self-Help Through Investment Clubs

Unlike other forms of self-help—i.e., the "I'm Okay but You Could Definitely Use Some Work" variety—investment clubs provide an enjoyable way to learn about money and, one hopes, make a profit or two here and there. The basic structure, which may differ slightly from club to club, essentially involves a group of friends and associates who get together and pool a preset amount of investment money on a regular basis (usually anywhere from $50 to $100 a month per person although, of course, that can range all over the place). The club's next step is to find a suitable place or places to invest its money, so members research stocks, mutual funds, and other sorts of investments, then offer their recommendations to the group, which then votes whether to invest and how much. That's basically it. Meeting on a regular basis, clubs track how their investments are performing and decide whether to buy new investments or discard ones that may not be performing up to snuff.

The advantages to the investment club idea are legion. For one thing, they can prove a wonderful learning experience in investing and portfolio management—after all, if all investing decisions are arrived at democratically, you better know your stuff if you want to win your fellow members over to an investment idea. And, whether meeting over coffee or pitchers of beer, investment clubs let you soak up all this investment knowledge in a comfortable social environment. And, the Beardstown Ladies notwithstanding (if you don't remember, they're the heralded all-women investment club that, despite a much-publicized brouhaha over their misreporting of their profits, continues to set the standard for self-aggrandizement), it's common to hear of investment clubs achieving fantastic investment records, with portfolios routinely exceeding $1 million. Even if the bulk of your own personal investing remains outside the purview of the group, an investment club can prove an effective—and enlightening—adjunct to your financial picture.

↗ *Useful Web Sites*

If the notion of an investment club appeals, set your browser to the National Association of Investors Corp. Web site (www.better-investing.org). This is probably as definitive a source of information as you'll be able to track down on investment clubs, since NAIC claims to have more than 34,000 clubs on its membership rolls. The site offers information on how to start a club, investing basics, software, model club structures and bylaws, and commonly asked questions. There's also an online bookstore. If your question has to do with investment clubs, you're going to find the answer here.

Don't assume that an investment club must, by definition, involve face-to-face meetings. Although the idea has yet to catch fire with investors, there are a few online investment clubs floating about in cyberspace. While many investment club essentials remain the same, these clubs transact all business via electronic mail. While the social feel may be lost, online members say there are advantages—not only can you include members from every part of the globe, but investment discussions and analysis aren't necessarily constrained by a set meeting limit, as they can be with live investment clubs. For a greater feel for what online clubs entail and some details on how to set up one if you're interested, check out the home pages of the Model On-Line Investment Club (www.better-investing.org/ molic) and the G.O.L.D. Investment Club (www.members.aol.com/aristotlem/gold.htm).

CHAPTER 10

Money Bytes

Many of you may be familiar with the classic film *Metropolis* by Fritz Lang, produced more than 70 years ago. In it, Lang warns of the seductive creep of technology and envisions a world supposedly rendered idyllic by machines but in reality a nightmarish prison for its human inhabitants. A dark vision, indeed.

It's probably a good thing that Lang never lived to see what computers—not to mention their fiendish coconspirator, the Internet—have become in our society, because he likely would have shed beads of sweat the size of CD-ROMs. It's genuinely hard to think of an area of everyday life where computing and its electronic communication sidekick haven't taken up a prominent role. The Internet lets us share reams of information with people halfway around the world whose faces we never see, five-year-olds are as comfortable using a computer mouse as their predecessors were with Slinkys, and the average car has a more sophisticated onboard computer than the Apollo rockets to the moon ("Detroit, we have a problem—my air conditioning just went out").

Computers have certainly affected our money management habits. We can use computers to help plan and maintain budgets, select investments, and project just how much money we may need come retirement. If what we have on our machines isn't adequate, we jump onto the Internet to sift through thousands of finance-related Web sites, covering everything from mutual funds to mortgages. If we see an investment we like, we can buy it online, but not before first tapping into an online bank account to make sure we have enough money to swing the deal.

Is technology's intrusion into our financial affairs Lang's vision realized, an ersatz environment where gigabytes and download times have supplanted human reason and sound judgment? Not from where I'm sitting. If anything, technology has enhanced our collective ability to make educated financial decisions, as is evident from the hundreds of Web sites, software programs, and other technology tools that we've discussed throughout this book. Not only are the mechanics of money made easier by technology, but also we now enjoy unprecedented access to financial products, information, analysis, and research—not to mention the means to act on those data quickly and efficiently.

Lang did raise a good point that you need to bear in mind when it comes to technology and the way you handle your money: Technology isn't necessarily a panacea, and nowhere might that hold greater truth than in our financial lives. Using technology intelligently without abandoning the notion that your money choices are ultimately up to you and not some machine or Web site are critical in ensuring that all these wonderful gizmos work for you and not the other way around. Put another way, take advantage of all that technology has to offer, but don't forget to use that incredibly sophisticated computer between your ears when it comes to making wise financial choices.

In this chapter we follow up on the technology references placed throughout the book and provide an overview of the broad category where technology and money cross paths, offering an idea of the various types of products and services that are available, some suggestions to help you select those that may prove helpful, and not a few caveats about keeping them in a healthy and useful perspective.

Cyberfunds

If banking online (as we'll see later in this chapter) can be compared to a sailboat slowly picking up speed in the wind, online stock trading is a sleek powerboat. It seems that everyone is trading stocks through an online brokerage account these days (admittedly, not exactly true, but not that far off, either. Estimates are that some 14 million investors will buy and sell securities online in the next five years or so. Put another way, roughly one in five American households will have an online investment account sometime early in the twenty-first century.)

All that may be well and good, but what about mutual funds online? Well, thanks to the booming interest in online investing in general, many online brokers now allow clients to buy and sell mutual funds through online services and the Internet. The reason is not that mutual funds are necessarily a huge cash cow for online brokers; unlike stocks, which can be traded often and generate a commission each time you buy or sell, mutual fund investors tend to be more of the buy-and-hold variety, which doesn't mean big bucks so far as commissions are concerned. Instead, it's more of a question of keeping up with the cyber-Joneses. As more and more customers asked about online mutual fund trading, online brokerages had little choice but to offer them this service or lose customers to someone who would.

Happily, that's paying off for mutual fund investors. As of this writing, there are dozens of sites online where you can buy and sell mutual funds, through autonomous discount brokers as well as mutual fund families that want to hawk their funds online. In many cases, it amounts to a veritable one-stop shopping experience. Some sites offer thousands of funds from hundreds of different families, eliminating the need to contact individual fund families if you want to find out about a fund or make a purchase.

Even better, more and more online mutual fund services are offering what's known as no-fee funds. As the name implies, it costs you nothing to buy these funds (except, of course, if the fund has a load). Moreover, it may also cost you nothing if you decide to dump it in the future (this can depend on individual policy; some fund families and brokerages require you to hold onto a fund for a certain amount of time before the sale fee is waived).

Even if a fee is imposed for an online mutual fund trade, it can be less expensive to buy over the Internet than the old-fashioned way, since some Web sites offer discounts for online trades. For instance, Charles Schwab offers a 20% discount on mutual funds purchased online that are not part of Schwab's OneSource program (these are no-fee funds from some 700 fund families). And that can cut your trading expenses. Whereas buying $10,000 in a mutual fund using a Schwab representative costs $70, the same trade online runs only $56 (bear in mind that these figures date from the writing of this book, so there's a very good chance fee structures have changed).

Although whatever savings you can nail down via online trading are nice, it's equally important to examine what other features an online service offers you as a mutual fund investor. While some sites are merely a bare-bones way to buy and sell, other sites offer comprehensive fund screening systems and other services that can help you choose the fund that's right for you. While almost any site will let you track the performance of your fund once you've bought it, some go a step further and establish a news service to automatically alert you about news about your fund or a company that may be a significant holding in your fund.

When shopping for an online mutual fund service, pay attention to these issues as well:

▶ *Check the minimum purchase requirement.* Some online mutual fund brokers don't require any minimum to start trading, while others mandate as much as a $5,000 minimum.

▶ *Look at the number of fund families a site offers.* Again, some offer hundreds, others merely a few. You're better off with a site that carries a reasonable selection of funds, which can only help you choose the one that best suits your needs.

▶ *Be sure you know just how much you have to pay if there's a fee.* Some brokers and fund families use a sliding fee scale based on the size of the purchase, while others impose other sorts of price structures. In particular, pay attention to the absolute maximum you may have to pay in fees for a transaction. Also, watch out for funds that are classified "no fee" but that in fact have a sales load—either way, it's money out of your pocket if you decide to buy the fund.

▶ *Check to see how much it costs to switch funds, whether within the same fund family or to another family of funds.* Compare what requirements you may have to meet to switch funds for free, such as having to hold onto a fund for a certain period of time.

▶ *Get a feel for how well the online service works.* Some online brokers and fund families have very smooth, responsive Web sites, while other sites can be painfully slow (and, occasionally, impossible to access). To gauge the site's accessibility, try logging on in the middle of a busy trading day. If things drag or fall apart completely, that may hint at a headache you would do well to avoid.

Cyberstocks

Although, as I've said ad nauseam, I'm a big believer in mutual funds as opposed to individual stocks—particularly for younger investors and others who may be new to investing—online stock trading may be the way to go if you hanker to get your feet wet in the world of individual equities. The most compelling reason is that it's a good deal cheaper than the old-fashioned way. For instance, as of mid-1998, if you used a big, full-service brokerage house to buy 500 shares of Microsoft, the commission was $525. The least expensive online brokerages were charging from $8 to $40 for the same trade.

The pluses don't end there. Not only is it cheaper to trade online, but you can also access your portfolio 24 hours a day and submit trades when the market is closed. Discounters are also starting to offer services that go beyond fast trades and cheap prices. Some provide online investment research and analysis, real-time stock quotes, and more extensive and reliable customer service if you have a problem. Online brokers are also toiling away to make their Web sites as easy to use and informative as possible; not only are they simple to get the hang of, but a good online brokerage site will also offer pluses beyond mere simplicity, such as news, chat rooms, articles, research, analysis, and other services designed to help you make intelligent investing decisions.

↗ Useful Web Sites

Check out the online investment guru Douglas Gerlach's article on online investing, (http://www.investorama.com/features/bits-onl.shtml), which spells out many of the functions, pluses, and minuses of investing online.

Still, all these wonderful attributes don't amount to an unqualified endorsement of online stock trading. For one thing, like other types of cyberfinance, online stock trading can lead to more fiddling with your investments than might be good for you, given the round-the-clock access most online brokers offer their customers. (As of this writing, there's a great deal of controversy surrounding the growing number of 'day traders'; investors who make dozens of trades in a single day, particularly with volatile Internet-related stocks. Some claim to make a killing, but many more may be losing their shirts). Not only can that interfere with achieving your long-term goals, but it can also end up costing you a lot more than you might have bargained for, since even dirt-cheap commissions can add up if you do a ton of buying and selling. Also, know full well that chintzy commissions come with a price—you're never going to get any specific buy and sell recommendations from any broker at an online house (they usually can discuss investing only in the most general terms). So, if you're looking to hook up with a financial pro to help you learn about the stock market, online brokers aren't the ones to do it.

That said, though, if you want to get your feet wet with individual stocks, online trading offers by far and away the cheapest way to pursue it. There's also something to be said for the ingrained autonomy online trading offers—rather than just sitting back and waiting for your stock broker to call with a recommendation, you're the one who has to do the research and other legwork that goes into making an investment decision. Ultimately, the call is yours, as well as any digging beforehand that leads up to that decision. In that sense, online trading really emphasizes the importance of solid education and research when making your financial choices, and that's never a bad thing. Granted, I would much rather push the positives of mutual funds, but you can get something out of online stock trading, provided you approach it with the right frame of mind (and, from my perspective, earmark a modest fraction of your investment dollars for the experience).

Choosing an online broker, however, is no simple task, and there are a few shopping considerations to bear in mind. First, no matter how much brokers may tout their super-low commission rates, don't choose a broker solely by price. Check out the services each offers, such as research reports, real-time stock quotes, and telephone backup systems; some brokers, for instance, offer little else except cheap rates, while others charge a bit more but provide a more complete array of customer options. But, by the same token, don't automatically choose an online service because of a recognizable name; some lesser-known houses are not merely less expensive but also offer better overall customer service than their larger competitors.

No matter which broker interests you, be sure to examine the fine print before opening an account. As with mutual funds, some online brokerages don't mandate any minimum deposit to open an account; others make you pony up thousands to start trading. Also, make sure that the broker doesn't require a certain minimum balance to qualify for a super-low commission rate. Watch out for surcharges; for example, one broker hits you with a $15 additional charge every time you make a trade by phone, while others charge more if you want real-time stock quotes. Some even levy extra charges if you place particularly large orders.

Access to a broker's Web site is even more important to stock traders than it is for mutual fund investors (nothing can be more frustrating than trying to get onto a Web site to buy or sell, only to suffer through erosion-speed download times or a complete inability to get in at all). Again, try logging onto a broker's Web site in the heart of an active trading day. If it seems to take forever or you can't get into the system at all, that may be a tip-off about what you could expect if you were actually trying to make a trade.

If you're interested in finding out more about online investing and which broker may be right for you, be sure to have a look at the Internet Broker Scorecard (www.quote.com/specials/gomez/index.htm). The product of Gomez Advisors, a Boston-based financial consulting concern, the site ranks some 25 online brokers according to several criteria, including cost, customer service, and all-around performance.

↗ Useful Web Sites

Gomez Advisors has also compiled a comprehensive alphabetical list of every online brokerage house up and running as of late 1998. Even better, the page ranks each house according to performance, cost, level of services, and other factors. The site is located at http://www.gomez.com. The page also links you directly to any brokerage house that may interest you.

For great, one-stop shopping for links to online brokerage houses as well as information to help you choose the one that best fits your needs, point your browser to http://www.investorama.com/brokrdir.shtml.

Smart Money has an online ranking of the best and worst online brokers (and, for that matter, of full-service brokers and discount brokers). It's worth a look at http://www.smartmoney.com/si/brokers/.

Money on the Web

Seven thousand. And counting.

Got a guess what that number refers to? If you said investment-related Web sites on the Internet, you're both right and wrong. Right in the sense that that's one recent estimate of just how many financial sites are floating around out there in cyberspace. And wrong since, in the time it took for you to read the preceding two paragraphs, who knows how many new financial sites have sprung from the fertile ether of the Internet. Moreover, that estimate is likely even further off if you take the broader perspective used in this book; when you take into consideration other types of money sites, such as insurance, real estate, budgeting, and so on, that initial estimate of 7,000 topples by the wayside.

Needless to say, the burgeoning world of money-oriented Web sites has advantages as well as a downside for those of you looking to use the Web to better manage your money. On the one hand, there's simply a ton of stuff to be had—most of it for free—and accessible to an extent that would make preceding investment generations gasp in awe. While our parents—and, to a certain degree, even some of our older siblings—had to troop down to the public library or, even slower, request information by mail, every-thing from government filings to sophisticated analysis to spirited discussion of financial issues can be had with the few clicks of a mouse, often in a matter of minutes.

Before you venture onto the Internet in search of financial pearls, however, do one thing first. Go down to the kitchen and lay your hands on the biggest shaker of salt you can find; you'll need it when it comes to sifting through financial Web sites, because there's a fine, often hazy line between the sites that are genuinely useful and reliable and the sites that are something less so. So, with your shaker firmly in one hand, there are several rules you should burn into your brain.

First, remember that you don't really know who is talking on the Internet. Faceless medium that it is, the Web is the ultimate venue that lets people say just about anything they like and to sound as informed as their ability to lay it on with a trowel can let them. Granted, this is less of an issue with larger sites that may have a well-known name attached to them, where attribution and cre-dentials are often more aboveboard than on other Web sites, but the fact remains that anonymity rules on the Internet. Therefore, take nothing you see or read as pure gospel, because you rarely know the true source. This is particularly true on message boards and in chat groups, which can be riddled with so-called informed discussion but which, in fact, can be nothing more than mindless blabber or carefully constructed discussions with an underlying agenda to them. People often use nicknames and can even appear under a variety of aliases to foster the idea that a bunch of different people are all enthusiastically talking about the same topic. Moreover, the growth of sites focused on money and investing on the Web has spawned a version of "marketspeak," a language unto itself that's bewildering to one not among the cognoscenti. (Know what someone means when they deride an investor for having "weak hands?" That's someone who bails out of an investment at the first sign of a problem.)

That's not to say that Web sites that purport to offer objective information can be any less shady. Although the law requires Web sites to disclose that they have been paid to promote a stock or some other investment, Web builders have become exceptionally good at making those sorts of disclaimers hard to find or, even if you do track them down, difficult to understand.

The bottom line: Use whatever you get on the Internet as nothing more than a basis for further investigation and discussion. If you hear of a mutual fund that you like, check it out on your own. If someone's touting a financial program or software package, the same applies. But don't ever take what you see on the Web on blind faith, because you don't ever truly know who's saying it or why it's there.

"Why are they telling me all this wonderful stuff?" Ask yourself that question repeatedly every time you read something that is finance related on the Internet. Just as you often don't know who's actually talking to you, you can never be sure of the person's true motivation. Are they merely filled with the unadulterated joy of sharing knowledge (assume a big-time no on that one, however jaded that may sound). Is the person interested in your buying something (not surprisingly, a lot of sites tout certain products and other stuff that, surprise, surprise, you can buy there and only there). Is there some other insidious reason behind what they're saying? (It's certainly possible. There was a case a few years back where a bunch of stockbrokers posed as "everyday" investors and went online to tout the glories of a particular stock that they were busy trying to sell. Fortunately, they were found out and summarily delivered to the proper authorities.)

The message here is clear: You can never be 100% certain as to what's driving almost anything you can find on the Internet, so treat the information you obtain with care. Take whatever you can find on the Web as a starting point from which you can conduct your own more objective and empirical research. That's not to say that the Internet is a font of misinformation—far from it. (I never would have included the number of Web sites I have in this book if I thought they weren't genuinely useful and informative.) Rather, treat the Web as you would any other source of financial information—as a piece of a much larger puzzle that makes up intelligent financial decisions.

Keep an eye on how much all this wisdom is costing you. In the early days of the Internet, virtually all sites were free, since their operators were eager to drive as much traffic their way as they possibly could. Now, however, the number of Web sites that levy some sort of charge or fee is increasing. Some charge an annual membership or subscription fee, while others charge for particular services or access. Make sure you understand whether a service is charging you in some way, and be sure you know how high that charge can go. Some sites are worth the money, even if it runs $30 or $40 a month, while others are an unadulterated rip-off, charging for information you can often find elsewhere for free.

Finally, if you're averse to having your name end up on everyone's mailing list, be aware that many Web sites record your visit and summarily sell information about you to other entities—credit card companies, mortgage lenders, and a host of others. That can be particularly true if you use an online calculator, since the site may turn around and sell the data that you entered. If you don't give a hoot about being solicited, fine. However, if this is an issue for you, check Web sites to see if they have any sort of declaration as to whether they'll pass your name along to someone else. While many do share data, some Web sites make it clear that you and information about you will stay within their borders.

⤴ *Useful Web Sites*

Here are a few Web sites that can help clue you in to financial scams on the Internet:

The National Fraud Center (http://www.fraud.com/) is a great clearinghouse on fraud of all types. In particular, the site maintains an Internet fraud watch to help you and other Web users determine what's legit and what's not.

If you come across something that seems suspicious or just too good to be true, consider letting Cybercops (http://www.cybercops.org/) know about it. Operated by the Utility Consumers' Action Network, the site lets you let others know about surreptitious Web goings-on.

ScamBusters (http://www.scambusters.org/) may focus much of its energies on spamming, but the site is also a great stopover for information on all types of cyber-skullduggery.

Web Central has a handy page that links you to other topnotch financial sites at http://www.cio.com/central/financial.html.

Cyberbanking

Think you're the only one on your block who's not using your computer and modem to pay bills and balance your checkbook? Guess again. As of this writing, online banking has yet to set the financial world aflame. According to a recent survey, only 7% of U.S. households have used online banking, while 25% have the technical means to use it.

But that's not to say that things aren't improving in the world of cyberbanking and that you should never give any serious thought to banking online yourself. In fact, the online banking industry is plugging away at many of the problems that have discouraged prospective online bankers. For instance, in the "old days" of online banking, the only software you could use was the proprietary software the bank gave you. Generally, it worked with that bank and that bank alone. Now, however, more and more banks are changing their systems to make them compatible with popular financial planning software programs. As a result, it's becoming more common that, provided you have a well-known program installed on your machine, you can hook right up with your bank to set up an online account. Additionally, many banks are setting up their own autonomous Web sites that let you obtain account information and other personal banking data without the need for you to have any one software program (in applicable terminology, this is known as Internet banking, as opposed to "dial in," where you use a particular software program).

Banks are also increasingly addressing system function and customer service. For instance, rather than limiting online accounts merely to banking, an increasing number of banks are beefing up Web sites to provide other functions such as financial planning tools and calculators. Banks have also come to realize—albeit slowly—that customers still want the human touch, whether they bank via a computer or face-to-face with a teller. Accordingly, more banks are amassing better-staffed customer support services to help consumers who have encountered a problem. In fact, some banks have gone so far as to dispatch customer services representatives to people's homes to help set up their online accounts and answer any questions the customers may have.

The technology itself is also making strides. Within a few years time, say the experts, you may be able to enjoy what the industry refers to as "bill presentment." In plain English, that means you'll get your bills online, where they can be paid online, without the use of a single shred of paper. For now, online check paying amounts to payment authorization—you tell the bank via your electronic system to pay a bill and the bank goes ahead and does it. (Ironically, banks still do this most frequently by cutting a paper check and mailing it. As of this writing, relatively few companies are equipped to receive electronic payments, although the number is increasing all the time.)

That said, does banking online make sense? That depends. It can certainly be cheaper than doing your banking the old-fashioned way. Certain large banks, for example, don't charge checking customers anything at all to access accounts and pay bills electronically. Other banks charge fees, but usually less than what you pay for a regular checking account. Typically, online customers get free access but have to pay $5 or $10 per month to pay bills electronically. Still, that's a bargain; it's less than many of us spend on stamps each month. So, if you find yourself cutting a bunch of checks and mailing them out each month—say, at least ten—then you'll likely save a few bucks by going online to pay those same bills.

Online banking also affords you a good deal more control. Most banks now give you round-the-clock access to account information, and not just checking—data on money market, credit cards, savings, and information from other accounts are also available. There's also a greater sense of immediacy—rather than waiting for the paper ledger to come every month, online bankers can balance their accounts each and every time they pay a bill. Online banking can also be particularly advantageous if you travel a good deal; rather than having to scramble to the bank every time you're in town for a few days, online banking lets you do your banking wherever you happen to be. That may prove especially handy if, for instance, you're waiting for a particular deposit to clear so you can pay a bill.

Still, online banking is not for everyone. If you're perfectly happy with the old checkbook and monthly statement—and don't feel you're spending too much time paying bills and making certain that everything jibes—there's no overwhelming reason to jump online, since cyberbanking isn't likely to save you a carload of cash or time. Finally, you may want to hold off on online banking if you're prone to overmanagement—all that access may just drive you nuts and offer little advantage in return.

If cyberbanking appeals, bear a few shopping considerations in mind:

▶ *See what this is all going to cost you.* Some banks charge to go online, some don't. Ask about extra fees for bill paying, which can range all over the board. Ask whether basic fees cover a certain number of electronic payments and what it'll cost you if you have to pay more bills than the preset maximum.

▶ *Find out what sort of software you need.* Some banks let you use popular financial planning programs, while others are still mired in their home-grown software. The latter can make banking a real pain if you want to transfer all your banking information to your budget software program.

▶ *Find out what you can do online.* Can you move money between accounts? How simple is it to reconcile your checks? Can you access every account you have with that bank? How far back can you go in your records (some banks let you go back only a single month)?

▶ *Ask precisely how you hook up with your bank.* Do you link up directly with the bank's computer, or can you access your account information via an Internet Web site that also offers other services and functions? The trend in online banking is toward Web sites; not only can you do more with a multifunction Web site, but you can also access it with a secured browser such as Netscape (as opposed to systems that limit you to a particular kind of financial planning or proprietary software program).

↗ *Useful Web Site*

For a great overview of how online banking works, its advantages and drawbacks, and other basics, check out the Bank Rate Monitor page at http://www.bankrate.com/brm/olbstep2.asp. A companion page at http://www.bankrate.com/brm/publ/onlifees.asp spells out which banks offer online banking and what the pertinent fees and charges are.

Gomez Advisors has compiled its own rankings of the top 20 banks offering Internet banking services at http://www.gomez.com. The rankings are based on cost, ease of use, available resources, and other criteria.

Financial Software Programs

There are countless financial planning programs available, from pricey monsters that can seemingly do everything except let the dog out at night to bare-bones freeware that you can yank right off the Internet. What kind of program is right for you depends on how much you want to spend, what you plan to use the program for, and, equally important, how disciplined you genuinely think you'll be in using the software on a consistent basis.

Bear in mind that what matters most in choosing software is what programs can do for you—what features are important, how you can get the most out of the program, and how easily the programs work. Moreover, what works for one person may well bomb with another, despite the fact that the program is a "big name" that everyone seems to be using. So let's turn the discussion around and pay attention to those things you should look for in choosing a financial software package (if, indeed, you should choose one at all). Once you know what you want, you'll be able to find that product that meets your needs.

For all the varied functions and neat little tricks many programs can do, one of the most important elements in choosing a suitable software package is its ease of use. Is it simple to get the program to do what you want it to do, or is it weighed down with a lot of convoluted instructions that don't seem to make any sense? To gauge this and other elements of a program, see if you can track down a friend or colleague who's using it, or go to the manufacturer's Internet site to see if it has an online demo or a program that you can download and try on a limited basis. Whether on a pal's machine or your own, see how quickly you become comfortable with the program's primary functions and features. Does the program have some sort of interactive tutorial that walks you through some of the major applications, or are you relegated to trial and error to learn the program? If you do experience a problem, how simple is it to get it solved? Is there free telephone support if you need to run your problem past another person? If there is free support, how long does it last? (More and more programs are offering limited support that runs out after a few months or a year. After that, you have to pay for the privilege.) In short, test-driving a program before you actually lay out the cash for it can help ensure that you'll hook up with a program that you'll use consistently rather than one that's just too hard to get the hang of and that will end up in a dusty corner of your computer's hard drive.

Here are some other major functions and considerations to take into account when shopping around for a program.

> ▶ *Budgeting and check paying.* This function is a mainstay with many programs. With it, you can set up and track your expenses, work on a savings program, plan for significant purchases, and receive a heads-up when your spending gets out of whack with how much money you have to go around. Depending on the program you choose, you can also get periodic reports on how your budget is doing, work out schedules to dig yourself out of debt, and even produce spiffy charts and graphs that summarize all this information.

At the heart of most systems is a ledger where you type in checks written and cash payments made for various expenses. While systems differ slightly, most then have you assign each payment to a budgetary category, such as housing, food, entertainment, and long-term savings. Then, the program earmarks a payment to that category and tracks how your spending—both within individual categories and overall—jibes with the budget that you set up. On top of that, most programs help you balance your checking account or any other similar account.

Budgeting and account tracking functions are probably the most important—and most widely used—feature in most financial software packages, so it won't hurt to be a bit anal when comparing how one program's features stack up against another's. While it doesn't make sense to pay for a ton of bells and whistles—for instance, charts and graphs—it's equally important not to shortchange yourself in features. With that in mind, know what sort of budgetary challenges and problems you face when checking out programs—for instance, if you chronically overspend in one area of your budget, make sure the software has a feature to let you know immediately about any overspending it detects. If you have trouble balancing your checkbook, see how well that particular function works. One handy element in many of the more popular programs automatically summarizes your spending for a month and compares it with spending in other months to see how you're doing over the long haul, within particular spending categories as well as overall. Likewise, if you want to skip a step in financial drudgery, see if the program allows you to print out checks; this function lets you enter the payment and produce the actual check in one step, all printed and ready to sign.

The reason that budget functions are probably the most popular feature of many software programs is that they're the most useful for the most people. If you're interested in watching where your money goes, you should have a budget, and budgetary software can be genuinely helpful in keeping you on course—it provides, if you will, the proverbial whack upside the head when you need to know that you're spending too much, somewhere. It provides a tangible record of your budgetary comings and goings, which is handy not only for the single user who needs a clear picture of what's going on but also for couples and roommates who chronically disagree over where their money goes—all it takes is a quick check of their computer records to find out exactly who spent what and where. Another plus is the ease of keeping tax records with these programs, since most allow you to track things such as deductible expenses.

However, a program's budget features, like any other function software can offer, are only as helpful as you're willing to make them. You need a real commitment to sitting down and pounding in all the data on a regular basis. Granted, online banking capabilities have made this less of a problem but, if you're not using any sort of automated function to let the program know what you're doing, know up front that it often takes a fair chunk of time to set up a budget and keep the program's information up to date. If you don't think you'll have either the discipline or the time to keep things current, then you're better off not wasting any money on a software program, since it won't do you much good. But, if you think you'll be able to keep up, the programs can prove genuinely useful.

▶ *Investment selection and tracking.* Most programs worth their salt will let you set up and follow your investments. Again, what you want and need will depend on your individual tastes and circumstances. Even the most skeletal program will let you establish an account to track a mutual fund, although you'll likely have to enter information such as price changes and buys and sells by hand so that you can see the overall value of your investment.

If that's adequate, good enough. But, if you want something above and beyond that, more involved programs let you do a bit more analysis of your investments. Some, for instance, help you select those investments that may suit your situation; for instance, they may offer "screens" that let you choose stocks and mutual funds according to any number of parameters. Often, these work in conjunction with a program's complementary Web site, letting you tap into research reports, news, and information on how a stock or mutual fund has performed over time. One thing to bear in mind—if you want to use a program to help choose investments, there are often additional surcharges for accessing online information (charges are above and beyond normal connection fees). Depending on how often you use the online service and what you do, these additional fees can easily hit $30 a month and more—so, when shopping, try to find out how much all a program's fabulous research and analysis functions may cost you.

Next, look at the program's investment and portfolio tracking capabilities. Some, for example, let you break down the investments and savings in your overall portfolio to see how each account is doing in terms of percentage gained or lost, current annual returns, and even more specific data such as price highs and lows over a given time period. Getting all the necessary data for all this fancy footwork can also be easier with more costly programs, as many download quotes and plug them into your investments, updating them automatically (if you regularly update your portfolio, this can be a wonderful time saver, so keep an eye peeled for this feature). For the more aesthetically inclined, some programs let you produce flowery charts and graphs that illustrate at a glance how your investments are performing. Again, it's a question of how much you want the program to do, how much you're willing to enter manually, and the price you're willing to pay to balance those two considerations.

↗ Useful Web Sites

When it comes to software, one's true love may be pure poison to another. As such, it behooves you to get as many opinions about the issues we've raised as well as any others you may think are important. Here's a few Web-based ways to do just that:

The Software Review Source (http://www.reviewsource.com/) lets you read product reviews for a variety of financial software. Enter the type of software you're interested in and the system returns compact, easy-to-read overviews, including price, system requirements, and other information. Depending on the particular review, there may also be links to more detailed reviews of performance and features. Here's a search tip: Be specific about what you want, whether it's financial planning software or programs for handling taxes, mutual funds, and so on. Otherwise, you may bypass a review that could prove handy.

PC Magazine published a piece awhile back that compared the features and performance of several top financial software programs. It's at http://www.zdnet.com/pcmag/features/finance/_open.htm. Some information may be dated (such as the prices), but the piece does raise some good shopping issues worthy of consideration.

For a great Web page that can give you an overview of dozens of investment software packages, as well as links to the package's own Web sites, have a look at http://www.investorama.com/software.shtml.

▶ *Calculators.* Almost any software program, whether from a box or the product of a freeware download, will give you a calculator to add, subtract, and perform other basic arithmetic functions. But don't sell yourself short when looking into the varied types of calculators a program offers, as some can really come in handy. Some of the more useful types of calculators include functions that let you figure mortgages and other types of loan payments; let you estimate the value of an investment, taking into account how much you're investing at what interest rate and for how long; and allow you to set up side-by-side comparisons of various loan programs and features.

In fact, calculators are something of an aberration in the world of financial software. While many of the more expensive financial programs have a bevy of fancy features, some—including some of the more popular—provide rather limited calculator functions. On the other hand, other so-called basic programs have a wide array of functions. Again, try to figure what you think you'll use and what may prove little more than a toy. When checking out calculators, pay attention to the various ways you can use them. Some, for instance, may limit savings projections to how much you can end up with, while others let you plug in elements such as monthly savings and various rates of return to see different scenarios.

> ► *Education.* This feature of financial software is frequently overlooked, but, in fact, it may be as valuable as any sort of number-crunching or record-keeping function. These days, any financial planning software that you buy from one of the big manufacturers will let you hook up with a Web site maintained by the manufacturer. Not only do these sites offer a carload of current financial information and data such as stock quotes and breaking financial news, but the better ones also have extensive libraries, message boards, analysis, and other features.

Don't bypass a program's companion Web site when considering which software is right for you, as a good site can prove a marvelous financial tutor. Before you drop good money on a financial program, try to track down its Web site to see what it offers (a general search will usually turn up these sorts of sites. You can generally get into them without the companion software, since companies are eager to make them as accessible as possible). Drop by the site and see what sort of libraries it has, how responsive its message boards are, and whether its material is useful for both novices and experienced investors. For instance, if you have a question about whether an index mutual fund suits your investing style, a good Web site will probably have an article or two that addresses that very topic. Post the question on a message board and watch what answers you get. If you find that a site lacks information on topics that interest you or that questions you put on its message board die on the vine without being answered, it may not be much of a Web site. Likewise, pay attention to a Web site's interactive and financial shopping services. The better ones will let you do such jobs as track down a mortgage, find the best paying CDs, and even hook up with a financial planner who lives near you. Again, focus on how easy it is to use all these features—they don't do a lick of good if they're too hard to learn.

For that matter, a good program's educational capabilities shouldn't be limited to cyberspace. Many programs include an extensive database of articles and features covering a variety of financial topics. Some, in fact, offer what amounts to an in-house "course", starting you off with some basics and systematically leading you through more advanced topics and concepts. Again, match yourself up with a program that fits. If all you see are articles that cover investing ideas that you wouldn't go near, you may want to keep looking. Likewise, if the articles sound as though Barney the Dinosaur would be at home singing them (Everybody: "Saving is good, saving is neat, or else you'll have no food to eat"), a more, shall we say, sophisticated reference library would be better suited to you. Finally, see whether the program lets you update its libraries; some hook up with the companion Internet site to download current articles and analysis. That can be essential with some topics, such as home buying, where conditions can change quickly enough to warrant different strategies.

↗ Useful Web Sites

Instead of heading out to the nearest software store to lay down your hard-earned money on financial planning software, which may offer features that are of no use to you or bypass things that you deem essential, try downloading some free software packages to get a feel for what's available, how they work, and what you want. One great place to do that is at http://www.e-analytics.com/soft2.htm, a page devoted exclusively to freeware for finance and investment applications.

CHAPTER 11

"No Man but a Blockhead..."

L anding a job is the ultimate goal for most of us, leaving out the self-anointed few who spend most of their lives in that half-purgatory, half-nirvana state known as "professional student." For the rest of us, once our school days are done—or, in many cases, while we're still getting a degree of some kind—finding satisfying, rewarding work and making the most of it are significant reasons we spent all that money and effort on education in the first place. Indeed, latching onto a career that's both enjoyable and fulfilling is far and away the most important element of our work life. Funny as it may sound in a book on money, things such as enjoying generous pay and benefits are decidedly less important than doing the kind of work that brings us joy.

That's not to say that salary and fringe benefits don't matter, because they certainly do. After all, financial compensation in its varied forms is, once we're past the psychological satisfaction of meaningful work, the reason most of us have to work (whenever I hear someone waxing poetic about the supposed existential rapture that comes from writing, I inevitably conjure up the response offered two centuries ago by Dr. Samuel Johnson: "No man but a blockhead ever wrote except for money"). Seeking the common ground between the two points, it's probably healthiest to conclude that we need to find work that we enjoy and that duly compensates us for the time and effort expended.

That being said, it's important to understand what compensation means these days, because it's taken on much broader significance than simply a paycheck. Getting the most money that you can is certainly important, but attendant forms of compensation—retirement programs, programs to cut your taxes, strategies to pay for medical expenses—should carry a good deal of weight as well. In fact, unlike our workplace predecessors, whose primary focus usually was the size of the paycheck and the rest be damned, we should pay almost as much attention to benefits and other forms of compensation as we do to the figure on the bottom line of our pay stubs. Here are some ideas to increase your chances of getting the best overall work package possible, including salary and all the other little goodies that, properly taken advantage of, can pay massive dividends in the long run.

⬈ Useful Web Sites

Of course, before you get to the particulars of salary, benefits, and the like, you have to track down a job. And, not suprisingly, the Internet can also prove helpful in that very task. Two of the larger job search Web sites are Monster Board (www.monsterboard.com), which touts some 50,000 domestic and international jobs, and Career Mosaic (www.careermosaic.com), which also offers tens of thousands of openings. The beauty of these and most other job sites is that you don't do the browsing—the computer does. You enter some basic data, including keywords that describe the job you're looking for and the region of the country in which you're interested and the database rousts out available openings that match your search parameters. In many cases, you can apply right away online. You usually have to complete a questionnaire detailing your work experience, education, and other pertinent information.

(Caveat: For all its wonders, online job hunting has its flaws. Postings can be sketchy, often failing to point out details that would disqualify many job seekers. Moreover, when responding to a posting, bear in mind you may well be one of thousands applying for the same job. Some estimates suggest that fewer than 5% of all responses actually result in a job offer.)

Cutting the Best Salary Deal You Can

Things just aren't the way they used to be in the insulated little world of salaries. Not very long ago, people coming out of college and those with limited time in the workplace pretty much took what they could get when it came to pay; experience and longevity were the keys to earning potential. My first job as a newspaper reporter at a tiny New England daily earned me the whopping windfall of $140 a week. Not only was I earning a pittance; it never occurred to me at the time to have the chutzpah to ask for more when I was hired (not that I would have gotten a thin dime out of it, but at least I would have tried).

Fundamental, sweeping changes in the labor market are pushing aside the old salary parameters of time and work experience. Instead, we're fast moving into an environment where skills are the determining factor in what you can earn, whether you've been in the workforce for years or are looking for your very first job. If you have a set of desirable, marketable skills—and that covers a very broad base of topics, from a Java programmer to a liberal arts graduate who has the intellectual wherewithal to learn valuable skills on the job—more and more companies are interested in seeking out your services, regardless of your level of experience. Moreover, in a world where the thought of staying with a single employer throughout your entire working life has gone the way of eight-tracks and carbon paper, companies are also interested in enticing qualified applicants and making it worth their while to stick around for longer than a couple of years.

↗ Useful Web Sites

Just how can you find out whether you have the skills or training that employers are chomping at the bit for? One way is through the federal government's Bureau of Labor Statistics employment projections Web site (http://stats.bls.gov/emphome.htm). There, among other goodies, the BLS identifies those occupations with the best job growth outlook. The site also explores which industries and regions of the country will enjoy the most expansion in the foreseeable future. Also, don't forget to check out the BLS's general homepage, which offers an exhaustive lineup of statistics, research, and information on employment and labor.

Today's recent graduates and young employees have an enviable amount of leverage when it comes to negotiating a solid salary package. But, whether dickering over pay from your first job or pursuing greater pay from a new or existing employer, landing the best deal you possibly can is a learned skill that takes in a variety of strategies and techniques:

First, get a dose of reality. Before you take the first step in salary negotiation, take the time to learn the constraints of the world in which you're operating. Find out what the accepted pay range is for a person with your job, your skills, your level of training, and your experience. That way, you're covered from both ends. If you know what others in your field are making, you'll know full well when a salary offer is a chintzy joke. By the same token, you'll save yourself the embarrassment of looking delusional when you demand an outlandish amount of pay.

↗ Useful Web Sites

Knowing your profession's accepted salary range can prove a huge boon to getting you the best pay package you can. So, take the time to research the numbers. Not surprisingly, the Internet offers a host of useful sites. One worth checking out is JobSmart (http://jobsmart.org). There, you're linked to more than 200 salary surveys on the Web, both general and profession-specific. JobSmart also provides other tools that can get you the best job with the best possible compensation, including negotiation strategies, tips on preparing resumes, and career guides.

The Bureau of Labor Statistics Occupational Outlook Handbook (found at http://www.bls.gov) also provides salary information on more than 250 occupations. Likewise, the National Business Employment Weekly gives an industry-by-industry breakdown of salaries (http://careers.wsj.com).

Implicit in all this discussion of salary data and other statistics is the importance of focusing purely on fact, not emotion. Keep your salary discussions on a fact-only basis. Don't try to finagle a better salary by coming off as a martyr or as some sort of misused genius who just isn't going to take anymore. All this kind of posturing does is back the other person into a corner from which the most plausible escape is the word "no". Moreover, if by some chance you do get more money this way, you may pay a price later on (employers who feel they've been shafted in salary negotiations can have remarkably long memories when, for instance, the ugly subject of personnel layoffs happens to come up). Instead, put the salary question back into the other court by raising questions rather than making demands. Cite your research on salary ranges, and, if an employer balks, simply ask why he or she doesn't feel a comparable amount of pay is warranted.

Have your own number in mind. On the basis of your research, come up with a salary with which you'd be satisfied. Don't keep pushing an employer up and up needlessly—again, even if you get more money than you ever dreamed of, you may end up paying for it more in the long run.

The preceding strategies are particularly important when lobbying for a raise with an existing employer: Do your homework, keep things factual, and don't back anyone into a corner. On top of that, be ready to cite your accomplishments within the company. That doesn't mean doing it in an obnoxious way with some blow-by-blow description of every little thing you've done ever since you first walked in the door, but have a few particularly glowing examples at the ready. Cite positive job reviews or projects that were completed well ahead of schedule. In particular, make the most of many companies' emphasis on positive teamwork. For example, if you're looking for a raise, it may not hurt to drop your boss a short memo outlining a recent example of a fellow employee who helped you iron out some sort of problem. That sets up a double positive—not only do you come off as a team player, but you're also pointing out another example of workplace success.

Finally, don't make the subject of salary the end-all to your job. While it's important to get a fair amount of compensation, bear in mind that you have a long career path ahead of you, one with ample time to make a good deal of money. As you work out salary questions in your own mind, don't overlook the importance of a variety of job experience, the compilation of credentials, and other things that may well prove more valuable in the long run than a bit more money now. So, if, by chance, you're looking at a couple of jobs—one where the money may not be as hot but the potential for growth and experience is great—give some serious consideration to putting salary on the back burner. Chances are you'll be a good deal happier and more satisfied down the road.

↗ Useful Web Sites

OK, you've got a great job offer, but you're going to have to move cross-country to take advantage of it. Unless your employer-to-be is footing the bill, moving costs are a definite issue. To get a feel for how much moving might cost you—and ways to shop for the most cost-effective deal—check out Mover Quotes (http://www.moverquotes.com/). A free service, Mover Quotes let you enter where you're moving from, where you're going to, and how much you want a mover to haul. The system then pops up a list of carriers with quotes on fees and insurance coverage.

401k Plans

Other than your salary—and, in some cases, even more than your paycheck—401k plans are perhaps the most important employee benefit you can tap into, because it offers myriad opportunities—retirement savings, lower taxes, the power of compounding, and the growth potential of any number of investments—all rolled into one absolutely amazing vehicle. So it pays to understand what a 401k is and how you can make the most of it.

A 401k is an employee benefit that has at its heart a salary reduction program. Before you gag on that last term, permit me to explain: A 401k lets you save for your retirement by automatically having a certain portion of salary deducted from every paycheck. Actually, it's not really from your paycheck, since the money is automatically removed before you ever have your check in your hot little hand. The money is placed into an investment vehicle of your choosing (depending on the type of 401k your company offers, that can take in everything from mutual funds to company stock to bonds to money market funds).

⤢ Useful Web Sites

For a great overview of all that a 401k plan can offer, as well as links to other handy 401k Web sites, point your browser to http://www.invest-faq. com/articles/ret-plan-401k.html.

The problem with many people—particularly younger ones, whose salaries may be a bit more modest than those of their older colleagues—is that they think they can't afford to have their paycheck reduced by one thin dime. Well, there are reasons to rethink that position. First, since your contributions to your 401k are taken out before you're actually paid, that money isn't subject to the state and federal taxes that bite into your income. Put another way, from the IRS's point of view, it's as though you never actually earned that money in the first place.

Therein lies the first big benefit. Since you're saving on your taxes by taking out money for your 401k, you're effectively earning a "return" on your money before it's ever invested. Here's an example: Say you put away $1,000 a year in your 401k and you're in the 15% federal tax bracket and the 6% state tax bracket. By excluding $1,000 of your income from your taxes, you're saving $150 on your federal taxes ($1,000 times .15) and an additional $60 on your state taxes. That's $210 back in your pocket, an effective return of 21% on that $1,000 you've socked away. Put another way, you've invested $1,000 but it's cost you only $790. A lot of investing professionals would be tickled pink if they could average that kind of investment return, year in and year out.

The next big plus is that your 401k has tax-deferred status. That means any sort of growth in value your 401k enjoys isn't subject to state or federal taxes, at least until you start withdrawing the money. As we discussed in Chapter 5, deferring taxes on an investment can make a big difference in how quickly your investment grows. To illustrate, if you set aside $100 a month for 20 years with an average return of 10% a year and you pay no taxes on the investment, you'll come out with nearly $76,000. However, if you pay 15% of your annual return in taxes each and every year, you'll be left with just $62,699. If you also pay state taxes, you'll lose even more.

↗ Useful Web Sites

Fidelity Investments has put together a nice page summarizing the varied tax advantages of 401ks. You can find it at http://www.401k.com/401k/pfp/rp/taxes.htm.

Juiced About Your 401k Yet?

Well, as they used to say in the old Ginsu knife ads, don't answer yet, because there's more. The first additional plus is what's known as a match. Depending on where you work and how generous your employer is, he or she may also contribute to your 401k. The usual arrangement is that your employer promises to pay a certain percentage of the amount you're contributing. That amount can range from next to nothing (some places may promise to contribute a whopping 2% or so) to $1.50 for every dollar that you as the employee contribute. Whether great or small, those matching funds serve as extra fuel for your 401k, because, like the tax savings you automatically enjoy, they mean that your 401k produces an effective return before your contribution is actually invested in anything. For instance, if you're saving 21% in taxes according to the example we just discussed and your boss, Diamond Jim—whose largesse has definite bounds—matches your contribution at a heady rate of 2%, that's still a 23% return on every dollar you stash away in your 401k. The message is clear: Whether your employer is dedicated to helping his or her workers achieve financial security or would sell snow in the winter if he or she could, a match adds a built-in return to your 401k before the money truly earns anything on its own.

Another plus, particularly important to those who fear they can't spare a penny from their salary, is that 401k plans are automatic. As we mentioned in earlier chapters, the best way to ensure financial discipline is to make things as mechanical as possible. Unlike other types of investing, where you have to sit down and cut a check to contribute, all you need do with a 401k is set up the plan and let it roll; your contributions are automatically deducted from your salary without your having to lift a finger. Not only does that make 401k participation easy from a practical standpoint, but it's easier to keep your program going when it all functions on autopilot. It's the easiest form of discipline you can find.

You can even get to your 401k money without incurring the sort of nasty early withdrawal penalties we'll discuss later. Many companies allow you to borrow from your 401k, usually up to half the money in the account up to a maximum of $50,000. Interest rates are usually only a point or two higher than what you'd incur for a conventional loan, and loan terms are usually for five years. Even better, any interest you repay just goes back into your account.

Bear in mind, however, that it's usually best to leave your 401k alone unless absolutely necessary. For one thing, if you leave your job or get canned, you have to pay the balance back in full in short order—otherwise, the IRS treats the loan as a withdrawal and you're socked with taxes and penalties. On top of that, shy away from borrowing from your 401k if the financial obligation of repaying the loan will discourage you from continuing to contribute as much as you can to your 401k.

Another way to get at the money early is through what's called a "hardship withdrawal." This applies when you're faced with a huge and immediate financial obligation and can't get the money from any other source except your 401k. Typical obligations include paying college tuition for yourself or a dependent, paying for medical expenses, buying your own home, and avoiding foreclosure. Unfortunately, hardship withdrawals can be an out-and-out pain. For one thing, you may have to prove in exhaustive detail that you can't get the money anywhere else. Moreover, it's essentially up to your employer to say yea or nay to your request; if he or she is, shall we say, a jerk, that may prove iffy for your request. And, of course, you'll be hit with taxes once you withdraw the money.

↗ Useful Web Sites

A nice article that goes into some detail about the pluses and minuses of accessing your 401k account can be found at http://www.phillynews.com/online/finance/pers10896.htm.

Fidelity has a page that spells out everything you should know before borrowing from your 401k at http://www.401k.com/401k/pfp/rp/proscons.htm.

Another of the myriad advantages of 401ks is that you can effectively take your 401k wherever you go. In the good old days of conventional company pensions, you usually had to stick with the same employer—often for more than 20 or 30 years—before you were eligible to tap into your company's pension. If you left before that, you could exit empty handed. Not so with 401ks. Unless you are not yet fully vested (we'll explain that term later), you can roll over all the proceeds from one 401k into another plan when you change jobs. That's particularly important to today's increasingly mobile workforce, whose members aren't nearly as likely to stay with the same company for as long as their parents and grandparents—whether by choice or because of some less palatable force—did.

↗ Useful Web Sites

Changing jobs? Check out the ramifications of taking your 401k along with you at http://www.401k.com/401k/pfp/rp/jobs.htm.

Of course, 401ks aren't a financial never-never land, and there are a few wrinkles to bear in mind. First, you can't sign up to take part in a 401k the minute you walk in the company's door—depending on your employer's policy, you may have to wait as long as a year to join. Moreover, there are usually only certain times of the year when you can join a company 401k, so if you suddenly get an urge to get on board your 401k outside your employer's designated sign-up period, you're SOL (Savings Obviously in Limbo—what were you expecting?) Additionally, short of the exceptions we discussed earlier, you can't get at the money before you reach age 59 1/2. If you do withdraw anything before that, you're subject to income taxes as well as a nasty 10% early-withdrawal penalty.

Another wrinkle is what's known as vesting. This is the time before the matching funds that your employer puts into your 401k become yours (of course, anything you contribute to the plan remains yours). Vesting is supposed to motivate you to stay with the company as long as possible. While the matching funds may seem a small price to pay for leaving a company when you see fit, a generous match from your employer may be a tough thing to sacrifice should you wish to leave before you're fully vested. More-over, vesting can happen in a couple of ways. In some companies, you have to work for several years before you become fully vested in your 401k. At other companies, vesting occurs incrementally; you may have to work at the company for a couple of years before you become partly vested, say 20%. After another year, you become vested in another 20%, and so on until the whole shooting match is yours. It's important to ask before you hook up with a 401k about the sort of vesting program you may be looking at. While a prohibitive vesting plan should not necessarily discourage you from taking part in your 401k—there are just too many other benefits to argue for that—it is food for thought if you are not sure how long you may want to stick around with a particular company.

↗ Useful Web Sites

The potential problems posed by vesting—and other issues that you should know about when it comes to your rights as a pension-plan partic-ipant—are covered in a great Web site called "What You Should Know About Your Pension Rights" at http://www.dol.gov/dol/pwba/public/pubs/youknow/knowtoc.htm.

The final consideration is how you invest the money in your 401k. As with individual retirement accounts, the decision of where to put your 401k dollars rests with you. Unfortunately, unlike IRAs, 401ks do not offer limitless choices. In fact, the range of investment choices is probably the aspect that most distinguishes one 401k plan from another. A good plan, for example, may offer you a range of a dozen or more investment choices, including mutual funds, bond funds, and money market funds. Other plans may be a good deal stingier, often limiting your choices to a mere handful (and, in very rare instances, a single choice, as we discuss at the end of this section.)

Whatever the range of options, it's important to approach your 401k as you would any other investment. Bear in mind your tolerance for risk, and research any investment option thoroughly; for instance, if your plan offers several mutual funds, jump over to a place such as Morningstar to see what their long-term performance and volatility have been. Bear in mind the importance of diversification—you always have the option of dividing your 401k contributions among as many investment choices as your plan offers. It's a good idea to look at your 401k as a portfolio in its own right, one where your investment choices should complement each other.

When choosing those investments that are best suited to you, bear in mind that 401ks are designated retirement accounts, since you usually can't touch the money until you're nearly 60 years old without getting nailed by a nasty penalty. That means you're looking at a long-term investment horizon, particularly if you're relatively new to the workforce. As we've discussed in prior chapters, that can argue for a fairly aggressive investment posture—the longer you can sock your money away, the more time you'll have to ride out any ups and downs in the investments and, theoretically, enjoy better returns than what you might get from more conservative choices. Again, however, don't go against your nature. If, say, a mutual fund offers a point or two less a year in return than a more aggressive option but isn't as subject to the roller-coaster ride as its more aggressive brethren, go with it if that makes you feel better. As we've said before, a slightly better return just isn't worth losing sleep over.

One last word about 401ks—there's really only one situation that offers a persuasive argument for bypassing your 401k plan altogether. In very rare instances, your only choice of 401k investments is your company's stock. If you happen to be one of these unfortunate few confronted with only this option, think carefully about whether your 401k is worth the risk. Granted, you'll still enjoy all the benefits that any other sort of 401k provides, but you'll be effectively hitching both your job and your retirement money to the same wagon. If, by chance, your company crashes, you stand to lose both your job and whatever you've contributed to your 401k. That lack of diversification can prove exceedingly dangerous, especially with companies whose futures may be touch and go. So if all you can do is buy your employer's stock, try to find out as much as you can about your company's prospects for survival. If the long-term outlook is anything short of rosy, you may want to stay on the 401k sidelines.

⤴ Useful Web Sites

There's no shortage of Web sites that offer basic information and guidance on 401ks. Here are a couple that are worth checking out:

The 401k Forum (www.401kforum.com) serves up a comprehensive overview of 401k plans, including 401k basics, the advantages of 401ks, the nuts and bolts of investing in 401ks, and almost any other issue or topic that touches on 401ks. Equally interesting—and, frankly, refreshing in the sales-oriented environment that many such Internet services espouse—is a discussion, albeit brief, of the drawbacks of 401ks.

Comfin (www.comfin.com), the Internet arm of Community Financial Planning Services, not only provides information and frequently asked questions about 401ks but also offers a free interactive calculator that lets you see how much a 401k can grow under various circumstances. Set up any number of plans you like—ones based on conservative, moderate, or aggressive investing—and immediately see how much you can accumulate over time. This is a great tool that lets you tinker with any number of variables.

NOTE: If you work for a nonprofit organization, such as a school or charitable group, you have access to a similar retirement vehicle known as a 403b, which is virtually identical to a 401k. The major difference is that with a 403b you can contribute a slightly larger percentage of your salary than you can with a 401k (a bit more than 16% with a 403b versus 15% with a 401k.) Other than that, 403bs offer the same features and advantages as 401ks, so it's always a great idea to make the most of them.

↗ Useful Web Sites

Perhaps the definitive source of information on 403bs is IRS Publication 571 (located online at www.benefitslink.com/403b/index.html). There, you'll get the word on what 403bs are, who offers them, who can partici-pate, the nuts and bolts of contributing, and even worksheets that you can print out to figure out your own 403b. Granted, it's not the liveliest read-ing in the world—this is the IRS, remember—but if you have a question about your 403b, this is as good a bet as you'll find in cyberspace.

Another nice source of information on 403bs—and a host of other financial subjects, for that matter—is The Investment FAQ (http://invest-faq.com). The site offers an article introducing readers to 403bs and also provides links to several other sites of interest to 403b participants.

Hit the Cafeteria

If you associate the word *cafeteria* with rather unpleasant things—meat cooked beyond recognition, stale bread, and salad bars whose sole source of green is mold—it's time to update your conscious-ness. In the workaday world, many companies employ what's known as a cafeteria plan when it comes to doling out employee benefits (such plans are now available to companies with 50 or more employees). At its heart, the system is simple—you as the employee are allocated a certain number of credits, which you can use to select the types of benefits you wish. The idea is that individ-uals can choose those benefits that match their situation best and bypass others that don't really meet their requirements.

If a cafeteria plan is in place where you work, it's important to understand what it covers and how to tailor it to your advantage. Generally, you're allowed to distribute your designated number of credits among four different areas—health coverage, dental cover-age, life insurance, and long-term disability insurance. What you do with those choices depends on your circumstances. If, for instance, you're young and in good health, you may opt for health insurance with a higher deductible and put the remaining credits into something else, such as dental or disability insurance. In making decisions about health insurance, the most important issue—as it is with investing—is your risk tolerance. Would you rather pay less in premiums but face a higher deductible if something serious happened or choose instead a lower deductible at the expense of other types of coverage? While the answer to that question will vary from person to person, many financial pros recommend that if you're at the low end of the salary scale, you should go for higher-cost health insurance with a lower deductible. Although that would leave you with less to spend elsewhere, you wouldn't run the risk of having to fork out a huge deductible on a more modest income. Moreover, don't shy away from comprehensive health coverage just because you're young and in good shape—doctors, orthopedic surgeons, and others who try to patch up weekend athletes and others like them can attest to the hefty medical bills "healthy" types can run up as a result of sports injuries and other similar maladies.

As we mentioned in Chapter 8, disability coverage is an essential, yet frequently overlooked form of insurance, so give that some serious thought when choosing benefits from your cafeteria plan. In many cases, employers offer disability coverage free of charge; if yours does not, weigh the cost of an in-house disability policy against what you may be able to get elsewhere. There's a decent chance that your company's policy will cost you less. The same holds true for life insurance (provided, of course, as we discussed in Chapter 8, that you need any sort of life insurance to begin with).

Flexible Spending Accounts

These innovative accounts—pardon the pun—really let you flex your benefits muscles to the max. Flexible spending accounts let you supplement your health care coverage, pay for kinds of coverage that conventional health insurance won't touch, and even lower your taxes. Flexible Spending Accounts—known as FSAs—are akin to 401ks in their scope of advantages and, in fact, function in something of a similar fashion.

Here's how FSAs work. At the beginning of each year, your employer asks you how much money you want subtracted from your salary for your FSA. As with 401k plans, the money is taken out before it's counted as income, which, in turn, reduces your taxes. The money is then placed in an account, which you can access to help pay for any number of benefits-related expenses. For instance, you can use money from your FSA to pay for costs that your health coverage won't, such as routine physical examinations, eyeglasses and contact lenses, cosmetic surgery, and even such things as faith healing, if you so choose.

FSA money can also go toward expenses that most medical plans only cover in part. Here, the perfect example is psychotherapy and other forms of mental health counseling, which many plans cover only up to 50%. The same holds true with other types of coverage that you may have passed on in your company's cafeteria program. If, for instance, you took a flyer on dental insurance because the coverage was too costly, you can use FSA money to pay for yearly exams, cleanings, fillings, and other procedures. Compared with monthly dental insurance premiums, an FSA can prove particularly cost-effective.

Of course, there are a couple of catches with FSAs (aren't there always?) For one thing, unlike 401ks, in which the money withdrawn from your salary is theoretically growing in value, an FSA produces no income or growth for you—the money just sits there (or in an account where your employer, not you, earns interest). More important, FSAs are a yearly use-it-or-lose-it deal. If any money is left in your FSA at the end of the year, it reverts to your employer, and you're left out in the cold.

That said, it's critical to be realistic—and perhaps a touch conservative—when trying to determine just how much money to put into an FSA. One way to do this is to go back for the past year or two and add up every sort of medical expense that you had to pay out of pocket—that should give you a reasonably good idea of what may be enough but not too much. Be exhaustive, and include everything from copayments to deductibles to expenses for procedures and treatments that your conventional health care coverage didn't address. That way, you won't spend December buying five pairs of eyeglasses or enduring acupuncture for the heck of it just so that your company doesn't get its mitts on your remaining FSA stash.

↗ Useful Web Sites

> A great site on flexible spending accounts is available at http://www. lipman.com/tlc/flexover.htm. There, you can access information on how FSAs work, how often you'll get reimbursed under such programs (you pay first, then the program pays you back), and even how much you can expect to save on taxes with an FSA.

On Your Own

If, by chance, you're one of the increasing hardy breed who has ventured out into that brave new world called self-employment, you're probably very familiar with the varied joys and headaches of working for one's self. On one hand, you enjoy the freedom of choosing what work you wish to do and, within reason, when you care to do it. On the other, you may have to deal with the uncertainty that comes from the absence of a regular paycheck. On the plus side, you may never have to deal with a paranoid, deluded boss hovering over your desk every minute. But that privilege, as we discuss in Chapter 12, comes at the price of higher taxes. And so on.

↗ Useful Web Sites

> If you're self-employed—or are merely tossing the notion around in your head—then make a mental note to check out the National Association for the Self-Employed's Web site at (www.nase.org). There, you'll find scads of resources on any number of issues that face the self-employed, such as benefits, insurance, and financial planning, along with valuable reference material. The site also provides breaking news on legislation and policy decisions that affect the self-employed. Granted, NASE is a membership organization—and you'll see plenty of pitches for you to join up—but the dues may be money well spent, since membership lets you tap into low-cost insurance and other perks. If nothing else, the site is definitely worth a stopover.

I'm not going to get into an exhaustive examination of every nuance of self-employment—that demands a book unto itself, and there are any number of very good ones on the market. For starters, I happily recommend the works of Paul and Sarah Edwards, who have written several books covering such topics as how to choose the ideal form of self-employment and how to make working for one's self work for you. The NASE Web site just mentioned may also prove helpful. However, self-employment does change the picture when it comes to the benefits you bestow upon yourself as both boss and employee:

Insurance

No great pearls of enlightenment here. Since you're self-employed, you need to go out and buy your own health insurance, disability insurance, and any other type of coverage. Although the kind of coverage you'll need will depend on individual circumstances, do not try to go without health insurance and long-term disability coverage. Your health and well-being are the lifeblood of your income—if you're sick or disabled, you can't earn dime one. It's therefore essential to track down reasonably protective health and disability coverage. To help hold down those costs as much as possible, try some of the strategies we outlined in Chapter 8. Those include shopping for coverage from professional organizations, alumni/ae associations, and fraternal and religious groups. And, as we noted earlier, don't forget to compare coverage from any of those sources with programs that a good insurance agent can come up with.

Moreover, self-employment will likely require other types of insurance, including liability insurance (this, for instance, protects you if you work from home and the Federal Express guy slips and breaks an ankle making a delivery), malpractice insurance (which shields you from legal action if someone for whom you've worked alleges you screwed up), and riders to cover business equipment and supplies. Again, a competent insurance agent and/or a comprehensive book on self-employment can help you sort out what you need. If you find the cost overwhelming, give some thought to getting the most bare-bones type of coverage you can afford. Then, as your business and, one hopes, your income grow, you can add additional coverage later.

Retirement Funding

The other primary consideration facing the self-employed is the need to set up and fund a retirement program. First, don't overlook your IRA. Depending on your income, your yearly contributions may be fully or partially tax deductible. Even if they're not deductible, having your IRA money growing tax-deferred until you withdraw it still makes IRAs a palatable retirement funding choice. Moreover, unlike other options, they're a breeze to set up—just fill out a modest amount of paperwork, choose the investment or investments you want for your IRA, and write the check. That's pretty much it.

Another attractive self-employment retirement option is what's known as a Simplified Employee Pension Individual Retirement Account, referred to as a SEP IRA or simply a SEP. These accounts let self-employed people stash away roughly 13% of their annual income up to $22,500 a year. SEPs are a great deal for the self-employed for a variety of reasons. First, as with an IRA, you can set up a SEP with limited paperwork and select any investment that you want. And, as is the case with IRAs, the money in your SEP will grow tax-deferred until you take it out.

SEPs, however, go IRAs one better in one important way: Every penny you contribute reduces your federal and state taxes. There are no income restrictions as there are with IRAs. SEPs are also inherently flexible—there's no requirement that says you have to contribute the maximum every year or, for that matter, sock away a single penny. That's particularly handy for self-employed people whose yearly income can suffer wide swings; if they so choose, they can contribute the maximum in the up years and pare back their contributions when things are a bit leaner.

However, as with a 401k, it pays to take as much advantage of a SEP as you possibly can. Again, it whittles down your taxes and puts your hard-won money into an account where it grows tax-free until you take it out. One way to make SEP contributions easier is to set up an automatic deposit system, which allows a certain amount to be pulled from a checking account and placed into your SEP at regular intervals. As we've noted repeatedly, that puts your savings on autopilot—the best way to go there is.

↗ Useful Web Sites

Quicken's online service offers a concise summary of SEPs (go to http://www.quicken.com/retirement/, then follow the prompts to SEPs and small business retirement programs). The service pulls no punches in its rather laudatory discussion of SEPs—one section is simply titled "Why We Like It." There's even a link to an easy-to-understand graph that shows how the "one-two punch" of a SEP's tax-deferred contributions and earnings helps your money grow rapidly.

A final retirement funding option is called a Keogh plan. These accounts let you put more money away than a SEP (20% of your income, up to a max of $30,000 annually). However, Keoghs are more involved to set up and administer than either IRAs or SEPs—in fact, most people require the services of a financial pro to establish and oversee a Keogh. Although their contribution limits are more liberal, a Keogh will certainly cost you more than a more simplified retirement program because of these administrative costs. To find out whether that additional expense may be worth it, talk to a tax professional or get your hands on IRS publication 560, which offers information on all types of retirement programs for the self-employed.

↗ Useful Web Sites

The brokerage firm T. Rowe Price has put together a few nice Internet pages offering the lowdown on Keoghs and describing how they compare with SEPs and simple IRAs (www.troweprice.com/retirement/). That address then links you to an expansive chart that compares the three major retirement plans so that you can decide at a glance which one might work best for you and why.

CHAPTER 12

The Ever-Dreaded "T" Word

A ll right, no more fun of any kind. It's high time we got ugly and started talking taxes—specifically, income taxes.

Granted, the subject of income taxes is never going to be number one on anyone's popularity list. Taxes are like the flu—if you're lucky, they show up only once a year, they're unpleasant as heck to be around, and they leave you drained after they do the noble thing and blow out of town.

But that's not to say taxes can't become somewhat less of a pain. All it takes is a basic understanding of how they work and various steps you can take to mitigate their sting. You can't get rid of them completely—unless, of course, you're a total hermit chanting away in some far-flung monastery or a so-called patriot busy seceding from the United States and printing up your own money—but you can make them a bit easier to live with.

NOTE: You've no doubt noticed that we have already covered other sorts of taxes in prior chapters, such as the property taxes you pay on your home. This chapter won't cover these or other types of taxes you pay, such as sales tax (you're probably all too familiar with that concept as it is), capital gains taxes (these, if you're interested, are taxes that you pay on a profitable investment), and other taxes. The focus of this chapter is the taxes you pay on the money you earn and ways you can limit them.

A Brief Foray Into History (Very Brief, I Promise)

Amazingly enough, until 1913, the U.S. Supreme Court said that income taxes were unconstitutional, and so the government didn't collect a single penny in income taxes. But, with the adoption of the Sixteenth Amendment, income taxes became one of the laws of the land. Even then, though, most Americans didn't file a tax return or even pay income taxes until just prior to the onset of World War II; the income at which reporting was required was $5,000, and most people didn't even come close to making that.

Real-Life Interlude

Who says the IRS doesn't have a sense of humor? Millions of people, but that's not important right now. A few years back, the service began selling Christmas tree bulbs as "collectors' items." If that doesn't strike you as odd, consider this: In the true spirit of Christmas giving, each ornament featured a replica of the original 1040 tax form that was first released in 1913. The ornament also sported the words "80 Years of Tax Returns" and "Many Happy Returns." That's a joke. To laugh at. Anyway, the ornaments go for $12 apiece and can be obtained through the Treasury Historical Association, P.O. Box 28118, Washington, D.C. 20038-8118; telephone 202-895-5250. Lest you think this is the sickest thing to come down the Beltway in some time, proceeds from all sales do go to a good cause— restoration of the old Treasury Building in Washington.

One development that continues to impact us to this day is the IRS's decision in the middle of World War II to begin withholding taxes from workers' paychecks (the rationale at the time was that the federal Treasury needed a steady flow of income to meet wartime expenses). The practice of withholding is still in use today; when you start a new job, you first have to complete a W-4 form in which you list withholding allowance information. The withholding allowance—which you figure on an accompanying worksheet—is your best guess as to the number of tax deductions and exemptions you'll be entitled to in the coming work year. Your employer then takes out taxes from every paycheck on the basis of this estimate.

Just how much of your salary is withheld for income taxes is reported on a form known as a W-2, which also lists salary and other earnings information. Your employer is required by law to give you one of these so that you can file your taxes every year.

Therein lies your first tax tip: Watch how much tax you end up paying every year, since that will give you a good idea of how close to the mark your withholdings are. If you're forking out a good deal of additional money come April 15, you're probably overstating your withholdings (even worse, you could be liable for interest or penalties for underpayment of taxes). By the same token, if you're getting a huge refund, you're probably not withholding enough, which means you're just loaning the government money that it must eventually give back to you.

↗ Useful Web Sites

One nice recent development in the world of taxes is the Internal Revenue Service's massive Internet site. The general address is http://www.irs.ustreas.gov. A big advantage to the IRS's online presence is that you can download almost any form or publication the service publishes, saving you a trip to the post office or bank. In the case of withholding allowances, if you're not sure if you're setting aside too much or too little, download IRA Publication 919, "Is My Withholding Allowance Correct?" You can find it listed at http://www.irs.ustreas.gov/prod/forms_pubs/form pub.html).

For further information on withholding, check out "Tax Withholding and Estimated Tax" at http://www.irs.ustreas.gov/prod/forms_pubs/pubs/p505toc.htm.

Who Has to File Taxes?

If you're a full-time student age 24 or younger and your parents claim you as a dependent on their taxes, you have to file a tax return if your combined unearned income (income from investments and the like) and earned income (income from wages, tips) exceed $700. Happily, though, if you don't have a single penny in unearned income, you don't have to file even if your total earned income is a good deal higher than that—up to $4,150. If your student days are in your past and you're single and not listed as a dependent on anyone else's return, you must file a return if your gross income (the amount you get before any taxes are subtracted) is $6,800 or more. For married couples, the minimum jumps to $12,200.

↗ Useful Web Sites

The topic of students and taxes can be perplexing, particularly if you're supplementing your studies with a job or are funding your education— even in part—with a scholarship. Check out IRS Publication 4, "Student's Guide to Federal Income Tax," located on the Web at www.irs.ustreas.gov/ prod/forms pubs/pubs/p4toc.htm. Information ranges from the most basic ("Where do my taxes go?") to the specific (the site offers detailed criteria for determining whether proceeds from a scholarship need to be treated as income).

Just How Does the Tax System Work?

The United States operates under what's called a progressive tax system: The more you make, the greater the percentage of your income you'll owe in taxes. The system breaks income into ranges, and the rate at which your income will be taxed is based on what portion of your income falls within each range (these are called marginal tax brackets). Naturally, since tax rates are established by the government, they're subject to a good deal of fiddling. However, as of this writing, here are the tax brackets for single people, couples who file a joint tax return, and couples who file separately:

Singles:

For Taxable Income:	Marginal Tax Rate:
Less than $25,350	15%
More than $25,350 but less than $61,400	28%
More than $61,400 but less than $128,100	31%
More than $128,100 but less than $278,450	36%
More than $278,450	39.6%

Married Couples Filing Jointly:

For Taxable Income:	Marginal Tax Rate:
Less than $42,350	15%
More than $42,350 but less than $102,300	28%
More than $102,300 but less than $155,950	31%
More than $155,950 but less than $278,450	36%
More than $278,450	39.6%

Married Couples Filing Separately:

For Taxable Income:	Marginal Tax Rate:
Less than 21,175	15%
More than $21,175 but less than $51,150	28%
More than $51,150 but less than $77,975	31%
More than $77,975 but less than $139,225	36%
More than $139,225	39.6%

Bear in mind that these are marginal rates, meaning that the tax you actually owe depends on your overall income and how many brackets your income happens to cross. Here's an example: Say you're a single person whose taxable income comes to $22,000. Your tax bracket would be 15%, and, on the face of things, you would owe $3,300 in federal taxes ($22,000 times .15).

However, if you make $27,000, your tax becomes a bit more complicated. First, since the 15% bracket goes up to $25,350, you would owe $3,802 in taxes on that part of your income. But that leaves $1,650 of your income that falls into the 28% bracket, so you would owe an additional $462 on that ($1,650 times .28).

In our example, you would be responsible for an overall tax of $4,264 (for math jocks, that works out to an effective tax rate of .1579259. That makes sense, since almost all of the taxable income falls into the 15% bracket, with only a relatively small slice falling within the 28% bracket). Keep in mind, too, that taxable income takes in a broad spectrum—it isn't just the money you earn on your job but also income from investments, gifts, and other sources.

NOTE: Bear in mind that federal and state income taxes aren't the only form of tax that take a bite out of your earnings. You're also liable for contributions to the Social Security system and to Medicare (Social Security taxes, as the name implies, cover your Social Security benefits after you retire, and Medicare is a federal health program that pays for certain medical and hospital expenses for the elderly and needy). If you're employed by someone else, 6.2% of your pay goes for Social Security and an additional 1.45% for Medicare, with your employer kicking in equal amounts. And, as we note in the section on self-employment later in this chapter, it's even worse for people who work for themselves, since they're liable for both the employer's and the employee's share of Social Security and Medicare.

↗ Useful Web Sites

For a handy worksheet that can help you get an idea of how much you may owe in taxes, have a look at http://www.dtonline.com/taxguide97/worksheet.htm.

The Easiest, Most Pain-Free Way to File a Tax Return

Many tax guides take you through an involved, lengthy discussion of ways to reduce your tax bill, only to mention at the very end that there's an exceedingly fast and simple way to figure your taxes and pay them, provided you qualify to use it. I'd like to reverse the process and tackle that subject first, given that a fair number of you will probably be able to use this expeditious choice (but give at least a quick look to the material that follows on exemptions, deductions, and similar subjects, because your simple tax-filing Nirvana isn't going to last forever).

And now for the name of this miraculous time-saver: Form 1040EZ (get it?) Like its name suggests, 1040EZ is, indeed, eeezy, because it provides certain taxpayers with the most simple and least time-consuming way to pay your taxes. You can use 1040EZ to file your taxes if you're single (or married filing jointly) and your total taxable annual income is less than $50,000. Unlike other types of returns, which seem to approach the Encyclopedia Britannica in size, Form 1040EZ is only a scant 12 lines long. First, fill in your name, address, and Social Security number, then enter your total income for the year.

From there, subtract a standard deduction and your personal exemption, if you can claim one (these two topics will be explained later). Then see how much tax you owe on the resulting amount by consulting a chart that comes with the form, and compare the tax due with how much you've already paid (listed in Box 2 on your W-2 form). If you've paid more than you owe, then you've got a refund coming; if you come up short, it's you who owes the feds.

That, as they say, is that. The obvious upside to Form 1040EZ is that it's quick and perfectly suited to someone whose tax situation is relatively simple (no dependents, not a host of deductions to report, and a relatively modest income). But there are drawbacks. For one thing, you cannot deduct IRA contributions on a 1040EZ. For another, you're not eligible to use this simple form if you've earned more than $400 in taxable interest from sources such as savings accounts, money market funds, and other investments. But if you qualify, by all means go for the 1040EZ. Sad to say, but there will be plenty of time later to make your tax life a good deal less simple and straightforward.

If you don't qualify for 1040EZ, there is something of a halfway point between that and the standard Form 1040. Form 1040A is a simplified version of the more involved Form 1040 and, in fact, isn't a good deal more complex than 1040EZ. Of course, there are limitations. For one thing, you can't use 1040A if you have more than $50,000 in taxable income. Nor are you allowed to itemize your deductions as you can on Form 1040. However, unlike 1040EZ, 1040A does allow you to deduct contributions to an IRA.

↗ Useful Web Sites

For more information on the various tax forms and help in determining which one you should use, go to http://www.irs.ustreas.gov and select Publication 17, "Your Federal Income Taxes." The information you want is listed under "Filing Information."

Taxes, Slash Thyselves!

The two most immediate and accessible ways to reduce your taxes are through exemptions and deductions. Exemptions are simple, off-the-top reductions to your taxable income that you may take for yourself, a spouse, and any dependents. For instance, if you're single and have no kids, you can claim yourself as an exemption, which, as of 1998, reduced your taxable income by $2,700. If you're married or claim a child, that effectively doubles your exemption reduction to $5,400. The more kids you have (I would also say spouses, but we'll go under the assumption that it's either one or none), the more exemptions you can claim.

↗ Useful Web Sites

For more information on exemptions and the various wrinkles contained therein—for instance, if you have questions about who qualifies as a dependent and other specific issues—check out the IRS's online section on exemptions at www.irs.ustreas.gov/prod/forms_pubs/pubs/p50104.htm). The site covers just about every question that you may pose about exemptions and also offers handy worksheets and illustrative examples. It's particularly useful if, for instance, you're wondering how exemptions apply when using the 1040EZ form.

The other way to cut your tax bill is through deductions. Essentially, these are expenses that the government permits you to subtract from your income. There are two types of deductions, standard and itemized. Standard is by far the most simple—rather than tallying up all the various expenses you incurred during the year, a standard deduction lets all taxpayers deduct a fixed dollar amount from their taxes. As of 1998, single persons could deduct $4,250 for a standard deduction; married couples filing a joint return could deduct $7,100, and married couples filing separate returns could deduct $3,550 on each return.

The other way to take advantage of deductions is through itemizing. As the name suggests, this involves adding up various deductible expenses and costs and then subtracting them from your income. While this obviously involves a good deal more work than merely taking the standard deduction, it can pay off if itemizing reduces your taxes more than the standard deduction would.

The trick, needless to say, is to figure out which option—standard or itemizing—will save you the most come tax time. To do this, you first need to identify which itemized deductions you qualify for, then the amount of the tax break each deduction will give you. To start off, here's a rundown of several major types of deductible expenses that you may be able to take advantage of:

▶ *Interest on your home mortgage and property taxes.* Remember back in Chapter 7 when we said you got some big-time tax breaks for owning your own place? You can usually deduct all the interest that you pay on a loan used to buy a home (remember, in the early years of a mortgage, almost all of your monthly payments are for interest), as well as every penny you pay in property taxes.

▶ *Donations to charities.* Here, the wrinkle is whether the IRS considers something a "qualified tax-exempt" organization, which includes most religious organizations, charities, and similar entities. Remember, too, that donations include items other than money, such as clothes donated to the Salvation Army. In general, it's a good idea to get a receipt when making these sorts of noncash contributions.

▶ *State and other forms of local income tax.* These are all deductible from your federal taxes.

Figuring out just how much these types of expenses may save you if you decide to itemize is fairly simple. Just take the amount of the expenses, multiply it by your marginal tax bracket, and you've got the actual amount of taxes that you'll save from that particular deduction. For instance, if you own your own home and you paid $3,000 in mortgage interest in one year, that's worth $450 in tax savings if you're in the 15% bracket ($3,000 times .15). If you are in the 28% bracket, the deduction is worth $840. That's all there is to it. Then, once you've added up all the deductions you may be entitled to, compare that figure with your standard deduction. If you save more by itemizing, it's worth the extra effort. If not, kick back and opt for the standard deduction.

By the way, don't think that your decision to itemize or not is cast in stone—if you choose one option and later discover that you would have been better off going with the other, you can change your return by filing Form 1040X.

The More Persnickety Types of Deductions

Of course, the tax code being what it is, there is also a rash of other sorts of deductions, some of which you may be able to take advantage of, others of which may be beyond your reach. Here's a sampling of these more mercurial deductions:

> *Medical costs.* You can deduct out-of-pocket medical costs that exceed 7.5% of your adjusted gross income (again, as we pointed out in Chapter 5, gross income is what you make before taxes. Adjusted gross income is that amount minus things such as deductible IRA contributions or moving expenses. For most of you, the most likely adjustment to gross income will come from contributions to an IRA or other types of retirement programs). That adds up to a healthy chunk of your income. For instance, if your AGI is $30,000, you would have to have paid out at least $2,250 in medical expenses to start deducting medical costs. But bear in mind that out-of-pocket costs can come from a variety of sources, such as medical copayments, deductibles, medical insurance premiums, and certain types of services not covered entirely by your medical plan (psychological counseling services, as we pointed out earlier, are often only partially covered by many medical plans). You can also add in the expense of transportation to and from medical care appointments.

▶ *Work-related deductions.* If your employer insists that you buy certain types of equipment such as a computer or cellular phone, you may be able to deduct those expenses. You can also deduct certain job-hunting expenses, provided you meet certain IRS requirements. (Bear in mind, however, that work-related expenses have their limits, as you can deduct only job-related expenses that exceed 2% of your adjusted gross income. In the case of someone making $25,000 a year, for instance, that means that anything you spend up to $500 on business expenses can't be deducted. After that, however, you can write off your costs. Other sorts of limits may also apply, depending on the specific type of work-related deduction.)

Then there are possible deductions that relate to less than pleasant situations in our lives. For instance, you can deduct the cost of goods lost due to some sort of disaster such as fire or burglary (these, too, have to exceed a certain value limit). You can also deduct the expense of bad debt. Suppose a "friend" skips town without repaying a loan owed to you— again, if you meet certain requirements pertaining to documentation and other information (for instance, you have to be able to show that you made a reasonable effort to collect the money owed you), you can write off your loss.

NOTE: If you'd rather defer to a living pro than do the digging yourself, a tax preparer such as an enrolled agent or accountant should certainly be able to walk you through your situation and identify any and all deductions to which you should be entitled (we covered the various pluses and minuses of using tax preparers in Chapter 9).

↗ *Useful Web Sites*

Given that deductions—both common and not so—are such an expansive topic, the best way to track down information on a specific deduction is to go to the main page of the IRS's online publications Web site at www.irs.ustreas.gov. There, you can scroll through a variety of publications that address any number of tax- and deduction-related subjects. Since the list is extensive, chances are good you'll find something of use.

Microsoft Money Central (www.moneycentral.msn.com) has a wonderful little calculator listed under "tools" known as the "tax deduction finder." This lets you identify qualified deductions by leading you through a series of questions. You start by identifying categories of deductions that you think may apply to you, then move on to designate the specific type of deduction you have in mind. The site then asks you certain questions that determine whether, in fact, you can take that deduction. Finally, the calculator lists all the deductions you're entitled to, the tax forms you'll need to file them properly, what they may be worth to you, and the IRS publication that addresses them. The site even has a "tax estimator" calculator that lets you plug in deductions and other information to get an idea of your tax liability. It's a great way to take much of the drudgery out of hunting down your deductions.

How to Prepare, How to File

In days gone by, the only way to file your taxes was on paper. Some of you may remember seeing one of your parents, sweating beneath the glare of the kitchen table light, painfully poring over reams of IRS forms, No. 2 pencils gnawed beyond recognition. If your sense of nostalgia carries over to the way you do your taxes, that option is still available to you. However, there are now immeasurably more pleasant and time-efficient ways of preparing your tax return and, for that matter, getting it into the IRS's hands.

(NOTE: Again, you'll remember we discussed use of a tax preparer in Chapter 9, reviewing what they can do for you and what kind of taxpayers may be best suited to using one. If the idea of paying someone else to take on the headache of your taxes strikes a responsive chord, jump back to that section of the book for further details on how to go about finding one.)

Take a Byte Out of the IRS

Once an anomaly tax preparation software provides a relatively inexpensive way to get help preparing your taxes. The two most popular programs are TurboTax (as of this writing, $49.95 for the deluxe version) and Kiplinger's Tax Cut ($39.95 for the deluxe model). Both programs effectively employ the same system—a detailed interview involving screen after screen of questions about your filing status, income, deductions, and other related information. Then, once the interview's finished, the program prints out completed versions of your tax return, all ready for you to sign and drop in the mail (or send electronically—see our discussion later in this chapter).

The nice thing about both these programs is that they not only lead you by the hand through the entire preparation process but also are designed to call your attention to tax items that you may have overlooked, such as deductions that could save you a few bucks. Likewise, they also give you a heads-up if some bit of information you've entered seems out of whack.

These sorts of programs are ideal for people whose tax situation is complicated enough to exceed the limits of the 1040EZ form but not so convoluted that a living, breathing tax pro is in order (e.g., if complicated investments, trusts, gifts between family members, and other elements are involved). Know, too, that tax preparation software is not without its flaws. For one thing, if you also intend to do your state taxes, you'll have to go out and buy the companion state program (in fact, as of this writing TurboTax and TaxCut don't even offer programs for a number of states, so, if you happen to live in one of those, it's back to the old No. 2 pencil whether you like it or not).

And, while the programs are designed to speed up preparation of your return, don't look to have things wrapped up in a heartbeat. It may take you anywhere from several hours to several days to complete the necessary interviews, depending on how complicated your return is. Nor is there any ironclad guarantee that you won't make a mistake—for one thing, you may enter incorrect information, something the program may not catch. For another, over the past several years, tax software manufacturers have, on occasion, caught mistakes in the programs themselves, although they've been very good about letting users know about snafus and taking fast steps to correct them. Finally, there are occasions where the program simply won't give you a definitive answer about a tax question—in one instance, a program identifies a home office deduction as a popular audit target, then leaves it up to the user to decide whether to take that chance.

All that said, there's no question that using tax software beats doing your taxes by hand, particularly if your return isn't very tricky. But if your situation is a bit muddier than that, it'll ultimately come down to your call whether the time you put into using tax software might be better spent elsewhere.

↗ Useful Web Sites

Computer Shopper put together a nice review package on tax software a couple years back—again, it's not entirely up-to-date, but it's very useful, nonetheless. It's at http://www.zdnet.com/pcmag/features/finance/_open.htm.

PC Magazine has also weighed in on tax software, and it pulls no punches in identifying which ones it thinks are best and why. Have a look at http://www.zdnet.com/pcmag/features/tax98/_open.htm.

Not to be outdone by its software counterpart, the Internet is also spawning several Web sites that allow you to prepare your taxes online. For the most part, they function pretty much the same way the software does—you log on, and the site leads you through an interactive interview (some sites also give you the option of filling out the actual tax forms, if that sort of thing appeals). Then, as you proceed, the site automatically calculates your return. Upon finishing, you can print out a paper version of your return and, if you wish, zap your return to the IRS via the Internet. Three sites now up and running to do this are SecureTax (www.securetax.com), TurboTax (www.turbotax.com), and Taxsoft (www.taxsoft.com).

Unfortunately, these sites are geared to only the most basic of tax returns—for the most part, you can use only the most elementary tax forms. And, in the case of TurboTax, the only state return you can do online is California, meaning everyone else has to opt for the old-fashioned paper return. Not only that, but you're also subject to the connectivity wiles of the Internet, which means that there's always a chance that you could be booted offline right in the middle of preparing your return.

Zap! Yer Filed!

You've no doubt noticed that our discussion of tax-related software and other forms of technology has been littered with the term "electronic filing." The phrase means just what you would expect—sending your return to the IRS via the Internet (or, in some cases, the telephone) in lieu of mailing a paper return. The purported benefits of filing electronically are legion. For one thing, returns filed electronically have less than a 1% error rate (which eliminates one bull's eye the IRS targets for audits). It's also supposed to be faster; if you file electronically and are expecting a refund, the IRS claims you'll get your money in no more than 21 days, about half the refund turnaround for paper returns. In fact, if you have your refund deposited directly into a bank account, it can happen in as little as two weeks (although, to be complete, direct deposit turnaround on conventionally filed paper returns usually takes two to three weeks as well).

The taxpaying public really hasn't caught on to filing electronically. Of more than 120 million individual tax returns filed in 1997, only some 19 million arrived electronically, most from professional preparers (in fact, only 367,000 returns were filed using home computers and tax prep software). Until recently, the problem has been added surcharges people were required to pay to shoot their returns to the IRS electronically, often more than $10. Taxpayers asked why they should lay out extra money when they could mail the return for a whole lot less. The good news is that programs such as TurboTax and Tax Cut have recently introduced free online filing as part of their tax preparation software programs. That, if nothing else, should spur greater use of electronic filing and, as a result, make its touted benefits available to more taxpayers.

(NOTE: Keep in mind that electronic filing isn't purely electronic. Once you've sent your return in electronically, you still have to get hold of, sign, and mail in IRS Form 8453. That validates the electronic transmission.)

↗ Useful Web Sites

For additional information on electronic filing and its potential benefits, have a look at the IRS's electronic services main page at http://www.irs.ustreas.gov/prod/elec_svs/index.html.

Another filing alternative is known as TeleFile, the IRS's system that lets certain taxpayers submit their tax returns over the phone. All you have to do is dial a toll-free number and enter the required information—wages, withheld taxes, and other data—on your telephone keypad. The process takes only several minutes, thanks in part to the fact that the system does whatever math is necessary and lets you know whether you owe any money or are due a refund. Like refunds for returns filed electronically, TeleFile refunds are supposed to arrive a good deal faster than those from conventional returns, particularly if you arrange a direct deposit into a bank account.

Unfortunately, TeleFile is limited to only the most rudimentary tax returns. For instance, you can't use the system if you're claiming any dependents. Moreover, eligible income is limited to wages, salaries, tips, taxable scholarships or fellowships, and unemployment insurance. On top of that, you're disqualified from using TeleFile if you earn more than $400 in interest. In fact, it's easy to know if you qualify, since the government sends out Telefile tax packages only to eligible taxpayers; if you don't get one in the mail, you can't access the system.

↗ Useful Web Sites

For the full story on TeleFile and its features and advantages, check out the IRS's TeleFile site at www.irs.ustreas.gov/prod/elec_svs/telefile.html. The site offers complete information about the system as well as commonly asked questions about the TeleFile network. In fact, look for the feds to possibly beef up this site in the future, as a big p.r. push to win qualified taxpayers over to the TeleFile way of doing things is in the wind.

When to Send All This Stuff In and (Gulp) What to Do If You Don't Have Enough Money

Although the popularly known deadline for tax filing is April 15, that doesn't necessarily mean that you have to line up with all those other unfortunate souls outside the post office at 11:55 P.M. on April 15. Instead, the decision about when to send in your return is dictated by what happens after the feds get your forms. If you owe them money, there's no rush—a week or so prior to the April 15 deadline is usually plenty of time. But if you have a refund coming, try to get your return in as soon after the first of the year as you can—you'll likely get your refund faster than if you wait until later in the year, when the increasing workload at the IRS tends to slow down taxpayer refunds.

Of course, there's always a chance (let's hope exceedingly small) that you just don't have enough money to pay the taxes that you owe. You should still go ahead and send in your return by the April 15 deadline (fail to do this and you can be socked with very heavy penalties). When you send in your return, include a request for an installment payment program (this is done by using IRS Form 9465, which allows you to propose what sort of monthly payment plan you'll be able to afford). The IRS then has 30 days to say whether it accepts or rejects your proposal or to ask for additional information. Unfortunately, even if the IRS accepts your installment payment proposal, you're going to end up paying a combination of late payment charges as well as interest on any unpaid amounts. Taken together, they amount to about 13% a year.

On Your Own

If you're one of the growing number of people who are self-employed, the joy and autonomy that can come from working for oneself is, sad to say, partially soured by what's known as self-employment tax. When you work for someone else, your employer pays half your Social Security and Medicare taxes. When you're out on your own, you're liable for the whole shooting match yourself.

That adds up to some hefty numbers: The self-employment tax rate on net earnings for 1997 was 15.3%, comprising 12.4% for Social Security and 2.9% for Medicare. Looked at another way, that means self-employed people are paying 7.65% more in taxes than folks who work for someone else.

That said, it behooves self-employed folks to approach their taxes more aggressively and comprehensively than their employed counterparts. First, you as a self-employed person are responsible for filing quarterly estimated taxes with both the feds and the state where you live. These, as the name suggests, represent an estimate of what you think you'll owe in taxes. You make estimated payments to the feds and to your state every three months. The estimated payment you make must be no less than 90% of the tax you actually owe (or 100% of the total tax liability you had the previous year), or you may face a penalty for underpayment.

↗ Useful Web Sites

A handy site we mentioned earlier in this chapter is the IRS's "Tax Withholding and Estimated Tax" page at http://www.irs.ustreas.gov/prod/forms_pubs/pubs/p505toc.htm.

The good news for the self-employed is that you can tap into deductions and other tax-cutting strategies that are unavailable to those who toil for someone else. For instance, if you work out of your home, you may be able to deduct home office expenses (be careful with this one, as the IRS is rather nasty when it comes to validating the fact that a home office is, indeed, used for that purpose. You usually have to use a specific room exclusively for your work, have clients visit you at your home office, and meet other requirements.) Similarly, you can deduct business materials, travel, health insurance premiums, and even a portion of the Social Security and Medicare taxes you have to pay. As a general rule, if you use something to help generate self-employment income, you can consider that a potential deduction.

That said, here are some general tax tips that can prove helpful to the self-employed:

▶ *Keep exhaustive records on things such as income, expenses, travel, and other elements connected with your work.* The more you can document, the more you'll be able to save come tax time.

▶ *Open up and fund a retirement account.* This is sound advice for anyone, but particularly so for the self-employed, who can tap into significant tax breaks. The simplest is the good old IRA, but since, as we noted back in Chapter 5, these limit you to just $2,000 a year, consider a SEP-IRA, which lets you stash up to 13% of your income (up to $22,500) into a retirement account, completely tax-deductible and tax-deferred until you start removing money from the account. If your circumstances warrant it, a Keogh plan ups your contribution maximums to 20% of your income or $30,000 annually (refer to Chapter 11 for more details). And, remember, not only does a retirement account cut your taxes; it's also critical to put away as much as you can. Since you don't have an employer perhaps matching part of your contribution, you're the only one responsible for funding your retirement.

▶ *Consider hooking up with a tax pro to help with tax issues related to running your own business.* While taxes are a bewildering subject for most people, they're even more complex for the self-employed. So, if you're confused or intimidated, check out a pro. It's money well spent (and deductible from your next year's taxable income to boot).

⤴ Useful Web Sites

Here's a sampling of some online IRS materials that address taxes and self-employment:

A nice overview of things to know when starting your own business and methods of record-keeping is at http://www.irs.ustreas.gov/prod/forms_pubs/pubs/p583toc.htm.

Information on self-employment tax, including ways to calculate it, is available at http://www.irs.ustreas.gov/prod/forms_pubs/pubs/p533toc.htm.

For general information on small business and taxes, have a look at the IRS's "Tax Guide for Small Business" at http://www.irs.ustreas.gov/prod/forms_pubs/pubs/p334toc.htm.

Information on travel, entertainment, and car expenses can be found at http://www.irs.ustreas.gov/prod/forms_pubs/pubs/p463toc.htm.

To help get a start untangling the rules governing your use of your home for business purposes, be sure to read http://www.irs.ustreas.gov/prod/forms_pubs/pubs/p587toc.htm.

Some Final—Thank Heaven—Thoughts on Taxes

The best advice to bear in mind about taxes is to constantly keep your eyes peeled for ways to cut them. Along those lines, here are a few thoughts and reminders on ways to do just that:

▶ *Try to make the most of tax-cutting ways to save, such as IRAs, 401ks, and SEPs.* Even if it seems you haven't money to spare for them, do your utmost to free up some funds. Not only are you stashing money away for your retirement, but you're also slashing your taxes along the way. The same is true for tax-cutting employee benefits, such as flexible spending accounts, which we covered in Chapter 11.

▶ *Once again, provided your personal situation warrants it, look into buying your own home.* Home ownership has a dual benefit. Not only are you building wealth by putting your money into something that's your own, but mortgage interest and property taxes provide some of the biggest tax-cutting opportunities around.

▶ *If your income has been particularly high in a given year, give some thought to making your January mortgage payment in December.* That way, you can apply an extra month's interest to the tax year where you may need the most help.

▶ *If you think you can itemize in some years but not others, try bunching.* This means taking the standard deduction in one year, then plowing as many deductible expenses as you can into the next year, where they can be itemized and help you save on your taxes.

▶ *Look into a home equity loan to help pay off high-interest credit cards if you own your own home.* Unlike credit card debt, home equity loan interest is usually deductible.

▶ *Keep good records.* This recalls the advice we gave at the beginning of the book. It's awfully hard to identify ways to cut your taxes if you can't find out how you spent your money quickly and efficiently. To that end, keep receipts, expense records, and other similar data in an orderly fashion. The effort may pay off in a big way come tax time.

↗ Useful Web Site

Careful planning and foresight are among the most important tools for lessening the pain of paying taxes. Have a look at the handy tax-planning calendar posted at http://www.inswebpro.com/carriers/nefe/archive/nov1.htm. This gives you a rundown on what you should do and when, which can go a long way to keeping your taxes in shape.

Another nice tax Web site is located at http://www.1040.com/txsubj.htm. The site offers tax forms, discussion, commonly asked questions, and information on a variety of tax-related issues.

CHAPTER 13

Top Ten Money Caveats

A dmittedly, money can be a rather dry topic. Try as I have to inject some readability into the text—and I dearly hope I have been able to achieve that—sometimes it's nearly impossible to discuss money matters without backsliding into a dull monotone ("Please press one on your touch tone keypad to hear more options . . . ").

Therefore, to wrap up this tome and to conclude on a lighter note, I'd like to borrow a page from David Letterman and present my own list of 10 things that you should be very, very, very careful about when it comes to your money. Bear in mind that, while you may find some of these amusing—and you may well not agree with all of them—I think they all contain at least a grain of truth.

Caveat Number 10: If you have to listen to a cassette, watch a videotape, or sit through an infomercial, make a run for it. Sensible money knowledge and habits are neither quantum physics nor proprietary information. Be terribly wary of any so-called courses or free introductory tapes that purport to pass along some sort of money magic. If, by chance, you're somehow roped into watching a video or television infomercial of some sort, watch out for opening scenes involving speedboats (often involving a grinning "captain" who's made it big-time, financially speaking, flanked by a couple of beauteous "mateys"), panoramic shots of castle-like homes, or Robin Leach sound-alikes promising that you, yes you, can attain this fabulous lifestyle if you will only put these simple principles to work. If any of these comes up, excuse yourself, head for the bathroom, and scramble out the nearest unlocked window. Otherwise, you may end up spending hundreds on some worthless "course" or, even worse, find yourself hawking cleaning products and shampoo to annoyed friends and coworkers. It's hard to say which of the two is the uglier fate.

Caveat Number Nine: Ignore money-making ads that have lots of dollar signs or too many exclamation points. Look at any advertisement for a solid mutual fund or brokerage house—numbers, statistics, calm explanations. Not exciting, but not a medicine show, either. Now, compare that ad with other money-making touts—lots of bold type, blurry pictures of so-called success stories, and lots and lots of $$$$$$$. Grab your wallet and run for cover. Legitimate investments don't need to shout to make their point. Sink your money into snake oil and the only exclamation points you may end up seeing are "Why the !!!#@&&!!! did I ever waste my money????"

Caveat Number Eight: Avoid financial pitches. Clever double meaning here. Call it a singular prejudice of mine, but since when are folks like Jim Palmer and Dan Marino money experts? Both are unquestioned Hall of Fame athletes in their respective sports, but what really makes them qualified to hawk debt consolidation programs? (In fact, that's a particular laugh. What with all the dough Palmer and Marino raked in during their playing days—not to mention other deals like the money Palmer made prancing around in his underwear—their biggest money problem is probably trying to find a warehouse big enough to hold their pocket change. Since when do they know what it feels like not to have enough money to make a car payment?)

The message here is that a well-known name doesn't necessarily make a financial product or service valid; the inherent workings and strengths of the product and service do that. Evaluate anything on its own merits, and don't be influenced by the talking head doing its fronting. In fact, the better the product, the less likely it is to need a famous face. For years Fidelity's Magellan Fund was *the* mutual fund, outperforming the market and its competitors year after year. Did you ever once see its manager, Peter Lynch, on the tube cajoling you to invest by dialing an 800 number? Of course not—the product was good enough that Fidelity didn't have to put him on TV. The same thing should apply to any financial buying decision you make. (Of course, since leaving Magellan, Lynch's face seems to be on every magazine and television ad imaginable, but you can't fault the guy for making the most of his reputation. It's only when Lynch starts hawking Ben Gay and Gatorade that I'll start to worry.)

Caveat Number Seven: Consider the Source. As a companion to tip number eight, pay attention to who's handing out money advice and why. As we've mentioned time and again, there's no shortage of financial advice to be had, but always bear in mind what your source of wisdom may be thinking while doling out all these pearls. As often as not, someone or something may be trying to get his or her hands into your wallet. It can be a stockbroker who calls you touting a particular stock—after all, he or she works on commission and doesn't get a red cent unless you buy something, and that's perfectly legitimate. On a more insidious level, not long ago a well-known credit card company sponsored a touring "Wheel of Fortune" game that zipped about the country hitting various college campuses. Complete with its own college-age Pat Sajak and a Vanna White-esque sidekick, the game purported to test college students' financial knowledge in return for scholarship money and other goodies. That may sound all well and good, but I wonder how often a credit card—one particular card, for that matter—may have been mentioned as part of a "sound" financial education? Hmmmmm....Bottom line—consider the source of investment advice, as it may not always have your best interests at heart.

Caveat Number Six: Do not ever, ever buy any sort of "investment" offered to you over the phone. If you think back to our discussion of credit cards, you'll remember that one or two of those plastic rectangles will probably shoot your name onto lists that literally dozens of companies of all sorts can buy. And that can lead to these sorts of interchanges:

> **Yours Truly** (*picking up the phone*): Hello?
> **Person at Other End** (*clearly struggling to pronounce my name right*): Mr....Mr. Wooo-orareaoo? Did I get that right?
> **Your Truly:** Close enough.
> **Person at Other End:** Well, Mr. Wooo-orareaoo, I'm from the Precious Metals Emporium based in the back of a moving pickup truck currently heading south on Interstate 95 at an exceedingly high rate of speed, and I'd like to bring your attention to the fabulous investment potential inherent in gold and silver doubloons. In these uncertain economic times, have you given any thought to diversifying your portfolio to include these invaluable commodities?
> **Yours Truly:** Yeah, I suppose I have, but certainly not with you, boyo. (*followed by the click of my phone being hung up*).

The message here is clear: Your name can end up just about anywhere, which can prompt every shyster in the book to call you up and make a sales pitch. Don't ever bite, particularly if the caller butchers your name (that's a dead giveaway that you're just another name on a list). Sad to say, but thousands of folks, particularly the elderly, get roped into over-the-phone investment scams every year. Make sure you're not one of them.

Caveat Number Five: Follow the herd and count on getting roped. Say you bought a car for $20,000, an unusual one that attracted any number of people's interest. All of a sudden, you're getting offers to buy the car—person after person is coming up to you making a pitch—only they're all offering no more than $5,000.

You certainly may feel popular, but would you sell? Of course not—you'd have to be out of your mind or desperate for the cash. But that's what can happen to a lot of people when they're making other financial decisions, because a large number of people all doing the same thing suggests that's the right thing to do. For instance, if the stock market takes a downturn (as it has as of this writing), a lot of people are probably going to abandon quality mutual funds and stocks for fear of greater losses. That may indicate that that's the right thing to do, but it's not necessarily so. Remember the example we cited in the mutual fund section, about how you would have made huge profits in certain funds if you had been willing to ride out the sliding stock market of the 1970s? A lot of "herd" investors who jumped ship undoubtedly wish they had had a second chance to climb back on board.

The bottom line here is that it's dangerous to assume that a money decision is right just because lots of other people are doing the same thing. Instead, develop your own money plan—one that's based on your goals and preferences, not someone else's—and stick by it.

Caveat Number Four: Treat money as money, no matter what. At the risk of piling too many illustrative anecdotes on, say you're walking down the street and see a $10 bill on the sidewalk. There's no doubt you would take a few seconds to pick it up. But, if you're buying a CD player and you know that the store down the street has the model you want for $10 less, would you take the time to walk over there?

You'd be surprised how many people would say the $10 savings isn't worth the extra block's hike, yet that $10 isn't a bit different from the $10 lying on the street. The dynamic at play is that we tend to interpret money on the basis of the circumstances. For instance, in the this example, the $10 on the street is "found money," something that people treat a good deal more cavalierly than, say, a $10 savings on a piece of electronic equipment. But they're not the least bit different.

It's important to treat money the same, no matter what form it takes and how you gain access to it. Not only can that help you make smarter money decisions in general, but it may also head off some serious problems. Just ask anyone how he or she racked up thousands in credit card debt and the person is likely to say that it didn't feel as if he or she were actually spending "real" money when charging things. Had the person treated credit as if it were cash—and, in the long run, credit card debt and cash boil down to the same element—the problem might have been averted.

Caveat Number Three: Know what you're getting into when you mix money with friends or family. Cold as it may seem, we all tend to make foolish money decisions when it comes to family and friends. Lending money to a buddy whom you know will probably never pay it back, cosigning a mortgage with a relative with a spotty work history—these acts arise from our feelings of affection toward our families and our friends, emotions that, however noble, cloud our better judgment and push us into situations that we would normally avoid.

That's not to put a blanket prohibition on helping friends and family financially—after all, risking destroying a relationship by saying no may cost you more than the money in question. Just go into these sorts of situations with your eyes open, and don't be shocked if things go south. On the other hand, if you know deep down that getting involved financially is the absolute wrong thing to do—for instance, the money in question is money you just can't afford to lose—don't be skittish about saying no. Instead, ask how else you may be able to help—finding a financial planner or debt counselor or providing a shoulder to cry on, if need be. Help genuinely offered may ultimately carry more value than mere money.

Caveat Number Two: Don't expect to hit home runs unless you're Mark McGwire. An underlying theme throughout this book has been that sensible money management and habits aren't made up of financials coups—the brilliant stock bought at just the right nano-second, the magnificent home snapped up at the very bottom of a down market at a sliver of its actual value, that wondrous, all-encompassing financial magic pill that makes everything click, time and again. Instead, money smarts consists of basic knowledge, consistently applied over time. That's it. With that in mind, watch for your financial successes—your savings, your investments, your assets in their varied forms—to grow slowly and steadily over time. It's the safest and most reliably time-tested way to go. Remember, McGwire in 1998 broke the single-season record for home runs with 70, but he also struck out 155 times. There's no need to take that approach with your money.

Caveat Number One: Never lose sight of what money is and isn't. This is perhaps the most important tip. Simply put, keep money in perspective. Don't ignore its importance, but remember that there are any number of other things in life that are a good deal more critical—your health, your self-respect, family, friends, a world that's not bent on tearing itself apart, to name just a sampling. Knowing how to handle your money sanely makes that healthy perspective a good deal easier to achieve. Equally important, I genuinely believe you'll get there one day.

APPENDIX

Websites Grouped By Category, with referring page for additional information:

Apartments, renting, tenant/landlord issues:
—http://www.springstreet.com
—http://www.abreak4students.com/
—http://www.law.cornell.edu/topics/landlord_tenant.html
—http://tenant.net/main.html
—http://www.bostonapartments.com/rentips.htm
—http://home.oit.umass.edu/~cshrc/housing/questions.html

Automobile (Buying):
—http://www.kbb.com/
—http://www.autopricing.com/
—http://www.aautomall.com
—http://www.autosite.com/
—www.carfax.com
—www.eauto.com/carbuyingsvc
—www.carpoint.com
—www.intellichoice.com
—http://fightingchance.com/
—http://www.handilinks.com/cat1/a/a1684.htm
—http://www.ford.com/us/collegegrad/

Automobile (Leasing):
—http://www.cslnet.ctstateu.edu/attygenl/reality1.htm
—http://www.carinfo.com/
—http://www.leasesource.com/workshop/leasewizard_jr.htm
—http://www.financenter.com/autos.htm

Automobile (Safety):
—http://www.nhtsa.dot.gov/cars/testing/
—http://www.hwysafety.org

Banking:
—www.bankrate.com

Banking (Online):
—http://www.bankrate.com/brm/olbstep2.asp

—http://www.bankrate.com/brm/publ/onlifees.asp
—http://www.gomez.com

Bond Ratings:
—www.moodys.com
—www.standardpoor.com

Bonds (General Information):
—www.bondsonline.com
—http://www.vanguard.com/educ/module1/m1_3_2.html
—http://www.cis.ohio-state.edu/hypertext/faq/usenet/investment-faq/general/part3/faq-doc-5.html
—http://www.franklintempleton.com/public/education/bond_mutual/bond_mutual.htm
—http://www.prusec.com/whyfi.htm

Bonds (Municipal):
—http://www.troweprice.com/mutual/insights/
—http://www.investinginbonds.com/info/igmunis/what.htm

Bonds (U.S. Savings Bonds):
—http://www.publicdebt.treas.gov/sav/sav.htm
—http://www.ny.frb.org/pihome/svg_bnds/sb_val.html

Budgeting:
—www.americanexpress.com/student/moneypit/budget/budget.html
—www.americanexpress.com
—www.financenter.com/budget.htm

Certificates of Deposit:
—http://www.bankrate.com/brm/rate/high_ratehome.asp
—http://www.bbb.org/library/cds.html

College Costs:
—http://www.collegeboard.org/press/cost97/970917.html

Consumer Information:
—www.consumerworld.org

Credit, Credit Reports:
—http://www.cccsdc.org/credit-road.html
—http://www.experian.com/personal/repair.html
—http://www.start-smart.com/creditrepairfaq.html

Credit Cards:
—http://www.smartcalc.com/cgi-bin/smartcalcpro/hel6.cgi/FinanCenter
—http://www.bankrate.com/universal/rate/content/cchome.asp
—http://www.financenter.com/cards.htm
—http://www.bankrate.com/brm/publ/rebate.asp

—http://www.nfcc.org

—http://members.aol.com/debtrelief/index.html

Employment:

—www.monsterboard.com

—www.careermosaic.com

—http://stats.bls.gov/emphome.htm

—http://jobsmart.org

—http://www.bls.gov

Financial News and Research:

—www.quicken.com

—http://moneycentral.msn.com

—www.money.com

—www.wsj.com

—www.investorama.com

—www.wsrn.com

—www.quote.yahoo.com

Financial Planners:

—http://www.efmoody.com/whouse.html

—www.efmoody.com

—http://www.worth.com/articles/Z9610F05.html

—http:///www.iafp.org

—http://www.investorhome.com/choosing.htm

—www.napfa.org

—http://www.icfp.org/

—http://www.pueblo.gsa.gov/cic_text/money/financial-planner/
10questions.txt

—http://www.investorguide.com/Advisors.htm

Financial Software:

—http://www.reviewsource.com

—http://www.zdnet.com/pcmag/features/finance/_open.htm

—http://www.investorama.com/software.shtml

—http://www.e-analytics.com/soft2.htm

—http://www.zdnet.com/pcmag/features/finance/_open.htm

—http://www.zdnet.com/pcmag/features/tax98/_open.htm

Flexible Spending Accounts:

—http://www.lipman.com/tlc/flexover.htm

401(k) Plans:

—http://www.invest-faq.com/articles/ret-plan-401k.html

—http://www.401k.com/401k/pfp/rp/taxes.htm

—http://www.phillynews.com/online/finance/pers10896.htm.

—http://www.401k.com/401k/pfp/rp/proscons.htm

—http://www.401k.com/401k/pfp/rp/jobs.htm

—www.401kforum.com
—www.comfin.com

403b Plans:
—www.benefitslink.com/403b/index.html
—http://invest-faq.com

Home Inspections:
—http://www.inspectamerica.com/
—http://www.ashi.com/

Home Buying (Agents):
—http://www.nnerealestate.com/
—http://www.homespot.com/r4main2w.htm

Home Buying (General Information):
—Http://www.realtor.com
—http://www.realtimes.com/
—http://www.ourbroker.com/
—http://www.homepath.com/hsp2.html
—http://www.homepath.com/hsp3.html
—http://www.interest.com/sa961029.htm
—http://www.bankrate.com/brm/green/mtg/mort7a.asp.

Home Buying (Loans and Mortgages):
—http://www.snws.com/loan-bin/credit/
—http://www.fanniemae.com/
—http://www.freddiemac.com/
—http://www.ewmortgage.com/scheng/fhaloans.htm
—http://detnews.com/cyberia/sites/970329/mortgage/mortgage.htm
—http://www.interest.com/
—http://www.loanpage.com/
—http://www.hsh.com/
—http://www.bankrate.com/brm/rate/mtg_home.asp
—http://www.ces.ncsu.edu/depts/fcs/docs/he437.html
—http://www.smartcalc.com/cgi-bin/smartcalcpro/HOM5.cgi/Finan-Center

Home Buying (State Housing Agencies):
—http://www.ncsha.org/

Inflation:
—http://www.putnaminv.com/frames/e101.htm
—http://www.fintrend.com/html/inflation.html

Individual Retirement Accounts (General):
—http://www.vanguard.com/educ/lib/retire/faqira.html
—http://www.prudential.com/retirement/rpzzz1009.html
—http://moneycentral.msn.com

Individual Retirement Accounts (Roth):
- —http://www.nbfunds.com
- —http://www.datachimp.com/articles/rothira/rothintro.htm
- —http://www.invest-faq.com/articles/ret-plan-roth-ira.html.
- —http://www.slfcu.org/slfcu_financial_life/roth_convert.html

Insurance (Agents):
- —http://www.tywell.com/tywell01/index.htm
- —http://www.dirs.com/insure
- —http://www.iiaa.iix.com/

Insurance (Auto):
- —http://www.insure.com/states/index.html
- —http://www.dtonline.com/insur/inauto.htm
- —http://www.insuranceman.com/auto.htm
- —http://www.infoseek.com/Topic/Personal_Finance/Insurance/For_individuals/Automotive_Insurance_Center?sv=N6&tid=15376
- —http://www.insweb.com/cgi-bin/bozellauto.exe?bid=16203

Insurance (Disability):
- —http://www.insweb.com/research/faq/disability-q.htm.
- —http://www.alldigins.com/distips.html
- —http://www.life-line.org/disability/calc/calcmsg.html

Insurance (General Information):
- —http://www.insure.com/
- —http://www.insuremarket.com/
- —http://insurance.yahoo.com/)
- —http://www.4insurance.com/

Insurance (Health):
- —http://www.ama-assn.org/insight/gen_hlth/ahcpr/ahcprfin.htm.
- —http://www.medhelp.org/ccf/insure.htm.
- —http://www.louisville.com/health/insurance.html
- —http://www.medicalsocieties.org/hmo.htm
- —http://www.charm.net/~jmevans/hmo.htm

Insurance (Homeowners):
- —http://www.bosbbb.org/lit/0072.htm
- —http://www.iii.org/individuals/
- —http://www.insure.com/home/index.html#basics
- —http://www.fema.gov/home/NFIP/answe2d.htm

Insurance (Life):
- —http://www.invest-faq.com/articles/ins-life.html
- —http://www.bygpub.com/finance/LifeInsCalc.htm
- —http://www.quickquote.com/fFaqTermLife.html
- —http://www.e-analytics.com/fp7.htm
- —http://www.insuremarket.com/basics/life/wholelifen.htm.

—http://www.safetnet.com/New_Site/www_directory/life/lifeTypesfrm.html
—www.quotesmith.com
—http://www.1stquote.com/front.htm
—http://www.ameritasdirect.com
—http://www.instaquote.com

Insurance (Renters):
—http://www.rentara.com/
—http://www.prudential.com/insurance/home/inhzz1007.html

Insurance (Temporary Coverage):
— http://www.charm.net/~roy/tem.html

Insurance (Umbrella):
—http://www.dtonline.com/insur/insurumbrella.htm

Investing (General Information):
—http://www.fundsinteractive.com/features/vuj07984.html
—http://www.investorhome.com/history.htm
—http://www.aaii.org
—www.invest-faq.com
—http://www.strong-funds.com/strong/LearningCenter/compound.htm

Investing (On-Line):
—http://www.investorama.com/features/bits-onl.shtml
—www.quote.com/specials/gomez/index.htm
—http://www.gomez.com
—http://www.smartmoney.com/si/brokers/
—http://www.fraud.com
—http://www.cio.com/central/financial.html
—http://www.cybercops.org/
—http://www.scambusters.org

Investment Clubs:
—www.better-investing.org
—www.better-investing.org/molic

Keough Plans:
—www.troweprice.com/retirement/

Money Market Funds:
—http://www.vanguard.com/daily/pricesyields.html#30
—http://www.vanguard.com/educ/module1/m1_2_0.html

Moving Expenses:
—http://www.moverquotes.com

Mutual Funds:
—http://www.jhancock.com/basics/principles/eight.html
—http://www.invest-faq.com/articles/mfund-a-basics.html

—http://www.fidelity.com
—http://www.troweprice.com
—http://www.morningstar.net
—http://pathfinder.com/money/funds/
—http://www.schwab.com
—http://www.investorama.com/features/piazza1.shtml
—http://www.fundsinteractive.com/
—http://www.sec.gov/consumer/inwsmf.htm
—http://www.fundspot.com/
—http://members.aol.com/plweiss1/mfunds.htm
—http://www.mfea.com/educidx.html

Private Mortgage Insurance (PMI):
—http://www.loanpage.com/morpmi.htm
—http://www.amo-mortgage.com/library/mortgageinsurance.html
—http://www.pmirescue.com/index.html
—http://www.ahahome.com/topics/finance/pmi.html

Retirement Planning:
—http://cgi.pathfinder.com/cgi-bin/Money/retire.cgi

Saving:
—http://ourworld.compuserve.com/homepages/Bonehead_Finance/-
bone4c_s.htm
—http://www.ed.gov/pubs/Prepare/chart8.html
—http://www.wfla.com/indepth/5.htm

Self-Employment:
—www.nase.org

Shopping On The Internet (General Information):
—http://www.pricescan.com/
—http://moneycentral.msn.com/home.asp

Shopping On The Internet (Travel):
—http://www.airlines.thelinks.com/
—http://www.all-hotels.com/
—http://www.bnm.com/
—http://www.sta-travel.com/
—www.bestfares.com

Simplified Employee Pensions (SEPs):
—http://www.quicken.com/retirement

Socially Responsible Investing:
—http://www.greenmoney.com/index.htm

Stock Brokers (Discount):
—http://www.sonic.net/donaldj/
—http://www.angelfire.com/biz/markettiming/discount.html
—http://www.invest-faq.com/articles/trade-disc-brok.html

Stock Brokers (General Information):
—http://www.investorhome.com/brokers.htm#info
—http://www.securitieslaw.com/main.html
—http://www.maxinvest.com/html/full-service_brokers_a_misunder-
stood_lot.html
—http://pdpi.nasdr.com/pdpi/helpfiles/faqs_frame.asp

Student Loans:
—http://www.irs.ustreas.gov/prod/forms_pubs/pubs/p970toc.htm
—http://www.ed.gov/DirectLoan/consolid.html
—http://www.ed.gov/DirectLoan/pubs/repabook/
—http://www.gsa.gov/fdac/data/p93908

Tax Deductions:
—www.irs.ustreas.gov/
—http://www.moneycentral.msn.com

Tax Exemptions:
—www.irs.ustreas.gov/prod/forms_pubs/pubs/p50104.htm

Tax Forms:
—http://www.irs.ustreas.gov/prod/forms_pubs/pubs/index.htm

Tax Professionals:
—http://www.cpalink.com
—http://www.naea.org/
—http://www.quicken.com/taxes/articles/889832439_2089
—http://hrblock.com/tax/

Taxes (Electronic Filing):
—www.securetax.com
—www.turbotax.com
—www.taxsoft.com
—http://www.irs.ustreas.gov/prod/elec_svs/index.html
—www.irs.ustreas.gov/prod/elec_svs/telefile.html

Taxes (General Information):
—http://www.irs.ustreas.gov
—http://www.irs.ustreas.gov/prod/forms_pubs/formpub.html
—http://www.irs.ustreas.gov/prod/forms_pubs/pubs/p505toc.htm
—www.irs.ustreas.gov/prod/forms_pubs/pubs/p4toc.htm.
—http://www.dtonline.com/taxguide97/worksheet.htm
—http://www.inswebpro.com/carriers/nefe/archive/nov1.htm.
—http://www.1040.com/txsubj.htm

Taxes (Self-Employed):

—http://www.irs.ustreas.gov/prod/forms_pubs/pubs/p505toc.htm
—http://www.irs.ustreas.gov/prod/forms_pubs/pubs/p583toc.htm
—http://www.irs.ustreas.gov/prod/forms_pubs/pubs/p533toc.htm.
—http://www.irs.ustreas.gov/prod/forms_pubs/pubs/p334toc.htm
—http://www.irs.ustreas.gov/prod/forms_pubs/pubs/p463toc.htm
—http://www.irs.ustreas.gov/prod/forms_pubs/pubs/p587toc.htm

Vesting and Pension Plan Rights:

—http://www.dol.gov/dol/pwba/public/pubs/youknow/knowtoc.htm

INDEX